UK Public Law and European Law

UK PUBLIC LAW AND EUROPEAN LAW

Gordon Anthony LLB, MSSc, PhD

Lecturer in Law
Queen's University Belfast

HART PUBLISHING

Oxford and Portland, Oregon
2002

Hart Publishing
Oxford and Portland, Oregon

Published in North America (US and Canada) by
Hart Publishing
c/o International Specialized Book Services
5804 NE Hassalo Street
Portland, Oregon
97213-3644
USA

Distributed in Netherlands, Belgium and Luxembourg by
Intersentia, Churchillaan 108
B2900 Schoten
Antwerpen
Belgium

Hart Publishing is a specialist legal publisher based in Oxford, England.
To order further copies of this book or to request a list of other
publications please write to:

Hart Publishing, Salters Boatyard, Folly Bridge, Abingdon Rd, Oxford,
OX1 4LB
Telephone: +44 (0)1865 245533 Fax: +44 (0) 1865 794882
email: mail@hartpub.co.uk
WEBSITE: http//:www.hartpub.co.uk

British Library Cataloguing in Publication Data
Data Available

ISBN 1-84113-148-2

Typeset by John Saunders Design & Production. Reading UK
Printed and bound in Great Britain by
Biddles Ltd www.biddles.co.uk

For
Jill, Emily and Louis

Preface and Acknowledgements

This is a book about UK courts and the manner in which they use European law – specifically EU law and the ECHR – to develop principle and practice in domestic public law. My argument in the book is simply that ongoing and more recent developments offer UK courts the opportunity to reassess their approach to the integration of domestic and European standards. Doctrinal debates about the constitutional role of the courts, the continuing institutional demands of EU law, and the coming into force of the Human Rights Act 1998 have, in different ways, each raised questions about the potential benefits of deeper integration. While the viability of legal integration is often contested in literature, I adopt and develop the competing arguments that favour a more open approach to domestic adaptation. I also suggest that, in the absence of the more open approach, the workings of UK public law will be characterised by a number of distinctions that are largely false and ultimately problematic.

Because the book has been written at a time of ongoing and far-reaching change, it has proven difficult to decide where to draw the line in terms of incorporating case law and academic commentary. The earliest Human Rights Act decisions appeared almost at the same time as the first draft of the text of the book, and there were new judgments virtually every other day. In order to finalise the text, therefore, I decided to wait for the first full Human Rights Act judgments of the House of Lords, *Alconbury* and *Daly*, and to structure my arguments accordingly. Where subsequent case law and commentary significantly added to, or detracted from, the more general argument in the book, I then referred to the point in footnotes. Future case law and commentary should likewise be read in that light.

My use of the terms "UK public law", "UK courts" and "EU law" should perhaps also be clarified. I have preferred the terms "UK public law" and "UK courts" because they better reflect the reality that it is the United Kingdom, rather than any of the legal systems within it, that is the constitutional order into which European law feeds. Although the book focuses almost exclusively on judgments in England and Wales, the cases considered raise issues relevant to courts throughout the UK, and I have included some references to judgments of the Northern Irish and Scottish courts (there is further the point that several House of Lords cases have been heard on appeal from Northern Ireland and Scotland). My use of the term "EU law", meanwhile, has been prompted by my wish to stop the text of the book becoming unnecessarily cluttered by abbreviations. While it is, of course, true that the courts have been dealing with "EC law" cases, I considered that, as EC law is ultimately a part of EU law, I could use the umbrella term. I also considered that use of the term was more in keeping with growing convention.

Much of the research that led to this book was conducted when I was a PhD student in the Institute of European Studies at the Queen's University of Belfast, and I owe a debt of gratitude to many people. My studies were supervised by Dr Robert Harmsen and Professor John Morison, and I want to thank them for their advice and for their immediate willingness to read and comment upon my work. My thanks are also due to the thesis examiners – Professor Evelyn Ellis, Professor Elizabeth Meehan, and Professor Barry Fitzpatrick – and to a number of other people who, in various ways, helped me formulate my arguments: Professor Patrick Birkinshaw, Dr John Curran, Professor Brice Dickson, Dr Scott Dixon, Dr Mark Elliott (who answered my unannounced emails), Dr Andrew Evans (who was effectively a third supervisor), Professor Brigid Hadfield, Professor Stephen Livingstone, Mrs Ruth McDowell, Dr Kieran McEvoy, Dr Søren Schønberg, and Professor Michael Smith. I also want to thank friends and colleagues who I met through the Academy of European Public Law in Greece: Dr John Allison, Dr Bernardo Ayala, Professor Sérvulo Correia, Professor Spirydon Flogaitis, Dr Eva Nieto Garrido, Mr John O'Dowd, Professor Luis Ortega, Dr Stephanie Palmer, Dr Julio Ponce Solé, Dr Jens Elo Rytter, Dr Francisco Sañchez Rodriguez, and Dr Tom Zwart.

I am also greatly indebted to Richard Hart of Hart Publishing. Richard is, in short, the most patient and understanding person I have met, and I am sure that he could by now write his own book about academics' excuses in the world of publishing. I want to thank Richard for his professionalism, flexibility, and friendliness. I also want to thank Hannah Young for the same reasons.

Finally, I want to thank family and friends for their more general support and interest: my parents; Peter Maginnis; and of course, my wife, Jill, and our children, Emily and Louis.

GORDON ANTHONY
December 2001

Contents

Table of Cases xi
Table of Legislation xxv

1. Issues, Concepts and Arguments 1
1. Introduction 1
2. Contextualising Legal Integration 3
3. Conceptualising Legal Integration 9
Legal transplants 9
Legal cross-fertilisation 12
Interacting dynamics 15
4. Arguments 17

2. The Dynamics of UK Public Law 23
1. Introduction 23
2. The Ultra Vires Debate and the Changing Nature of Judicial Review 26
3. The Royal Prerogative 30
4. The Public–Private Divide 35
Expanding the reach of judicial review – *ex p Datafin* 37
The Human Rights Act and judicial review 39
The Human Rights Act and the ultra vires debate 42
5. Conclusion 44

3. The Dynamics of European Law 47
1. Introduction 47
2. European Union Law 48
The loyalty doctrine and principles of judicial review 50
Indirect effect 54
State liability 58
Fundamental rights 62
3. The European Convention on Human Rights 66
Effectiveness, legality, proportionality 68
The margin of appreciation 71
4. Conclusion 73

4. The Reception of EU Law 75
1. Introduction 75
2. Constitutional Orthodoxy and Supremacy 77

3. Constitutional Revolution and Supremacy 86
4. Orthodoxy, Indirect Effect and the Dualist Parameters of Integration 92
The limited approach 94
The revised approach 96
5. Conclusion 100

5. EU Law and Principles of Judicial Review 103
1. Introduction 103
2. The Dualist Divide 105
3. Proportionality 110
4. Substantive Legitimate Expectations 117
5. The Duty to Give Reasons 125
6. Conclusion 130

6. Remedies 133
1. Introduction 133
2. Remedies and the Individual 134
Restitution 135
Injunctive relief 139
3. Remedies, the Courts and Institutional Balance 142
State liability in EU law 144
State liability and damages actions in domestic law 145
Barrett v. *Enfield*, public authority liability and the interim impact of the ECHR 147
4. Conclusion 153

7. The Human Rights Act 1998 and Cross-fertilisation 157
1. Introduction 157
2. Domestic Law, the ECHR and Fundamental Rights Pre-Human Rights Act 160
3. The Human Rights Act: An Overview 165
4. The Human Rights Act and the Limits to Cross-fertilisation 169
5. Conclusion 177

8. The Dynamics of Legal Integration? 179

Select Bibliography 183

Index 195

Table of Cases

EUROPEAN UNION

Case 199/82, *Amministrazione delle Finanze dello Stato* v. *San Giorgio* [1985] 2 CMLR 658 135, 136, 138
Case 326/88, *Anklagemyndigheden* v. *Hansen & Sons I/S* [1990] ECR I–2911 51, 135
Case 309/85, *Barra* v. *Belgium* [1998] ECR 355 135
Case C–173/99, *BECTU* v. *Secretary of State for Trade and Industry*, 8 Feb 2001 65
Case C–62/93, *BP Supergaz* v. *Greek State* [1995] ECR I–1883 135
Joined Cases C–46 and 48/93, *Brasserie du Pêcheur SA* v. *Germany*, *R* v. *Secretary of State for Transport, ex p Factortame Ltd* [1996] ECR I–1029 50, 60, 61, 89, 143, 144, 145, 146
Case 127/73, *BRT* v. *SABAM* [1974] ECR 51 55
Case C–194/94, *CIA Security International SA* v. *Signalson and Securitel SPRL* [1996] ECR I–2201 58
Joined Cases C–192/95–218/95 , *Comateb* v. *Directeur Général des Douanes et Droits Indirects* [1997] ECR I–165 135
Case 47/76, *Comet* v. *Produktschap voor Siergewassen* [1976] ECR 2043 51, 60, 134
Case C–178/84, *Commission* v. *Germany* [1987] ECR 1227 144
Case 61/81, *Commission* v. *UK* [1982] ECR 2601 93
Case 6/64, *Costa* v. *ENEL* [1964] ECR 585 48, 49, 134
Case C–377/89, *Cotter and McDermott* v. *Minister for Social Welfare* [1991] ECR I–4269 60
Case C–177/88, *Dekker* v. *Stichting Vormingscentrum voor Jonge Volwassenen (VJV-Centrum) Plus* [1990] 1 ECR 3941 96
Case 240/87, *Deville* v. *Administration des Impôts* [1988] ECR 3513 135
Joined Cases C–178–179 & 188–190/94, *Dillenkofer* v. *Germany* [1996] 3 CMLR 469 50, 61, 135, 143, 144
Case 12/78, *Eggers* v. *Freie Hansestadt Bremen* [1978] ECR 1935 111
Case C–192/94, *El Corte Inglés* v. *Cristina Blázques Rivero* [1996] ECR I–1281 57
Case C–260/89, *Elliniki Radiophonia Tileorassi AE* v. *Dimotiki Etairia Pliroforissis and Sotirios Kouvelas* [1991] ECR I–2925 64
Case C–208/90, *Emmott* v. *Minister of Social Welfare* [1991] ECR I–4269 51, 60, 135
Case C–91/92, *Faccini Dori* v. *Recreb Srl* [1994] ECR I–3325 57, 58, 59

Case 98/78, *Firma A Racke* v. *Hauptzollamt Mainz* [1979] ECR 69 51
Case 314/85, *Firma Foto-Frost* v. *Hauptzollamt Lübeck Ost* [1987] ECR 4199 51
Case C–188/89, *Foster* v. *British Gas plc* [1990] ECR I–3313 41, 56, 168
Case 259/85, *France* v. *Commission* [1987] ECR 4393 106
Joined Cases C–6 & 9/90, *Francovich and Bonifaci* v. *Italy* [1991] ECR I–5357 50, 51, 58, 59, 60,61, 135, 143, 144, 146
Case C-468/93, *Gemeente Emmen* v. *Belastingdienst Grote/ Ondernemingen Amsterdam* [1996] ECR I–1721 57, 96
Case 24/22, *Germany* v. *Commission* [1963] ECR 63 126
Case 8/77, *Germany* v. *Sagulo, Brenca and Bakhouche* [1977] ECR 1495 60
Case 9/70, *Grad* v. *Finanzamt Traunstein* [1970] ECR 825 55
Case 249/96, *Grant* v. *South-West Trains Ltd* [1998] ECR I–621 166
Case 179/88, *Handels-og Kontorfunktionaerenes Forbund i Danmark* v. *Arbejdsgiverforening* [1990] ECR I–1979 96
Case 44/79, *Hauer* v. *Land Rheinland-Pfalz* [1979] ECR 3727 51, 106
Case 11/70, *Internationale Handelsgesellschaft* v. *Einfuhr-und Vorratsstelle fur Getreide und Futtermittel* [1972] CMLR 255 21, 48, 62, 63
Case 222/84, *Johnston* v. *Chief Constable of the RUC* [1986] ECR 1651 5, 60, 63
Case C–237/82, *Jongeneel Kaas* v. *Netherlands* [1984] ECR 483 52
Case 80/86, *Kolpinghuis Nijmegen* [1987] ECR 3969 57
Case 168/95, *Luciano Arcaro* [1996] ECR I–4705 57, 96
Case C–106/89, *Marleasing SA* v. *La Commercial Internacional de Alimentacion SA* [1990] ECR I–4153 50, 51, 57, 93, 96, 97, 98, 99, 166
Case 152/84, *Marshall* v. *Southampton and South West Area Health Authority* [1986] ECR 723 54, 55, 93, 94
Case 271/91, *Marshall* v. *Southampton and South West Hampshire Area Health Authority (No 2)* [1993] ECR I–4367 51, 57, 135
Joined Cases C–104/89 &37/90, *Mulder* v. *Council and Commission* [1992] ECR I–3061 118
Case 120/86, *Mulder* v. *Minister van Landbouw en Visserij* [1988] ECR 2321 51, 106, 118
Case 157/86, *Murphy* v. *An Bord Telecom Eireann* [1988] ECR 673 54
Case 4/73, *Nold* v. *Commission* [1974] 2 CMLR 338 5, 63
Case 374/87, *Orkem* v. *Commission* [1989] ECR 3283 63
Case 240/83, *Procurer de la République* v. *Association de Défense des Brûleurs Usagées* [1985] ECR 520 62
Case C–213/89, *R* v. *Secretary of State for Transport, ex parte Factortame* [1990] ECR I–2433 7, 51, 60, 87, 135

Case C–331/88, *R* v. *The Ministry of Agriculture, Fisheries and Food and the Secretary of State for Health, ex parte Fedesa* [1990] ECR I–4023 111
Case C–5/94, *R* v. *Ministry of Agriculture, Fisheries and Food, ex parte Hedley Lomas (Ireland) Ltd* [1996] ECR I–2553 61, 145
Case 158/80, *Rewe Handelsgesellschaft Nord mbH* v. *Hauptzollamt Kiel* [1981] ECR 1805 51, 59, 60, 126, 134
Case 33/76, *Rewe-Zentralfinanz eG and Rewe-Zentral AG* v. *Landwirtschaftskammer für das Saarland* [1976] ECR 1989 51, 60, 134
Case 2/74, *Reyners* v. *Belgium* [1974] ECR 631 48
Joined Cases 75 & 117/82, *Razzouk and Beydoun* v. *Commission* [1984] ECR 1509 51, 106
Case 2/70, *Riva* v. *Commission* [1971] ECR 97 107
Case 36/75, *Rutili* v. *Minister for the Interior* [1976] 1 CMLR 140 5, 63
Case C–70/95, *Sodemare SA* v. *Regione Lombardia* [1997] ECR I–3395 127
Case C–152-88, *Sofrimport Sarl* v. *Commission* [1990] ECR I–2477 118
Case 29/69, *Stauder* v. *City of Ulm* [1969] ECR 419 62
Case C–338/91, *Steenhorst-Neerings* v. *Bestuur van de Bedrijfsvereniging voor Detailhandel, Ambachten en Huisvrouwen* [1993] ECR I–5475 51, 135
Case 1/58, *Stork* v. *High Authority* [1959] ECR 17 62
Case T–51/89, *Tetrapak Rausing SA* v. *Commission* [1990] ECR II–309 50
Case 17/74, *Transocean Marine Paint Association* v. *Commission* [1974] ECR 1063 3, 51
Case 222/86, *UNECTEF* v. *Heylens* [1987] ECR 4097 51, 106, 125, 127, 129, 130
Case 41/74, *Van Duyn* v. *Home Office* [1974] ECR 1337 55
Case 26/62, *Van Gend en Loos* v. *Nederlandse Aministratie der Belastingen* [1963] EC 1 48, 49, 55, 134
Case C–165/91, *Van Munster* v. *Rijksdienst voor Pensionen* [1994] ECR I–4661 54
Case C–316/93, *Vanteeveld* v. *SA Le Foyer* [1994] ECR I–763 57
Case 34/73, *Variola* v. *Amminstrazione delle Finanze dello Stato* [1973] ECR 981 55
Case 14/83, *Von Colson* v. *Land Nordrhein-Westfalen* [1984] ECR 1891 50, 51, 54, 56, 60, 93, 94, 95, 98, 166
Case C–334/92, *Wagner Miret* v. *Fondo Garantia Salarial* [1993] ECR I–6911 57
Case 5/88, *Wauchauf* v. *Germany* [1989] ECR 2609 6, 51, 157
Case 32/93, *Webb* v. *EMO Air Cargo (UK) Ltd* [1994] ECR I–3567 97
Case T–105/95, *WWF (World Wide Fund for Nature)* v. *EC Commission* [1997] ECR II–313 126

EUROPEAN CONVENTION OF HUMAN RIGHTS

Airey v. *Ireland* [1979] 2 EHRR 305 68
Albert and Le Compte v. *Belgium* [1983] 5 EHRR 533 175
B v. *France* [1993] 16 EHRR 1 67
Barthold v. *Germany* [1985] 7 EHRR 383 68
Bryan v. *UK* [1995] 21 EHRR 342 175
Cossey v. *UK* [1991] 13 EHRR 622 66, 67
Costello-Roberts v. *UK* [1993] 19 EHHR 112 42
Dudgeon v. *UK*, A/45 [1982] 4 EHRR 149 69
Engel v. *Netherlands* [1976] 1 EHRR 647 66
F v. *Switzerland*, A/128 [1988] 10 EHRR 411 69
Goodwin v. *UK*, Appl No 17488/90 [1996] 22 EHRR 123 69
Halford v. *UK* [1997] 24 EHRR 523 68
Handyside v. *UK* [1976] 1 EHRR 737 71
Hatton v. *UK* [2002] 34 EHRR 1 177
Ireland v. *United Kingdom* [1979-80] 2 EHRR 25 66
Jordan v. *UK* judgment of 4 May 2001 69, 172
Klass v. *Germany* [1979-80] 2 EHRR 214 169
Kokkinakis v. *Greece*, A/260-A [1994] 17 EHRR 397 70
Loizidou v. *Turkey*, A/310 [1995] ECHR 67
Malone v. *UK* [1985] 7 EHRR 14 69
Nasri v. *France*, A/324 [1996] 21 EHRR 458 69
National Provincial Building Society v. *United Kingdom* [1997] 25 EHRR 127 138
Open Door Counselling and Dublin Well Woman v. *Ireland* [1993] 15 EHRR 244 65, 69
Osman v. *UK* [1999] 1 FLR 193 22, 143, 147, 148, 149, 150, 151, 152, 153
Piersack v. *Belgium* [1982] 5 EHRR 169 154, 180
Rees v. *UK* [1976] 9 EHRR 56 67
Ringeisen v. *Austria* [1979-80] 1 EHRR 455 67
Sheffield and Horsham v. *UK* [1999] 27 EHRR 163 67
Smith and Grady v. *United Kingdom* [2000] 29 EHRR 493 70, 115, 153, 175, 177, 180
Sunday Times v. *UK* [1979-80] 2 EHRR 245 68
Swedish Engine Drivers' Union v. *Sweden* [1979-80] 1 EHRR 617 41
Vogt v. *Germany*, A/323 [1996] 21 EHRR 205 69
W v. *UK* [1988] 10 EHRR 29 153, 175
Wemhoff v. *Germany* [1979-80] 1 EHRR 55 66
X Union v. *France*, Appl No 9900/82 [1983] 32 DR 261 169
X, Y and Z v. *UK* [1997] 24 EHRR 143 67
Young, James and Webster v. *UK*, A/44 [1982] 4 EHRR 38 69
Z v. *UK*, judgment of 10 May 2001 22, 148, 149, 151

NATIONAL

Germany

Alcan, decision of 17 February 2000 (2001) 38 *CMLRev* 791 64
Brunner v. *European Union Treaty* [1994] 1 CMLR 57 63, 64
Wünsche Handelsgesellschaft, Re [1987] 3 CMLR 225 21, 48, 63
Internationale Handelsgesellschaft v. *Einfuhr -und Vorratstelle für Getreide und Futtermittel* 21, 48, 63

Ireland

Doyle v. *Commissioner of An Garda Síochána* [1999] 1 IR 249 66
Society for the Unborn Child (Ireland) Ltd v. *Grogan* [1990] 1 CMLR 689 64, 65

Italy

Frontini v. *Ministero delle Finanze* [1974] 2 CMLR 372 64

United Kingdom

A, In the Matter of an Application, judgment of the NIHC, 20 June 2001 171
Abbott v. *Sullivan* [1952] 1 KB 189, 22 22, 133, 141
Adv-Gen for Scotland v. *McDonald* [2001] SLT 819 166
Aero Zipp Fasteners v. *Fasteners (UK) Ltd* [1973] CMLR 819 80
Ahmad v. *Inner London Education Authority* [1978] QB 36 157
Alcock v. *Chief Constable of South Yorkshire* [1992] 1 AC 310 150
Alconbury v. *Secretary of State for the Environment, Transport and the Regions* [2001] JPEL 291 158, 175
Alexandrou v. *Oxford* [1993] 4 All ER 328 143, 150
Allgemeine Gold-und Silberscheideanstalt v. *Customs and Excise Commissioners* [1978] 2 CMLR 292 66, 158
American Cynamid v. *Ethicon Ltd* AC 396 140
Anisminic v. *Foreign Compensation Commission* [1969] 2 AC 147 23
Anns v. *Merton LBC* [1977] 2 All ER 492 148
Application des Gaz SA v. *Falks Veritas Ltd* [1974] 2 CMLR 75 60, 145
Ashby v. *White* [1703] 2 Ld Raym 938 22, 133
Associated Provincial Picture Houses v. *Wednesbury Corporation* [1948] 1 KB 223 15, 18, 26, 70, 71, 77, 105, 106, 110, 111, 113, 114, 115, 116, 117, 118, 119, 122, 124, 125, 142, 143, 154, 161, 162, 171, 172, 173, 176, 177
Attorney-General v. *De Keyser's Royal Hotel Ltd* [1920] AC 508 30, 33
Attorney-General v. *Guardian Newspapers* [1987] 1 WLR 1248 2

Attorney-General v. *Guardian Newspapers Ltd (No 2)* [1988] 3 All ER 545 162

Barrett v. *Enfield London BC* [1999] 3 All ER 193 22, 143, 147, 148, 151, 152, 153, 158, 174, 180
Beswick v. *Beswick* [1968] AC 58 99
Blackburn v. *Attorney General* [1971] 2 All ER 1380 31
Board of Education v. *Rice* [1911] AC 179 178
Bourgoin SA v. *Ministry of Agriculture, Fisheries and Food* [1986] 1 QB 716 143
British Steel Corporation v. *The King* [1935] AC 500 89
Brocklebank v. *R* [1925] 1 KB 52 137
Bromley LBC v. *Greater London Council* [1983] 1 AC 768 26
Brown v. *Stott (Procurator Fiscal, Dunfermline)* [2001] 2 All ER 97 171
Bulmer v. *Bollinger* [1974] 3 WLR 202 18
Caparo Industries plc v. *Dickman* [1990] 1 All ER 568 148
Chief Constable of the North Wales Police v. *Evans* [1982] 3 All ER 141 105
Chung Chi Cheung v. *The King* [1939] AC 160 78
Council of Civil Service Unions v. *Minister for the Civil Service* [1984] 3 All ER 935; [1985] 1 AC 374 7, 14, 18, 23, 30, 31, 32, 53, 105, 114
Davy v. *Spelthorne* [1984] AC 262 133
Derbyshire County Council v. *Times Newspapers Ltd* [1992] QB 770; [1993] AC 534 2, 162
Doughty v. *Rolls Royce plc* [1992] 1 CMLR 1045 41, 56
Douglas v. *Hello! Ltd* [2001] 2 WLR 992 41, 56, 165, 168
Duke v. *GEC Reliance Ltd* [1988] 1 All ER 626 94, 95, 97, 98
Duport Steels Ltd v. *Sirs* [1980] 1 WLR 142 26, 77
Ellen Street Estates v. *Minister of Health* [1934] 1 KB 590 75, 82, 89
Ellerman Lines v. *Murray* [1931] AC 126 6, 78
Entick v. *Carrington* [1765] 19 St TR 1030 162
Equal Opportunities Commission v. *Secretary of State for Employment* [1994] 1 All ER 910 24, 91, 100, 167
Factortame Ltd v. *Secretary of State for Transport* [1990] 2 AC 85 7, 86, 87, 140
Felixstowe Dock & Railway Co v. *British Transport Docks Board* [1976] 2 Lloyd's Law Reports 656 80
Findlay, Re [1985] AC 318 122
Finnegan v. *Clowney Youth Training Ltd* [1990] 2 AC 407 95
Garden Cottage Foods Ltd v. *Milk Marketing Board* [1984] AC 130 145
Garland v. *British Rail Engineering* [1983] 2 AC 751 82, 83, 84, 85, 86, 94, 98, 161, 165

Gough v. *Chief Constable of Derbyshire Constabulary* [2001] 4 All ER 289 20, 173
Gouriet v. *Union of Post Office Workers* [1977] 3 All ER 70 30
Griffin v. *South West Water Services Ltd* [1995] IRLR 15 41, 56
Heather v. *The Leonard Cheshire Foundation* [2001] EWHC Admin 429 42, 168
Hill v. *Chief Constable of West Yorkshire* [1989] AC 53 142-3, 150
Hoffman-La Roche v. *Secretary of State for Trade and Industry* [1975] AC 295 142
Kaur v. *Lord Advocate* [1980] SC 309 157
Kingdom of Spain v. *Christie, Manson & Woods Ltd* [1986] 1 WLR 1120 22, 133
Kirkham v. *Chief Constable of Greater Manchester* [1990] 3 All ER 246 150
Kirklees Borough Council v. *Wickes Building Supplies Ltd* [1992] 2 CMLR 765 143
Kruse v. *Johnson* [1889] 2 QB 291 178
Laker Airways Ltd v. *Department of Trade* [1977] 2 All ER 182 31
Larner v. *Solihull MBC* [2001] LGR 255 142
Law v. *National Greyhound Racing Club Ltd* [1983] 1 WLR 1302 36, 39
Litster v. *Forth Dry Dock & Engineering Co* [1990] 1 AC 546 93
Lloyd v. *McMahon* [1987] AC 625 128
Lonrho plc v. *Tebbit* [1991] 4 All ER 973 148
M v. *Home Office* [1993] 3 WLR 433 1, 3, 4, 7, 8, 22, 23, 47, 74, 133, 139, 140, 141, 180
Macarthys Ltd v. *Smith* [1979] 3 All ER 325 18, 76, 80, 82
Macarthys Ltd v. *Smith* [1981] 1 QB 180 82
MacCormick v. *Lord Advocate* [1953] SC 396 45
MacDonald v. *Ministry of Defence* [2001] 1 All ER 620 162, 166
McDonald v. *Secretary of State for Scotland* [1994] SC 234 141
McInnes v. *Onslow-Fane* [1978] 1 WLR 1520 125
Madzimbamuto v. *Lardner-Burke* [1969] 1 AC 645 26, 77
Malone v. *Metropolitan Police Commissioner* [1979] 2 WLR 700 157
Meadows v. *Grand Junction Waterworks* [1905] 21 TLR 538 137
Medicaments and Related Classes of Goods (No 2) [2001] 1 WLR 700 153, 180
Mercury Ltd v. *Director General of Telecommunications* [1996] 1 WLR 48 36
Metcalfe v. *Chief Constable of the RUC* [1995] NI 446 143, 150
Millar & Bryce Ltd v. *Keeper of the Registers of Scotland* [1997] SLT 1000 141
Minister of National Revenue v. *Wrights' Canadian Ropes Ltd* [1947] AC 109 125
Molyneaux , ex parte [1986] 1 WLR 331 31

Nagle v. *Fielden* [1966] 2 QB 633 178
National Pari-Mutuel Association v. *R* [1929] 46 TLR 594 137
Northern Ireland Human Rights Commission, In the Matter of an Application by, [2001] L NI 271 14
NUT v. *Governing Body of St Mary's Church of England (Aided) Junior School* [1997] IRLR 242 41, 56
O'Reilly v. *Mackman* [1983] 2 AC 237 36
O'Rouke v. *Camden LBC* [1998] AC 188 142
Osman v. *Ferguson* [1993] 4 All ER 344 143, 149, 151
Padfield v. *Minister of Agriculture* [1968] AC 997 23
Pepper v. *Hart* [1993] AC 593; [1992] WLR 1032; [1993] 1 All ER 42 98, 99
Phelps v. *Hillingdon LBC* [2000] 4 All ER 504 152
Pickstone v. *Freemans plc* [1989] AC 66 93, 98
Poplar Housing and Regeneration Community Association v. *Donoghue* [2001] 3 WLR 183 (CA) 42, 166, 168
R (on the application of Alconbury Developments Ltd) v. *Secretary of State for the Environment, Transport and the Regions* [2001] 2 All ER 929 20, 107, 114, 154, 158, 171, 174, 176, 180
R (on the application of H) v. *Mental Health Review Tribunal for North and East London Region,* [2001] 3 WLR 512 158
R v. *Advertising Standards Authority, ex parte The Insurance Service plc* [1990] 2 Admin LR 77 38
R v. *Barking and Dagenham LBC, ex parte Lloyd* [2001] LGR 86 124
R v. *Board of Visitors of Hull Prison, ex parte St Germain* [1979] QB 425 163
R v. *British Pharmaceutical Industry Association Code of Practice Committee, ex parte Professional Counselling Aids Ltd* [1991] COD 228 38
R v. *Cambridge Health Authority, ex parte Child B* [1995] 25 BMLR 5; [1995] 2 All ER 129 14, 18, 19, 44, 70, 104, 115, 163, 171
R v. *Chief Constable of Sussex, ex parte International Trader's Ferry Ltd* [1997] 2 All ER 65; [1998] 3 WLR 1260 107, 112, 113, 176
R v. *Chief Immigration Officer, Heathrow Airport, ex parte Salamat Bibi* [1976] 3 All ER 843 2, 157
R v. *Chief Magistrate, ex parte Choudhury* [1991] 1 All ER 306 162
R v. *Chief Rabbi of the United Hebrew Congregations, ex parte Wachmann* [1993] 2 All ER 249 38
R v. *City of London Corporation, ex parte Matson* [1997] 1 WLR 765 125, 130
R v. *Civil Service Appeal Board, ex parte Cunningham* [1991] 4 All ER 310 125, 127, 128, 129, 172

R v. *Coventry Airport, ex parte Phoenix Aviation* [1995] 3 All ER 37 18, 70, 171
R v. *Criminal Injuries Compensation Board, ex parte Lain* [1967] 3 WLR 348 31, 33
R v. *Criminal Injuries Compensation Board, ex parte P* [1995] 1 All ER 870 33
R v. *Criminal Injuries Compensation Board, ex parte Thompson and Crowe* [1984] 1 WLR 1234 33
R v. *Devon CC, ex parte Baker* [1995] 1 All ER 73 117
R v. *Disciplinary Committee of the Jockey Club, ex parte His Highness the Aga Khan* [1993] 2 All ER 853 36, 38, 39, 168
R v. *DPP, ex parte Kebeline* [2000] 2 AC 326 72, 170, 171, 174
R v. *Durham CC, ex parte Huddleston* [2000] 1 WLR 1484 93
R v. *Education Secretary, ex parte Avon County Council* [1991] 2 WLR 702 140
R v. *Fernhill Manor School, ex parte Brown* [1993] 5 Admin LR 159 39, 41, 168
R v. *Football Association Ltd, ex parte the Football League Ltd* [1993] 2 All ER 833 38
R v. *Gough* [1993] AC 646 153
R v. *Governors of Haberdashers' Aske's Hatcham College Trust, ex parte Tyrell* [1995] COD 399 39
R v. *Higher Education Funding Council, ex parte Institute of Dental Surgery* [1994] 1 All ER 651 126, 130, 172
R v. *HM Treasury, ex parte British Telecommunications plc* [1996] ECR I-1631 61, 145
R v. *Home Secretary, ex parte Duggan* [1994] 3 All ER 277 125, 129
R v. *Home Secretary, ex parte Follen* [1996] COD 169 129
R v. *Home Secretary, ex parte Murphy* [1997] COD 478 129
R v. *Home Secretary, ex parte Leech* [1994] QB 198 14, 44, 163
R v. *Horseferry Road Magistrates Court, ex parte Bennett* [1993] 3 All ER 138 108
R v. *Imam of Bury Park James Masjid Luton, ex parte Sulaiman Ali* [1992] COD 132 38
R v. *Immigration Appeal Tribunal, ex parte Marchon* [1993] Imm AR 98 66, 158
R v. *Inland Revenue Commissioners, ex parte National Federation of Self-Employed and Small Businesses Ltd* [1982] AC 617 24
R v. *Inland Revenue Commissioners, ex parte Unilever and Related Application* [1996] STC 681 117, 121
R v. *Inland Revenue Commissioners, ex parte Woolwich Building Society* [1987] STC 654; [1989] STC 463; [1990] 1 WLR 1400 137
R v. *Inspectorate of Pollution, ex parte Greenpeace Ltd (No 2)* [1994] 4 All ER 328 14, 24, 169

R v. *Jockey Club, ex parte RAM Racecourses* [1991] 3 Admin LR 292 39
R v. *Jockey Club, ex parte Massingberd-Mundy* [1990] 2 Admin LR 609 39
R v. *Legal Aid Board, ex parte Donn & Co* [1996] 3 All ER 1 39
R v. *Licensing Authority Established under the Medicines Act 1968, ex parte Smith, Kline & French Laboratories Ltd (No 2)* [1990] 1 QB 574 140
R v. *Liverpool Corporation, ex parte Liverpool Taxi Fleet Operators' Association* [1972] 2 QB 299 120
R v. *Lloyds of London, ex parte Briggs* [1993] 1 Lloyds Rep 176 36
R v. *Lord Chancellor, ex parte Hibbit & Sanders (a firm)* [1993] COD 326 39
R v. *Lord Chancellor, ex parte Lightfoot* [1999] 4 All ER 583 163
R v. *Lord Chancellor, ex parte Witham* [1997] 2 All ER 778 14, 44, 163
R v. *Lord Saville, ex parte A* [1999] 4 All ER 860 18, 44, 70, 104, 171
R v. *Ministry of Agriculture, Fisheries and Food, ex parte First City Trading Limited* [1997] 1 CMLR 250 3, 18, 46, 52, 76, 94, 108, 109, 110, 117, 131, 154
R v. *Ministry of Agriculture, Fisheries and Food, ex parte Hamble Fisheries* [1995] 2 All ER 714 1, 4, 46, 52, 53, 76, 120, 121, 122, 123, 124, 131, 154, 165, 180
R v. *Ministry of Agriculture, Fisheries and Food, ex parte Monsanto plc* [1998] 4 All ER 321 140
R v. *Ministry of Defence, ex parte Murray* [1998] COD 134 130, 172
R v. *Ministry of Defence, ex parte Smith* [1995] 4 All ER 427 14, 18, 32, 44, 70, 115, 162, 166, 171
R v. *Muntham House School, ex parte R* [2000] LGR 255 39
R v. *North and East Devon Health Authority, ex parte Coughlan* [2000] 2 WLR 622 3, 74, 123, 124, 165, 173, 180
R v. *Panel on Take-overs and Mergers, ex parte Datafin plc* [1987] QB 815 14, 23, 36, 37, 38, 40, 41, 168
R v. *Radio Authority, ex parte Bull* [1997] 2 All ER 561 19
R v. *Secretary of State for Education and Employment, ex parte Begbie* [2000] 1 WLR 1115 124
R v. *Secretary of State for Employment, ex parte Seymour Smith* [1997] 2 All ER 273 93
R v. *Secretary of State for the Environment, ex parte Nottingham CC* [1986] 1 AC 240 107, 174
R v. *Secretary of State for Foreign and Commonwealth Affairs, ex parte Everett* [1989] 1 All ER 655 14, 32
R v. *Secretary of State for Foreign and Commonwealth Affairs, ex parte Rees-Mogg* [1994] 4 All ER 457 14, 18, 24, 31, 76, 88, 169
R v. *Secretary of State for Foreign and Commonwealth Affairs, ex parte World Development Movement Ltd* [1995] 1 WLR 386 8, 14, 23, 24, 107, 169, 174

R v. *Secretary of State for Health, ex parte Imperial Tobacco Ltd* [2000] 1 All ER 572;1 All ER 850 99, 110, 131

R v. *Secretary of State for Health, ex parte US Tobbacco International Inc* [1992] 1 All ER 212 114, 120, 171

R v. *Secretary of State for Health, ex parte Imperial Tobbacco* [2000] 1 All ER 572; 1 All ER 850 99, 110, 131

R v. *Secretary of State for Home Affairs, ex parte Bhajan Singh* [1976] QB 198 157

R v. *Secretary of State for the Home Department, ex parte Adams* [1995] All ER (EC) 177 112, 164

R v. *Secretary of State for the Home Department, ex parte Anderson* [1984] QB 778 163

R v. *Secretary of State for the Home Department, ex parte Bentley* [1993] 4 All ER 442 14, 32, 33

R v. *Secretary of State for the Home Department, ex parte Brind* [1991] 2 WLR 588 2, 6, 18, 19, 78, 107, 114, 115, 131, 157, 160, 161, 162, 179

R v. *Secretary of State for the Home Department, ex parte Bugdaycay* [1987] AC 514 14, 18, 44, 70, 104, 115, 117, 161, 171

R v. *Secretary of State for the Home Department, ex parte Daly* [2001] UKHL 26; [2001] 2 WLR 1622; [2001] 3 All ER 433 20, 70, 114, 171, 174, 177, 180, 181

R v. *Secretary of State for the Home Department, ex parte Doody* [1994] 1 AC 531 108, 125, 127, 128, 129, 172

R v. *Secretary of State for Transport, ex parte Factortame (No 7)* [2001] 1 CMLR 1191 145

R v. *Secretary of State for the Home Department, ex parte Fayed* [1997] 1 All ER 228 125, 130, 172

R v. *Secretary of State for the Home Department, ex parte Fire Brigade's Union* [1995] 2 WLR 275; [1995] 2 WLR 464 8, 14, 23, 24, 33, 34, 35, 169

R v. *Secretary of State for the Home Department, ex parte Hargreaves* [1997] 1 All ER 397 19, 121, 122, 123, 124, 162, 165

R v. *Secretary of State for the Home Department, ex parte Herbage* [1987] QB 872 140

R v. *Secretary of State for the Home Department, ex parte Khan* [1985] 1 All ER 40 120

R v. *Secretary of State for the Home Department, ex parte McQuillan* [1995] 4 All ER 400 2, 3, 4, 20, 53, 66, 76, 112, 124, 158, 163, 164, 165, 174, 180

R v. *Secretary of State for the Home Department, ex parte Mahmood* [2001] 1 WLR 840 (CA) 173

R v. *Secretary of State for the Home Department, ex parte NALGO* [1993] Admin LR 785 19, 162

R v. *Secretary of State for the Home Department, ex parte Pierson* [1998] AC 539 163
R v. *Secretary of State for the Home Department, ex parte Ruddock* [1987] 1 WLR 1482 120
R v. *Secretary of State for the Home Department, ex parte Simms* [1999] 3 All ER 400 154, 158, 162
R v. *Secretary of State for the Home Department, ex parte Stroud* [1993] COD 75 178
R v. *Secretary of State for the Home Department, ex parte Venables and Thompson* [1997] 3 All ER 97 23, 129
R v. *Secretary of State for Social Security, ex parte Joint Council for the Welfare of Immigrants* [1997] 1 WLR 275 108
R v. *Secretary of State for Transport, ex parte Factortame (No 2)* [1991] 1 All ER 70 1, 7, 18, 74, 76, 86, 88–91, 139, 140
R v. *Secretary of State for Transport, ex parte Richmond Upon Thames LBC* [1994] 1 WLR 74 120
R v. *Servite Houses, ex parte Goldsmith* [2001] LGR 55 37, 168
Raymond v. *Honey* [1983] 1 AC 1 163
Ridge v. *Baldwin* [1964] AC 40 3, 23
Rigby v. *Chief Constable of Northamptonshire* [1985] 2 All ER 985 150
Rowling v. *Takaro Properties Ltd* [1988] 1 All ER 163 148
Roy v. *Kensington and Chelsea and Westminster Family Practitioner Committee* [1992] 2 WLR 239 36
S v. *Gloucestershire CC* [2001] 2 WLR 909 152
Salomon v. *Commissioners of Customs and Excise* [1967] 2 QB 116 78, 85, 161, 166
Schmidt v. *Secretary of State for Home Affairs* [1969] 2 Ch 149 119, 120
Sebel Products v. *Commissioners of Customs and Excise* [1949] Ch 409 137
Sherlock and Morris, Re [1996] NIJB 80 23, 36, 41, 56
Shields v. *E Coomes (Holdings) Ltd* [1978] 1 WLR 1408 80
Slater v. *Burnley Corporation* [1988] 59 LT 636 136
Slater v. *Burnley Corporation (No 2)* [1989] 3 JP 535 136
Smith v. *Inner London Education Authority* [1978] 1 All ER 411 140
Stoke-On-Trent CC and Norwich CC v. *B & Q plc* [1991] Ch 48 104, 112, 131
Stovin v. *Wise* [1996] 3 All ER 801 149
Tesco Stores Ltd v. *Secretary of State for the Environment* [1995] 1 WLR 759 19, 105, 131
Thoburn v. *Sunderland CC* [2002] EWHC 195 18, 82, 88
Three Rivers DC v. *Bank of England (No 3)* [2000] 2 WLR 1220 143
Twyford v. *Manchester Corporation* [1946] Ch 236 137
Vauxhall Estates Ltd v. *Liverpool Corporation* [1932] 1 KB 733 89

Venables and Thompson v. *News Group Newspapers* [2001] 2 WLR 1038 41, 56, 168
W v. *Essex CC* [2000] 2 All ER 237 152
Wandsworth London Borough Council v. *Winder* [1985] AC 461 108
Webb v. *EMO Air Cargo (UK) Ltd* [1992] 2 All ER 96
Webb v. *EMO Air Cargo (UK) Ltd (No 2)* [1995] 4 All ER 577 98
William Whitely v. *R* [1910] 101 LT 101 137
Wilson v. *First County Trust Ltd (No 2)*, [2001] 3 WLR 42 158
Woolwich Building Society v. *Inland Revenue Commissioners* [1989] 1 WLR 137 137, 138
Woolwich Building Society v. *Inland Revenue Commissioners (No 2)* [1992] 3 WLR 366 1, 3, 4, 7, 22, 47, 74, 133, 137, 138
X v. *Bedfordshire CC* [1995] 3 All ER 353 133, 149, 151

Table of Legislation

CONVENTIONS AND TREATIES

Convention on Valuation of Goods for Customs Purposes 1950 78

European Convention on Human Rights (ECHR) 1, 2, 5, 6, 13, 17, 19, 20, 21, 41, 47–8, 65, 66, 67, 70, 71, 114, 153, 154, 161–81
- Art. 2 66, 71, 164, 165
- Art. 3 66, 68, 71, 151, 152, 164, 165
- Art. 4 71, 165
- Art. 5 66, 68, 165
- Art. 6 66, 67, 68, 149–52, 165, 174–5
- Art. 7 165
- Art. 8 66, 68, 69, 71, 165, 177
- Art. 9 66, 68, 69, 71, 165
- Art. 10 66, 68, 69, 71, 114, 161, 162, 165
- Art. 11 66, 68, 69, 71, 165
- Art. 13 68, 150, 152, 165, 178
- Art. 14 66, 165, 178
- Art. 16 165
- Art. 17 165
- Art. 18 165
- Art. 34 169

Prot. 1
- Art. 1 66, 165
- Art. 2 165
- Art. 3 165

Prot. 2
- Art 1 66

Prot. 6
- Art. 1 165
- Art. 2 165

Prot. 12 66, 178

EC Treaty 88, 95
- Art. 10 50, 57, 59
- Art. 12 106
- Art. 13 106, 178
- Art. 14 178
- Art. 28 112
- Art. 29 113
- Art. 30 67, 113
- Arts. 32–38 108
- Art. 39 127
- Art. 43 87
- Art. 48 87
- Art. 50 64, 65
- Art. 141 80–4, 91, 92, 93, 106, 178
- Art. 230 106
- Art. 234 49, 51, 64, 79
- Art. 249 55, 58
- Art. 253 106, 126
- Art. 255 126
- Art. 288 145
- Art. 294 87

EU Charter of Rights 6, 48, 65
- Art. 52.3 65

Treaty on European Union (TEU)
- Art. 6 5, 48, 65
- Art. 7 5, 48, 65

Title V 88

Protocol 17 65

European Secondary Legislation

Directive 75/117/EEC OJ 1975 L45/19 (equal pay) 83, 91, 93

Directive 76/207/EEC OJ 1976 L39/40 (equal treatment) 55, 56, 83, 91, 94, 96
Directive 77/187/EEC OJ 1977 L61/27 (acquired rights) 93
Directive 80/987/EEC OJ 1980 L283/23 58, 59
Directive 85/577/EEC OJ 1985 L372/31 (contracts outside business premises) 58
Regulation 804/68/EEC JO 1968 L148/13 135
Regulation 805/68/EEC JO 1968 L148/24 135
Council Decision 93/731 OJ 1993 L340/43 (access to Council Documents) 126
Commission Decision 94/90 OJ 1994 L46/58 (access to Commission Documents) 126

NATIONAL

Germany

Biersteuergesetz 144

Ireland (Constitution 1937)

Art. 40.3.3 64

Italy

Decree-Law 430 of 10 July 1982, Gazzetta Ufficiale No 190 of 13 July 1982 136

United Kingdom

Acquisition of Land Act 1981 175
Broadcasting Act 1981
s. 29 (3) 114
Child Care Act 1980 149
Children Act 1989 149
Children and Young Persons Act 1969 149
Criminal Justice Act 1988
s. 171(1) 33
Criminal Justice Act 1991
s. 35 128
Crown Proceedings Act 1947
s. 21 87, 139, 140
Customs and Excise Act 1952 78
Employment Protection (Consolidation) Act 1978 91, 92
Equal Pay Act 1970 80, 81, 82, 93, 94
European Communities Act 1972 1, 13, 75, 78, 79, 80, 82, 85, 87, 93-4, 109, 145, 169, 170
s. 2 84
(1) 79, 81, 145
(4) 79, 80, 81, 85, 87
s. 3 79, 94
Finance Act 1985
s. 40 137
Finance Act 1991
s. 53 138
Finance (No 2) Act 1992
s. 64 138
Government of Wales Act 1998 159
Sch 8 1(1)(d) 167
Highways Act 1980 175
Human Rights Act 1998 1, 2, 3, 6, 8, 9, 13, 17, 19, 20, 21, 22, 40, 41, 42, 43, 45, 56, 67, 69, 74, 115, 117, 147, 152, 153,154, 157-78, 179, 180
s. 2 67, 158, 166, 169, 170, 173, 179
s. 3 166, 168, 169
(1)(c) 167
s. 4 42, 158
(2) 167
(5) 167
(6) 167
s. 5 166, 167
s. 6 40, 41, 43, 168, 169, 170
(2) 40, 168

(3) 40, 168, 169
(5) 41
s. 7 168, 169
(7) 169
s. 10 42, 167
s. 21 167
Medicines Act 1947 140
Merchant Shipping Act 1988 86, 87, 88, 144
Part II 87
Merchant Shipping Act 1894 86
Merchant Shipping (International Labour Conventions) Act 1925 78
Merchant Shipping (Registration, etc) Act 1993
Sch. 5 89
Northern Ireland Act 1998 14, 159
s. 6 167
s. 75 178
Race Relations Act 1976 178
Scotland Act 1998 159
s. 28(7) 181
s. 29 167
Sex Discrimination Act 1975 55, 80, 83, 93, 94, 95, 97, 166
s. 1(1) 96
s. 6 (2), (4) 83, 95
Sex Discrimination Act 1986 94
Shops Act 1950
s. 47 112
Supreme Court Act 1981
s. 31(2) 140
s. 130(1) 163
Town and Country Planning Act 1990 175
Transport and Works Act 1992 175

Statutory Instruments

Aliens Order 1953 (SI 1953/1671) 119
Equal Pay (Amendment) Regulations 1983 (SI 1983/1794) 93
Income Tax (Building Societies) Regulations 1986 (SI 1986/482) 137
Merchant Shipping Act 1988 (Amendment) Order 1989 (SI 1989/2006) 89
Rules of the Supreme Court 1965 (SI 1965/1776)
Ord. 53, r. 3(10)(a) 140
Sex Discrimination (Northern Ireland) Order 1976 (SI 1976/1042) 95
Supreme Court Fees Amendment Order 1996 (SI 1996/3191) 163
Transfer of Undertakings (Protection of Employment) Regulations 1981 (SI 1981/1794) 93

1

Issues, Concepts and Arguments

1. INTRODUCTION

The study of UK public law's relationship with European law has, in previous years, typically focused on the manner in which European Union (EU) law has effected a process of change and realignment within the domestic order. EU law feeds into the UK legal order by virtue of the European Communities Act 1972 and it is, as such, widely understood to have impacted upon UK public law in a number of ways and at a number of levels. It has, for example, almost become axiomatic to state that the doctrines of the supremacy and direct effect of EU law have strained the fundamental assumptions that underpin the UK constitutional tradition.[1] And beyond the constitutional question, it is equally apparent that UK courts have sometimes borrowed from their experience with the EU legal order by way of developing more generally the principle and practice of domestic law.[2] EU law has, therefore, entered the UK legal order in a manner that has both demanded and fostered a process of legal change. Even more significantly, it has, in doing so, recast the balance of domestic institutional relations.[3]

The passage of the Human Rights Act 1998 has, however, now added a new dimension to any study of UK public law's relationship with European law. The Human Rights Act gives effect in domestic law to most of the European Convention on Human Rights (ECHR).[4] Although it is unclear whether the Act goes so far as to incorporate the ECHR in domestic law,[5] the passage of the Act means that the ECHR will increasingly be central to the evolution of UK legal standards for the protection of fundamental

[1] See, e.g., H W R Wade, "What Has Happened to the Sovereignty of Parliament?" (1991) 107 *LQR* 1 and "Sovereignty – Revolution or Evolution?" (1996) 112 *LQR* 568. But see T R S Allan, "Parliamentary Sovereignty: Law, Politics and Revolution" (1997) 113 *LQR* 443.

[2] See, e.g., *Woolwich Building Society* v. *Inland Revenue·Commissioners (No 2)* [1992] 3 WLR 366; *M* v. *Home Office* [1993] 3 WLR 433; and *R* v. *Ministry of Agriculture, Fisheries and Food, ex p Hamble Fisheries* [1995] 2 All ER 714.

[3] See, e.g., the progression from *R* v. *Secretary of State for Transport, ex p Factortame (No 2)* [1991] 1 All ER 70 to *M* v. *Home Office* [1993] 3 WLR 433.

[4] The Act gives effect to Arts 2–12 and 14 ECHR, Arts 1–3 of Prot 1 and Arts 1 & 2 of Prot 6 to the ECHR, as read with Arts 16–18 ECHR.

[5] J Coppel, *The Human Rights Act 1998: Enforcing the European Convention in the Domestic Courts* (Wiley, Chichester, 1998), p 4.

rights.[6] That is not to say that the ECHR was devoid of influence in domestic law prior to the passage of the Human Rights Act as it clearly had some impact through the medium of EU law[7] and methods of domestic judicial reasoning.[8] But beyond these limited channels of influence, the ECHR was primarily viewed by UK courts as an external and unenforceable body of international law.[9] It is this understanding which the passage of the Human Rights Act will change.

In the following pages and chapters, this book examines in greater depth the relationship which UK public law has had, and now likely will have, with EU law and the law of the ECHR. It does so by focusing on the role which UK courts play in the development of the relationship. More specifically, this book considers the question of how far UK courts have used, and are likely to use, European law for purposes of developing the domestic legal order. The understanding that national courts use European law in this way is central to arguments that there is ongoing in Europe a process of legal convergence and integration.[10] Although the elements of the integration thesis are much contested,[11] the suggestion that national courts may borrow from the principle and practice of European law is of particular resonance in the context of the UK legal order. UK courts have, for many years, been reinventing domestic public law.[12] This process of

[6] See, e.g., B S Markesinis (ed.), *The Impact of the Human Rights Bill on English Law* (Clarendon Press, Oxford, 1998); J Wadham and H Mountfield, *Blackstone's Guide to the Human Rights Act 1998* (Blackstone, London, 2nd edn, 2000); and S Grosz, J Beatson and P Duffy, *Human Rights: The 1998 Act and the European Convention* (Sweet & Maxwell, London, 2000).

[7] For example, *R* v. *Secretary of State for the Home Department, ex p McQuillan* [1995] 4 All ER 400.

[8] See, e.g., as an aid to statutory interpretation in the event that a domestic statute was ambiguous (*R* v. *Chief Immigration Officer, Heathrow Airport, ex p Salamat Bibi* [1976] 3 All ER 843, 847); as a means of delimiting the reach of common law standards for the protection of fundamental rights (*Derbyshire County Council* v. *Times Newspapers Ltd* [1992] QB 770, 812 and 830); and as a guide to the exercise of judicial discretion (*Attorney-General* v. *Guardian Newspapers* [1987] 1 WLR 1248).

[9] See, most famously, *R* v. *Secretary of State for the Home Department, ex p Brind* [1991] 2 WLR 588.

[10] See, e.g., M Cappelletti (ed.), *New Perspectives for a Common Law of Europe* (EUI, Florence, 1978); J Schwarze, *European Administrative Law* (Sweet & Maxwell, London, 1992); B S Markesinis, (ed.), *The Gradual Convergence* (Clarendon Press, Oxford, 1994); and J Beatson and T Tridimas (eds), *New Directions in European Public Law* (Hart Publishing, Oxford, 1998). It should be noted that the process of European legal integration also engages the legal systems of some countries that are not (yet) EU Member States. See further A Evans, "Voluntary Harmonisation in Integration between the European Community and Eastern Europe" (1997) 22 *ELRev* 201.

[11] See, e.g., P Legrand, "European Legal Systems are not Converging" (1996) 45 *ICLQ* 52 and G Teubner, "Legal Irritants: Good Faith in British Law or How Unifying Law Ends Up in New Divergences" (1998) 61 *MLR* 11.

[12] J Rozenberg, *Trial of Strength: The Battle Between Ministers and Judges Over Who Makes the Law* (Richard Cohen, London, 1997).

reinvention has been prompted, on the one hand, by the reception of EU law and, on the other hand, by a series of domestic developments which have been driven by "internal" legal and political considerations. On some occasions, the courts have seemingly viewed the processes of change attributable to European law and domestic law as separate and distinct.[13] However, on other occasions, the courts have permitted a fusion of domestic and European legal standards to occur.[14] It is the primary purpose of this book, therefore, to identify the dynamics that have governed any instances of fusion and to suggest how far the dynamics may, in light of the passage of the Human Rights Act, be said to be open to change.

2. CONTEXTUALISING LEGAL INTEGRATION

The understanding that national courts may wish to use EU law to develop their domestic orders has been said by one commentator to stem from the "paradox" that requires courts to function within "two paradigms of law".[15] The accession of the UK to the European Communities in 1973 carried with it a series of institutional obligations foremost among which was the requirement that UK courts act as "EU courts" when hearing cases concerning provisions of EU law.[16] In the "EU law paradigm", the first paradigm, the national courts are obliged to give precedence to various principles, standards and norms drawn from the supranational order. Although some of the principles, standards and norms have much in common with the existing principle and practice of UK domestic law[17], others do not. EU law does, for example, incorporate some principles of judicial review which are different from those traditionally used by UK courts[18], and there likewise exists within EU law a

[13] See, e.g., *R* v. *Ministry of Agriculture, Fisheries and Food, ex p First City Trading Limited* [1997] 1 CMLR 250.

[14] See, e.g., *Woolwich Building Society* v. *Inland Revenue Commissioners (No 2)* [1992] 3 WLR 366; *M* v. *Home Office* [1993] 3 WLR 433; *R* v. *Ministry of Agriculture, Fisheries and Food, ex p Hamble Fisheries* [1995] 2 All ER 714; *R* v. *Secretary of State for the Home Department, ex p McQuillan* [1995] 4 All ER 400; and *R* v. *North and East Devon Health Authority, ex p Coughlan* [2000] 2 WLR 622.

[15] M L Fernandez Esteban, "National Judges and Community Law: The Paradox of the Two Paradigms of Law" (1997) 4 *MJ* 143.

[16] See further J Temple-Lang, "The Duties of National Courts under Community Constitutional Law" (1997) 22 *ELRev* 3.

[17] See, e.g., the ECJ's application of the right to a fair hearing in administrative proceedings in Case 17/74, *Transocean Marine Paint Association* v. *Commission* [1974] ECR 1063 as compared with the domestic standard exemplified by *Ridge* v. *Baldwin* [1964] AC 40.

[18] For example, EU law's proportionality principle as compared with the domestic standard of *Wednesbury* review.

series of remedial obligations which depart from core UK public law understandings.[19] Indeed, it has been the obligation to give effect to EU law's remedies regime which has led some commentators to suggest that EU law has strained the core constitutional constructs of the UK legal order.[20] Other commentators have gone even further and argued that domestic constitutional orthodoxy can no longer offer a satisfactory reference point for understanding the impact of EU law's remedies requirements.[21]

The second paradigm within which national courts must function is the "national law paradigm". Here, the issues raised before the courts do not concern EU law and the proceedings may be classified as purely domestic. In such cases, national courts are not under any obligation to have regard to EU law and proceedings are governed solely by domestic principle and practice. Under these circumstances, a process of borrowing occurs when national courts subsequently choose to apply in domestic proceedings a modified version of a legal standard they were previously introduced to in the EU law paradigm. The reasons for the borrowing may be varied. National courts may merely consider that the EU legal standard is of informative value,[22] or they may consider that it is imperative for there to exist a greater degree of symmetry between the national and supranational legal orders.[23] Either way, it is understood that the experience courts gain working within the EU law paradigm will present a new perspective on legal thinking in the national paradigm: "(W)hen lawyers have understood what remedies they can have against (EU) acts and institutions they will start to ask why they should not have the same against the public acts of their own governments".[24]

The assumption that norms of European law and national law can interact in this manner is of central importance to the European legal integration thesis. Jürgen Schwarze has argued with particular vigour that there is emerging within the framework of the wider EU legal order a

[19] On remedies in EU law see further R Craufurd Smith, "Remedies for Breaches of EC Law in National Courts: Legal Variation and Selection" in P Craig and G de Búrca (eds.), *The Evolution of EU Law* (Oxford University Press, Oxford, 1999), p 287.

[20] See, e.g., Wade n. 1 above.

[21] M Hunt, *Using Human Rights Law in English Courts* (Hart Publishing, Oxford, 1997), chs. 1–3.

[22] See, e.g., Sedley J's rulings in *R* v. *Ministry of Agriculture, Fisheries and Food, ex p Hamble Fisheries* [1995] 2 All ER 714 and *R* v. *Secretary of State for the Home Department, ex p McQuillan* [1995] 4 All ER 400.

[23] See, e.g., *Woolwich Building Society* v. *Inland Revenue Commissioners (No 2)* [1992] 3 WLR 366, 395–6 (Lord Goff) and *M* v. *Home Office* [1993] 3 WLR 433, 463 (Lord Woolf)

[24] J D B Mitchell, "'What do you want to be inscrutable for, Marcia?' The White Paper on the Legal and Constitutional Implications of UK Membership of the European Communities" (1967) 5 *CMLRev* 112, 122. It is interesting to note that these comments were made before the UK even acceded to the European Communities.

common, or integrated, body of administrative law.[25] Schwarze's argument holds, at source, that integration is occurring as a result of a two-way exchange of norms of administrative law between national legal systems and the EU legal order. At the level of the EU legal order, the interaction of norms and ideas has occurred by virtue of the European Court of Justice's (ECJ's) attempts to fashion a body of administrative law suited to the EU process. Schwarze argues that the ECJ has, in developing more fully the body of supranational administrative law, openly borrowed from the legal experience and tradition of various Member States.[26] But more significantly in the present context, Schwarze also suggests that these norms have, once formulated, permeated back through national legal orders. The result has been for EU law "to exercise an influence upon national legal systems and, as a medium and catalyst . . . to contribute to a convergence and approximation of administrative laws in Europe".[27]

A further source of law which Schwarze identifies as playing an integrating role within the EU legal order is the ECHR. Although Schwarze focuses on the impact which the ECHR has had in each of the Member States as an independent body of law[28], the ECJ has, since the 1970s, stated that the ECHR also informs the workings of the body of EU law which feeds into domestic systems.[29] The reasons underlying the ECJ's development of a body of fundamental rights jurisprudence around the ECHR have caused much academic debate, and some commentators have suggested that the ECJ's motivation lay more in the need to integrate an economic community than to pursue the ideal of protecting fundamental rights.[30] Despite these criticisms, the ECJ has long maintained that national courts are under an obligation to have regard to the general

[25] See, "Tendencies towards a Common Administrative Law in Europe" (1991) 16 *ELRev* 3; *European Administrative Law* (Sweet & Maxwell, London, 1992); (ed.), *Administrative Law under European Influence* (Nomos, Baden Baden and London, 1996); and "The Convergence of the Administrative Laws of the EU Member States" (1998) 4 *EPL* 191.

[26] See further G Nolte, "General Principles of German and European Administrative Law – A Comparison in Historical Perspective" (1994) 57 *MLR* 191.

[27] *European Administrative Law*, p 1465.

[28] See, "The Convergence of the Administrative Laws of the EU Member States" (1998) 4 *EPL* 191, 200: "(T)he ECHR . . . has a broader effect as regards the Europeanization of domestic legal orders, although it is focused on constitutional rather than administrative law. Nevertheless, influences of the ECHR on national administrative law are discernible, though to a different extent in each Member State".

[29] See, e.g., Case 36/75, *Rutili* v. *Minister for the Interior* [1976] 1 CMLR 140 and Case 222/84, *Johnston* v. *Chief Constable of the RUC* [1986] ECR 1651. Similar statements have also been made about the relevance of national constitutional standards to the workings of the EU legal order. See, e.g., Case 4/73, *Nold* v. *Commission* [1974] 2 CMLR 338. And see now also Arts. 6 and 7 (ex F1 and 2) TEU.

[30] J Coppel and A O'Neill, "The ECJ: Taking Rights Seriously?" (1992) 29 *CMLRev* 669. But see J H H Weiler, and NJS Lockhart, "'Taking Rights Seriously' Seriously: The ECJ and Its Fundamental Rights Jurisprudence" (1995) 32 *CMLRev* 51 and 579.

principles of EU law, including those derived from the ECHR.[31] And, while it is true that the validity of the obligation may be questioned on account of the fact that the EU institutions have not formally acceded to the ECHR,[32] it is recognised that the ECHR guides judicial rulings at both the supranational and national levels.[33] Consequently, it can be said that the legal standards which UK courts might wish to borrow from within the EU law paradigm have been born of a complex process of interaction engaging national, international and supranational standards. More significantly, it might now also be said that the process of interaction will, with the passage of the Human Rights Act, assume a greater intensity.

One feature of the UK legal tradition that has been said to limit the scope for borrowing from European law, however, is constitutional dualism. Ian Ward has argued that dualism necessarily militates against the idea of integration because it causes UK courts to view European law as "a component, or subspecies of our legal order".[34] This dualist understanding, which is attributable to UK public law's historic emphasis on the continuing and absolute sovereign power of the Westminster Parliament,[35] has manifested itself most obviously in the courts' refusal to have recourse to international standards that have not been incorporated in domestic law.[36] But the limiting influence of orthodoxy has also been apparent in other ways. This is particularly true of the courts' approach to the reach of international standards that have been incorporated. Although the courts have had due regard for incorporated international standards, they have been reluctant to allow them to have an influence beyond that specified in the parent legislation.[37] In other words, the courts have only permitted international law to impact on the domestic order in closely defined categories of cases. For one commentator, such an approach has, in the context of European integration, the clear potential to cause "a drifting apart from within" of domestic and European norms.[38]

[31] Case 5/88, *Wauchauf* v. *Germany* [1989] ECR 2609.

[32] For the ECJ's view of the prospects of such accession see Opinion 2/94 on "Accession by the Community to the ECHR" [1996] ECR I-1759. And see now also the "complicating" factor of the recently adopted EU Charter of Fundamental Rights, OJ 2000 C364/01.

[33] On the influence that the ECHR has had on ECJ jurisprudence see E Guild and G Lesieur, *The European Court of Justice on the European Convention on Human Rights: Who said what, when?* (Kluwer, London, 1998).

[34] "Dualism and the Limits of European Integration" (1995) 17 *Liverpool LRev* 29, 36.

[35] On which see, most famously, AV Dicey, *An Introduction to the Study of the Law of the Constitution* (Macmillan, London, 10th edn, 1959).

[36] *R* v. *Secretary of State for the Home Department, ex p Brind* [1991] 2 WLR 588.

[37] For example, *Ellerman Lines* v. *Murray* [1931] AC 126.

[38] W Van Gerven, "Bridging the Gap Between Community and National Laws: Towards a Principle of Homogeneity in the Field of Legal Remedies" (1995) 32 *CMLRev* 679, 700. This consequence of UK dualism can be contrasted with that of Spanish constitutional monism: "Spanish administrative law has many common principles and institutions, even at a constitutional level, with other European countries, especially with France, Germany and

Yet, while dualism might limit the scope for integration, there is, as implied above, some evidence that the co-existence within the UK legal system of different bodies of law has given rise to judicial expectation of a deeper enmeshing of domestic and European standards. In the *GCHQ*[39] case, for example, Lord Diplock, having identified the domestic grounds of judicial review (illegality, irrationality and procedural impropriety), proceeded to state that the grounds should not be seen as exhaustive and, moreover, that they may come to be joined by the European proportionality principle.[40] And the most notable example of actual overlap occurred in *M* v. *Home Office*.[41] In the case, the House of Lords ruled for the first time that injunctive relief should be available against a minister of the Crown in domestic proceedings. Their Lordships' decision, which had far-reaching institutional implications, made specific reference to a previous preliminary ruling from the ECJ which stated that injunctive relief should be available in EU law cases where the measure was considered necessary to ensure effective protection of EU law rights.[42] Related cross-referencing to EU standards has also been apparent in other domestic cases.[43]

The fact that some borrowing has occurred within the limiting framework of dualism then gives rise to the question of how far the UK legal order may truly be said to be open to a process of borrowing and change.[44] It was stated above that UK courts have, independent of the influence of European law, already been reinventing the body of domestic public law, hence it might be expected that borrowing would be prompted as much by the "internal" needs of the domestic order as by the "external" influence of European law. The internal process of change within UK law has, most recently, been

Italy. This is why most of the principles of EC law are not foreign to our legal system . . . The monist system that makes international or supranational legislation part of our domestic legislation . . . facilitates the general acceptance of the supremacy, precedence and direct effect principles of EC law". See E Garcia de Enterria and L Ortega, "Spanish Report" in J Schwarze (ed.) n. 25 above, p 731.

[39] *Council of Civil Service Unions* v. *Minister for the Civil Service* [1985] 1 AC 374.

[40] "That is not to say that further development on a case-by-case basis may not in the course of time add further groups. I have in mind particularly the possible adoption in the future of the principle of "proportionality" which is recognised in the administrative law of several of our fellow members of the European Economic Community" [1985] 1 AC 374, 410.

[41] [1993] 3 WLR 433.

[42] This was the outcome of the *Factortame* litigation. See *R* v. *Secretary of State for Transport, ex p Factortame* [1990] 2 AC 85; Case C-213/89, *R* v. *Secretary of State for Transport, ex p Factortame* [1990] ECR I-2433; and *R* v. *Secretary of State for Transport (No 2)* [1991] 1 All ER 70.

[43] For example, *Woolwich Building Society* v. *Inland Revenue Commissioners (No 2)* [1992] 3 WLR 366.

[44] The point has been made by Beatson and Tridimas: "If we are seeing a slow process of the "Europeanisation" of public law, a regional version of the "globalisation" so often talked about, it becomes important to know which principles, doctrines and structures are properly susceptible to the process and which are not". See n. 10 above, p 1.

caused by the reforming manifesto of the New Labour government.[45] New Labour's reform programme has, in addition to the passage of the Human Rights Act, centred around several key initiatives which have included the devolution of power to the constituent parts of the UK, and these are, quite clearly, developments that will raise new constitutional challenges for the courts.[46] And running prior to New Labour's reform package, there is also the ongoing process whereby UK courts have been developing a more active body of domestic judicial review. This process, which has sometimes seen the courts push legal developments beyond the boundaries of orthodoxy, has led to an active academic debate about the nature of the institutional role performed by the courts.[47] Although opinion has been divided as to the practical impact and significance of the growth in applications for judicial review,[48] there nevertheless exists a consensus opinion that the development of a more active supervisory jurisdiction has performed something of a "democratising" function.[49] The process of democratisation has been characterised by a series of high-profile cases concerning central government, with one of the most prominent in this regard being *M* v. *Home Office*.[50] An initial question which needs to be asked, therefore, is one of emphasis: to what extent has the UK courts' willingness to borrow from EU law been dependent upon a pre-existing active internal dynamic for change,

[45] On new Labour's reform package, see R Brazier, "New Labour, New Constitution" (1998) 49 *NILQ* 1. For critical analysis see J Morison, "The Case Against Constitutional Reform" (1998) 25 *JLS* 510.

[46] T Jones, "Scottish Devolution and Demarcation Disputes" [1997] *PL* 283; V Bogdanor, "Devolution: The Constitutional Aspects" in J Beatson, C Forsyth and I Hare (eds.), *Constitutional Reform in the United Kingdom: Practice and Principles* (Hart Publishing, Oxford, 1998), p 9; P Craig and M Walters, "The Courts, Devolution and Judicial Review" [1999] *PL* 274; and G Anthony and A Evans, "Northern Ireland, Devolution and the European Union" in C Harvey (ed.) *Human Rights, Equality and Democratic Renewal in Northern Ireland* (Hart Publishing, Oxford, 2001), p 53.

[47] See C Forsyth (ed.), *Judicial Review and the Constitution* (Hart Publishing, Oxford, 2000).

[48] See, e.g., The Public Law Project, *Judicial Review in Perspective: An Investigation of Trends in the Use and Operation of the Judicial Review Procedure in England and Wales* (London, 1993).

[49] Lord Irvine of Lairg, while being concerned to ensure that the judiciary should not usurp the proper function of the legislature or administration, has valued the growth of domestic judicial review in the following terms: "Let me begin with a recognition that the consequences of the "democratic deficit", the want of parliamentary control of the executive in recent years, have been, to an important degree, mitigated by the rigours of judicial review. I pay tribute to the high quality of judicial review in this country. It has so often rightly held the executive to account and improved the quality of administrative decision-making". See, "Judges and Decision-Makers: The Theory and Practice of *Wednesbury* Review" [1996] *PL* 59.

[50] [1993] 3 WLR 433. Other leading cases include *R* v. *Secretary of State for Foreign and Commonwealth Affairs, ex p World Development Movement Ltd* [1995] 1 WLR 386 and *R* v. *Secretary of State for the Home Department, ex p Fire Brigade's Union* [1995] 2 WLR 275.

and to what extent has the dynamic of EU law itself created the demand for a more responsive domestic legal system? A related point of inquiry goes to the issue of how far New Labour's reform package, in particular the passage of the Human Rights Act, might be expected to lessen the limiting influence which can be said to inhere in dualist public law orthodoxy.

3. CONCEPTUALISING LEGAL INTEGRATION

The argument that European law can provide a suitable reference point against which to develop domestic legal orders has, as noted, given rise to an active debate about the theoretical and practical viability of legal integration.[51] Academic opinion is divided among those scholars who consider that borrowing between legal systems is possible, those who consider that borrowing is not possible, and those who consider that borrowing might be possible subject to various institutional considerations being afforded due regard. The point of division between the schools of thought has concerned, at least implicitly, the viability of the "transplantation" of legal standards. Although legal transplantation can assume many forms,[52] it is, at its most basic, a concept and process which involves "the transposition of a doctrine from one jurisdiction to another".[53] Accordingly, while some commentators consider transplantation and borrowing to be relatively unproblematic,[54] others are much more circumspect: "Anyone who takes the view that 'the law' or 'the rules of the law' travel across jurisdictions must have in mind that law is a somewhat autonomous entity unencumbered by historical, epistemological, or cultural baggage".[55]

Legal transplants

The commentator who has been the most prominent and consistent proponent of the viability of legal transplantation is Alan Watson. Watson has

[51] Note 11 above. Debate has also been conducted in contexts other than that concerned with European integration. See, e.g., W Wiegand, "The Reception of American Law in Europe" (1991) 39 *AJCL* 229; D Wright, "Rethinking the Doctrine of Legitimate Expectations in Canadian Administrative Law" (1997) 35 *Osgoode Hall Law Journal* 139; and J W Bridge, "Judicial Review in Mauritius and the Continuing Influence of English Law" (1997) 46 *ICLQ* 787.

[52] G Ajani, "By Chance and Prestige: Legal Transplants in Russia and Eastern Europe" (1995) 43 *AJCL* 93.

[53] J Bell, "Mechanisms for Cross-fertilisation of Administrative Law in Europe" in J Beatson and T Tridimas (eds), n. 10 above, p 147.

[54] For example, Schwarze, n. 25 above and P Craig, "Once More Unto the Breach: The Community, The State and Damages Liability" (1997) 113 *LQR* 67.

[55] P Legrand, "The Impossibility of Legal Transplants" (1997) 4 *MJ* 111, 114.

argued, in a substantial body of work,[56] that there exists a rich history of the successful transplantation of legal ideas across legal borders. He notes in particular how elements of the English common law and Roman law have been transplanted around the globe. The transplantation of the English common law, for example, is said have occurred in Canada, the United States, Australia, New Zealand and India (among others). And the influence of Roman law is likewise said to be found in various European legal orders as well as in parts of Canada, South America, Africa and Japan: "What was received was not everywhere the same, and very substantial modifications took place. But that there was a reception of massive proportions cannot be gainsaid".[57]

Watson justifies his argument that the successful transplantation of legal principle and practice is possible by reference to an understanding of law as a largely autonomous entity which is created and developed in an environment free from wider societal pressures.[58] The separation of "law" from "society" is said by Watson to have arisen from the manner in which law has historically been made. Arguing that rulers and governments have historically been reluctant to formulate canons of law, Watson notes how the law-making function was delegated to jurists. These jurists subsequently "developed their own legal culture which was . . . distant from social reality. This culture determined the parameters of their legal reasoning, the systems of law that they would borrow from, and even the extent to which they would borrow".[59] For Watson, therefore, there exists no necessary relationship between law and its institutions and the "needs and desires and political economy of the ruling élite or of the members of (a) particular society".[60] Rather, law is developed in accordance with needs and desires which are identified by expert lawyers. Thus, while Watson concedes that there are various factors which may limit the extent of borrowing,[61] he emphasises the likelihood of successful transplantation should attempts at borrowing occur:

[56] See, e.g., *Legal Transplants: An Approach to Comparative Law* (Univ of Georgia Press, 2nd edn, 1993); "Legal Transplants and Law Reform" (1976) 92 *LQR* 79; "Comparative Law and Legal Change" (1978) 37 *CLJ* 313; "From Legal Transplants to Legal Formants" (1995) 43 *AJCL* 469; and, "Aspects of the Reception of Law" (1996) 44 *AJCL* 335. These contributions, and the broader body of Watson's work are summarised and evaluated in W Ewald, "Comparative Jurisprudence (II): The Logic of Legal Transplants" (1995) 43 *AJCL* 489. It should be noted that Alan Watson's work does not address explicitly the process of European legal integration. Nevertheless, his work is widely cited in literature that does address the European process. See, e.g., G Teubner, n. 11 above.

[57] "Comparative Law and Legal Change" 313, 313–14.

[58] *Ibid*, 313–16.

[59] "From Legal Transplants to Legal Formants" , n. 56 above, 469.

[60] Note 57 above, 315.

[61] *Ibid*, 321–36.

> "(L)egal rules may be very successfully borrowed where the relevant social, economic, geographical and political circumstances of the recipient are very different from those of the donor system . . . the recipient system does not require any real knowledge . . . of the origin and growth of the original rule".[62]

Watson's arguments have been fundamentally rejected by other commentators. The principal critic in this regard is Pierre Legrand.[63] Indeed, Legrand has been critical of the notion of borrowing and integration both as a general construct and as a construct related to the more specific process of European legal integration. As a general criticism, Legrand states that Watson's thesis is premised upon an erroneous understanding that "law" can be reduced to a series of "rules" and that these rules amount to nothing more than "bare propositional statements".[64] For Legrand, there exists instead an inextricable and all encompassing link between a body of law and its environmental surround.[65] In the first instance, the environment gives rise to a rule. But more than that, any rule must subsequently be interpreted and applied, and such interpretation as may be given to the rule necessarily incorporates further cultural and historical understandings:

> "No form of words purporting to be a 'rule' can be completely devoid of semantic content, for no rule can be without meaning. The meaning of the rule is an essential component of the rule; it partakes in the ruleness of the rule. The meaning of the rule, however, is not entirely supplied by the rule itself; a rule is never completely self-explanatory . . . meaning is also – and perhaps mostly – a function of the application of the rule by its interpreter . . . This ascription of meaning is predisposed by the way the interpreter understands the context within which the rule arises . . . The meaning of the rule is, accordingly, a function of the interpreter's epistemological assumptions which are themselves historically and culturally conditioned".[66]

Turning to the question of the viability of legal integration within the framework of the EU legal order, Legrand highlights how "irreducibly distinctive modes of legal perception and thinking" render the successful integration of different legal traditions unlikely.[67] Although Legrand's

[62] "Legal Transplants and Law Reform", n. 56 above, 80–1.

[63] See, e.g., n. 11 above; "Against a European Civil Code" (1997) 60 *MLR* 44; and "The Impossibility of Legal Transplants" (1997) 4 *MJ* 111. It should be noted that Legrand's arguments are primarily made by reference to private law. Nevertheless, many of the points raised are of equal relevance to debate about public law.

[64] (1997) 4 *MJ* 111, 114.

[65] Although the question of how a body of law evolves to reflect its environmental surround (i.e. historical, societal, economic, political forces etc.) is more complex. See N Luhmann, "Operational Closure and Structural Coupling: The Differentiation of the Legal System" (1992) 13 *Cardozo LRev* 1419.

[66] (1997) 4 *MJ* 111, 114.

[67] See generally n. 11 above.

arguments in this regard are developed by reference to differences between the common law and civil law traditions of the various Member States of the EU, his analysis may equally be said to be of value relative to the integration of national, international and supranational legal standards. Renaud Dehousse has cautioned that any comparison of EU law and domestic law should not lose sight of the fact that the EU, "because it is a systemic body, has to accommodate a number of requirements that are without equivalent in national systems . . . comparison and evaluation should be carried out keeping in mind that the same yardsticks should not lightly be used for the EU as for classical nation-states".[68] In keeping with the core logic of Legrand's reasoning, therefore, it might be expected that that there will exist many different functional perspectives between European law and national law and that these different perspectives, in addition to those differences which arise from a body of law's wider environmental surround, will act as a bar to any process of effective European legal integration.

Legal cross-fertilisation

The difficulty with accepting Legrand's arguments in their entirety, however, lies in the fact that they fail satisfactorily to account for such instances of borrowing as have occurred within the framework of the EU legal order. It has already been stated above that the body of EU law which has been developed by the ECJ has, at different times, borrowed from the experience of the Member States' legal orders[69] as well as that of the ECHR.[70] Likewise, there also exists empirical evidence which indicates that national orders have borrowed from EU law for purposes of developing domestic principle and practice.[71] Consequently, while Legrand's arguments are provocative and insightful, they ultimately may not enjoy full explanatory force.

It is in light of the fact that legal borrowing does occur that John Bell has latterly infused the transplantation debate with the more flexible language and imagery of legal cross-fertilisation.[72] For Bell, the value of the concept of legal cross-fertilisation lies in the fact that it assumes a point of reasoning and expectation somewhere between the contrasting theses forwarded by Watson and Legrand. While legal transplantation is

[68] "Comparing National and EC Law: The Problem of the Level of Analysis" (1994) 42 *AJCL* 761, 777–8. See further K Mortelmans, "EC Law: More than a Functional Area of Law, Less than a Legal System" (1996) *LIEI* 23.

[69] T Koopmans, "The Birth of European Law at the Cross-roads of Legal Traditions" (1991) 39 *AJCL* 493.

[70] But see also J Coppel and A O'Neill n. 30 above.

[71] See, e.g., each of the national reports in J Schwarze (ed.), n. 25 above.

[72] Note 33 above. For an earlier contribution which pursues similar themes see O Kahn-Freund, "On Uses and Misues of Comparative Law" (1974) 37 *MLR* 1.

suggestive of a rigid and potentially problematic process, legal cross-fertilisation implies:

> ". . . a different, more indirect process. It implies that an external stimulus promotes an evolution within the receiving legal system. The evolution involves an internal adaptation by the receiving legal system in its own way. The new development is a distinctive . . . product of that system rather than a bolt-on".[73]

Defined in these terms, legal cross-fertilisation is particularly appropriate as a means of conceptualising the relationship between UK public law and European law. The UK's dualist constitutional tradition requires that Parliament pass suitable enabling legislation before a body of international/supranational law can have effect within the domestic order. To that extent, EU law and the ECHR might be described as "external stimuli" which enjoy a direct channel into the domestic order by virtue of the European Communities Act 1972 and the Human Rights Act 1998. Furthermore, and once incorporated, EU law and the ECHR may, within the "European paradigm", oblige the courts to apply legal standards which are different from those of domestic law. Should it then be perceived that EU law and ECHR represent a superior standard of law to that of the domestic order, the judiciary may feel compelled, or at least the desire, to adapt the domestic system. Indeed, such correctional development of the law has been alluded to by other commentators, with Paul Craig referring to the "spill-over" of EU standards into domestic practice.[74]

A further feature of legal cross-fertilisation which is illuminating is its capacity to accommodate the internal dynamics of the receiving legal order. Bell's emphasis on internal evolution and adaptation has been welcomed by John Allison who stresses the imperative of structuring any process of borrowing around the established doctrinal, institutional and theoretical understandings of the receiving order.[75] This regard for internal

[73] Bell, n. 53 above, 147. It should be noted that Bell's contribution to the transplantation debate is concerned primarily with the process of interaction and integration between national legal orders. He does, however, acknowledge that there can be a process of legal cross-fertilisation whereby domestic courts borrow from EU law: "Such national developments illustrate the way in which cross-fertilisation takes place . . . The national legal order tries to find the most appropriate way to accommodate the new insight into its own conceptual structure and legal culture. As a result, the national solutions are not identical in form, even if they may be broadly similar in result". *Ibid*, 161.

[74] Note 54 above. See also G Anthony, "Community Law and the Development of UK Administrative Law: Delimiting the 'Spill-over' Effect" (1998) 4 *EPL* 253.

[75] See, "Transplantation and Cross-fertilisation" in J Beatson and T Tridimas (eds) n. 10 above, p 169. Although it might also be noted that, while Allison endorses Bell's approach, he is much more sceptical about the extent to which borrowing between legal systems is possible. See further J W F Allison, *A Continental Distinction in the Common Law: A Historical and Comparative Perspective on English Public Law* (Oxford University Press, Oxford, 2nd edn, 2000).

institutional considerations is the characteristic which allows legal cross-fertilisation to maximise the relative strengths of the various contributions to the transplantation debate. On the one hand, legal cross-fertilisation clearly recognises that borrowing between systems can happen and, more significantly, that it can be beneficial. But, on the other hand, it equally recognises that there must exist some identifiable limits to the transplantation of legal standards.[76] The function of national institutional considerations in a process of legal cross-fertilisation, therefore, is not to act as an absolute bar to integration, but rather to act as a filter mechanism which allows courts to identify those external standards which may, with suitable adaptation, properly inform domestic legal developments.

The requirement that national institutional considerations be afforded due regard does, however, beg the question of which institutional considerations might be said to be the defining considerations of the UK legal order. It has already been stated above that there has emerged in UK law a body of jurisprudence which has strained various established institutional understandings. The jurisprudence has typically concerned the liberalisation of the rules governing standing to bring an application for judicial review;[77] the expansion of the scope of the courts' supervisory jurisdiction;[78] and the assertion of a much more pronounced judicial role relative to the protection of the fundamental rights of individuals.[79] Although the jurisprudence may not yet be representative of a new orthodoxy, it is indicative of the internal

[76] See further O Kahn-Freund, n. 72 above.

[77] See, e.g., *R* v. *Secretary of State for Foreign Affairs and Commonwealth Affairs, ex p Rees-Mogg* [1994] 1 All ER 457; *R* v. *Inspectorate of Pollution, ex p Greenpeace Ltd (No 2)* [1994] 4 All ER 328; *R* v. *Secretary of State for Foreign and Commonwealth Affairs, ex p World Development Movement Ltd* [1995] 1 WLR 386; and *R* v. *Secretary of State for the Home Department, ex p Fire Brigade's Union* [1995] 2 WLR 275. It should be noted that the Scottish courts have interpreted standing rules more narrowly than the courts in England and Wales and Northern Ireland (although see now also the related judgment of the Northern Ireland CA in, *In the matter of an application by the Northern Ireland Human Rights Commission for judicial review*) [2000] NI 271, denying that the Northern Ireland Act 1998 gives the NIHRC a right of third party intervention in human rights cases). For commentary on the differences between Scotland and England see Lord Hope of Craighead, "Mike Tyson Comes to Glasgow – A Question of Standing" [2001] *PL* 294.

[78] See, e.g., with regard to the review of exercises of the royal prerogative, *Council of Civil Service Unions* v. *Minister for the Civil Service* [1985] 1 AC 374; *R* v. *Secretary of State for Foreign and Commonwealth Affairs, ex p Everett* [1989] 1 All ER 655; *R* v. *Secretary of State for the Home Department, ex p Bentley* [1993] 4 All ER 443; and *R* v. *Secretary of State for the Home Department, ex p Fire Brigade's Union* [1995] 2 WLR 646. See further the extension of the courts' supervisory jurisdiction to non-statutory bodies in, e.g., *R* v. *Panel on Take-overs and Mergers, ex p Datafin plc* [1987] QB 815.

[79] See, e.g., *Raymond* v. *Honey* [1983] 1 AC 1; *R* v. *Secretary of State for the Home Department, ex p Bugdaycay* [1987] AC 514; *M* v. *Home Office* [1993] 3 WLR 433; *R* v. *Home Secretary, ex p Leech* [1994] QB 198; *R* v. *Ministry of Defence, ex p Smith* [1995] 1 All ER 427; *R* v. *Cambridge Health Authority, ex p Child B* [1995] 25 BMLR 5; and *R* v. *Lord Chancellor, ex p Witham* [1997] 2 All ER 778.

institutional tensions which can increasingly be seen to underpin the workings of UK public law.[80] While UK public law was previously associated with the ultra vires doctrine and principles of judicial review that reflected one accepted understanding of the institutional role of the courts[81], there now exists widespread doubt about the continuing relevance of more orthodox assumptions.[82] Reduced to the language of the cross-fertilisation problematic, then, the central point of inquiry becomes apparent: if there are within the UK legal order competing understandings of the proper institutional role of the courts and of the nature of domestic public law, which of these understandings has been emphasised in any process of borrowing and integration?

Interacting dynamics

The above emphasis on the need to identify internal institutional limits to legal borrowing may lead to the inference that legal integration is a process that is governed solely by domestic factors and forces. Such an inference would, however, be contestable. The question of whether it is national or supranational considerations which ultimately govern the broader process of European integration has long vexed social and political scientists,[83] and it is likely that attempts to isolate a single governing dynamic in the more specific process of legal integration would similarly prove problematic. It is clear from Jürgen Schwarze's work, for example, that European law, by its very presence in domestic legal orders, sometimes enjoys a hortatory force which occasions change. But beyond any self-sustaining influence that European law may have, it is equally clear that national court borrowing from European law does not follow a set pattern either in terms of the extent of any borrowing or in terms of the specific principle and practice adopted.[84]

[80] Compare, e.g., Lord Irvine of Lairg's opinions in n. 49 above with those of other leading members of the judiciary, e.g., Sir Harry Woolf, "Droit Public – English Style" [1995] *PL* 57; Sir John Laws, "Law and Democracy" [1995] *PL* 72; and Sir Stephen Sedley, "Human Rights: A Twenty-First Century Agenda" [1995] *PL* 386.

[81] In particular, *Wednesbury* unreasonableness. See *Associated Provincial Picture Houses* v. *Wednesbury Corporation* [1948] 1 KB 223.

[82] See further the various contributions in C Forsyth (ed.), n. 47 above.

[83] See, most famously, the contrasting accounts of "neo-functionalism" and "liberal intergovernmentalism". For neo-functionalist approaches see, e.g., E Haas, *The Uniting of Europe: Political, Economic and Social Forces, 1950-57* (Stevens, London, 1958); L Lindberg, *The Political Dynamics of European Economic Integration* (Stanford University Press, 1963); and J Tranholm-Mikkelsen, "Neo-functionalism: Obstinate or Obsolete? A Reappraisal in the Light of the new Dynamism of the EC" (1991) 20 *Millennium* 1. On "liberal intergovernmentalism" see A Moravcsik, "Preferences and Power in the European Community: A Liberal Intergovernmentalist Approach" (1993) 31 *JCMS* 473 and, *The Choice for Europe: Social Purpose and State Power from Messina to Maastricht* (Cornell University Press, 1998).

[84] A point which, paradoxically, is evident from the various national reports in J Schwarze (ed.), n. 25 above.

The governing dynamic in any process of fusion, it would seem, may alternate between the national and supranational levels.

The respective influences of the European and domestic dynamics have been identified, albeit inadvertently, in existing literature on the reception of European law into the UK legal order. In an article entitled "The Europeanization of the British Legal Style",[85] Jonathon Levitsky suggests that the initial pressure for change in UK law might be seen to come from within the European order. Noting how accession to the EU served to bring UK judges into contact with "an alien judicial order" which incorporates different principles of judicial review as well as a series of interpretative obligations, Levitsky alludes to the existence of a subsequent process of osmosis:

> "There is significant evidence that British courts are applying techniques and judicial approaches that they were introduced to primarily as a result of Community membership in purely domestic cases. This phenomenon suggests the possibility of deep, long-term change in the British judicial role as a result of their experience".[86]

Levitsky's comments in this regard do, of course, share much in common with Jürgen Schwarze's understanding. Yet, beyond this initial point of agreement, it is striking to note how far Levitsky's conclusions about the final impact of EU law depart from those offered by Schwarze. In short, Levitsky moves towards an understanding of the reception of EU law which emphasises how the UK courts structure the process of assimilation around domestic, rather than European, legal considerations. For Levitsky, this has the corresponding effect of preventing the UK order from "simply evolving towards the synthesis some have predicted between civil and common law systems. Instead, (it seems) slowly, tentatively, to be moving toward an American version of a common law system".[87] Perhaps the most appropriate point that may be made in the present context, therefore, is that the dynamics of legal integration should not be seen as driven solely by either European or domestic legal considerations. Rather, it seems that they may best be conceived of as driven by a subtle and sequential process of interaction in which European law feeds into an already changing domestic legal

[85] (1994) 42 *AJCL* 347. Other contributions on the relationship between UK law and European law include J Jowell and P Birkinshaw, "English Report" in J Schwarze (ed.), n. 25 above, p 273; P Craig, "Substantive Legitimate Expectations in Domestic and Community Law" (1996) 55 *CLJ* 289; P Craig, "The Impact of Community Law on Domestic Public Law" in P Leyland and T Woods (eds), *Administrative Law Facing the Future: Old Constraints and New Horizons* (Blackstone, London, 1997) p 271; and G de Búrca, "Proportionality and *Wednesbury* Unreasonableness: The Influence of European Legal Concepts on UK Law" (1997) 3 *EPL* 561.

[86] Note 85 above, 348.

[87] *Ibid*, 380.

order, thereby raising questions about the possible need for further change and realignment. The extent of any subsequent adaptation is then determined in accordance with domestic institutional considerations. The relevant domestic considerations may have a limiting effect, or they may, where they are inherently open to the prospect of change, have an integrating effect. Either way, the need to have recourse to domestic considerations is prompted in the first instance by the very presence within domestic orders of the wider body of European law.

4. ARGUMENTS

Given these points of emphasis, this book forwards two main arguments about the process whereby UK courts borrow principle and practice from European law. First, the book argues that the process of borrowing has, in previous years, been more restricted than might logically have been expected. Although the ongoing internal process of change in domestic public law would suggest that UK law would have had much to gain from a rich process of cross-fertilisation, the book argues that the courts have, on balance, structured borrowing around orthodox public law understandings that have served to limit the scope for integration. Second, however, the book argues that the domestic institutional considerations that mediate the integration of UK and European legal standards may now be on the verge of far-reaching change. More specifically, the book argues that the Human Rights Act should coalesce with emerging internal institutional assumptions about the role of the courts to greatly invigorate the process of integration. While the process of borrowing has previously been limited, therefore, the book contends that there should be significantly increased assimilation of standards drawn from UK public law, EU law and the law of the ECHR.

The argument that UK courts have previously structured the process of legal cross-fertilisation around orthodox domestic considerations is traced to the manner in which UK courts have legitimated their rulings within the "EU law paradigm". It will be recalled that the EU law paradigm governs all domestic cases that raise EU law issues and that, in this context, the domestic courts have come into contact with a series of new and potentially insightful European principles and doctrines. More significantly, it will also be recalled that the UK courts' discharge of their obligations in the paradigm has been said by some commentators to have strained the core assumptions of constitutional orthodoxy.[88] Despite such arguments, UK courts have, for their part, consistently held that all decisions taken within the EU law paradigm have accorded fully with the elements of domestic orthodoxy and, in particular, the constitutional *grundnorm* of

[88] See, e.g., Wade at n. 1 above.

parliamentary sovereignty.[89] This point of emphasis, which has been much criticised in academic literature,[90] will be seen to have given rise to a sharp distinction, or "dualist divide", between the respective spheres of influence of EU law and domestic law.[91] And, although it is true that EU law itself conceives of domestic courts working within two paradigms of law, it will be argued that dualist orthodoxy has served to exaggerate presumed and actual differences between domestic and EU standards. It is this point of exaggeration that will be argued to have frustrated deeper integration.

The area in which the limiting influence of the dualist divide will be seen to have been most pervasive is principles of judicial review. In UK public law orthodoxy, the defining principle of judicial review has, for many years, been *Wednesbury* unreasonableness.[92] This principle is famously designed to minimise judicial involvement in the administrative decision-making process by allowing courts to impugn a decision only where that decision is ". . . so outrageous in its defiance of logic or of accepted moral standards that no sensible person who had applied his mind to the question could have arrived at it".[93] It is, however, a principle which has been subject to much criticism,[94] and one strand of the "internal" body of UK jurisprudence has seen the courts suggest that they will modify its application whenever administrative decisions impact upon an individual's fundamental rights.[95] This willingness to modify *Wednesbury* has been accompanied by

[89] See, e.g., *Macarthys Ltd* v. *Smith* [1979] 3 All ER 325, 329 (Lord Denning); *R* v. *Secretary of State for Transport, ex p Factortame (No 2)* [1991] 1 All ER 70, 107–8 (Lord Bridge); *R* v. *Secretary of State for Foreign and Commonwealth Affairs, ex p Rees-Mogg* [1994] 1 All ER 457, 470 (Lloyd LJ); and *R* v. *Ministry of Agriculture, Fisheries and Food, ex p First City Trading Limited* [1997] 1 CMLR 250, 268–9 (Laws J). And see now also Laws LJ's judgment in *Thoburn* v. *Sunderland CC* [2002] EWHC 195, para. 69 – "The fundamental legal basis of the United Kingdom's relationship with the EU rests with the domestic, not the European, legal powers" (although note further that Laws LJ's judgment should be read in the light of domestic debates about the relationship between Parliament and the courts. On the debates see ch. 2).

[90] For example, M Hunt n. 21 above.

[91] See, e.g., *Bulmer* v. *Bollinger* [1974] 3 WLR 202, 209 (Lord Denning); *R* v. *Ministry of Agriculture, Fisheries and Food, ex p First City Trading Limited* [1997] 1 CMLR 250 (Laws J); and *R* v. *Secretary of State for Health, ex p Imperial Tobacco Ltd* [2001] 1 All ER 850, 856 ff (Lord Hoffman).

[92] *Associated Provincial Picture Houses* v. *Wednesbury Corporation* [1948] 1 KB 223.

[93] *Council of Civil Service Unions* v. *Minister for the Civil Service* [1985] AC 374, 410–11 (Lord Diplock). The original formulation of *Wednesbury* was given by Lord Greene MR: "It is true to say that, if a decision on a competent matter is so unreasonable that no reasonable authority could ever have come to it, then the courts can interfere." See [1948] 1 KB 223, 230. On *Wednesbury* see further Irvine at n. 49 above.

[94] For example, J Jowell and A Lester, "Beyond *Wednesbury*: Substantive Principles of Administrative Law" [1987] *PL* 368.

[95] See, e.g., *R* v. *Secretary of State for the Home Department, ex p Bugdaycay* [1987] AC 514, 531 (Lord Bridge); *R* v. *Secretary of State for the Home Department, ex p Brind* [1991] 2 WLR 588, 592 (Lord Bridge); *R* v. *Ministry of Defence, ex p Smith* [1995] 4 All ER 427, 445 (Simon Brown LJ – see also Simon Brown LJ's ruling in *R* v. *Coventry City Council, ex p*

debate about how far, or whether, the UK courts should formally recognise the proportionality principle as a ground of review in domestic law. The proportionality principle, which is central to the workings of both the EU and ECHR legal orders,[96] is understood to afford courts greater opportunity for scrutinising decisions. Despite the potentially informative value of the principle, the courts have previously demonstrated a reluctance to allow proportionality formally to spill over into domestic practice.[97] This reluctance may, at one level, be attributed to the fact that not all judges would wish to see their institutional role developed through the importation of the proportionality principle.[98] But beyond individual judicial preferences, the courts' reluctance may more generally be understood with reference to the dualist divide. The process of legal cross-fertilisation requires courts to structure the process of borrowing around set institutional considerations. By identifying dualist orthodoxy as the basis for their decisions within the EU law paradigm, the courts have, either by design or default, emphasised that domestic law and EU law occupy functionally different spheres and perform institutionally separate tasks. The consequence has been that the process of borrowing has remained unduly constrained, even though internal processes of change may have had much to gain from the comparative experience of European law.[99]

It is in this context that the passage of the Human Rights Act and the emergence of debate about the institutional role of the courts will be argued to be of significance. At an obvious level, the significance of the Act will be seen to lie in the fact that it gives domestic effect to (most of)

Phoenix Aviation [1995] 3 All ER 37); *R* v. *Cambridge Health Authority, ex p Child B* [1995] 25 BMLR 5 (Laws J); and *R* v. *Lord Saville, ex p A* [1999] 4 All ER 860 (Lord Woolf MR).

[96] On its position in EU law see G de Búrca, "Proportionality in EC Law" (1993) 13 *YEL* 105. On its position in ECHR jurisprudence see, e.g., M A Eissen, "The Principle of Proportionality in the Case-Law of the European Court of Human Rights" in R StJ Macdonald *et al* (eds), *The European System for the Protection of Human Rights* (Martinus Nijhoff, Dordrecht, 1993), p 125.

[97] See, most famously, *R* v. *Secretary of State for the Home Department, ex p Brind* [1991] 2 WLR 588. For other judicial statements endorsing the enduring centrality of *Wednesbury* see, e.g., *R* v. *Secretary of State for the Environment, ex p NALGO* [1993] Admin. LR 785; *R* v. *Secretary of State for the Home Department, ex p Hargreaves* [1997] 1 All ER 397; *R* v. *Radio Authority, ex p Bull* [1997] 2 All ER 561; and *Tesco Stores Ltd* v. *Secretary of State for the Environment* [1995] 1 WLR 759.

[98] See, e.g., *R* v. *Secretary of State for the Home Department, ex p Brind* [1991] 2 WLR 588, 609–10 (Lord Lowry) and *R* v. *Cambridge Health Authority, ex p Child B* [1995] 2 All ER 129 (Sir Thomas Bingham MR, overturning Laws J's ruling at first instance).

[99] Although this is not to suggest that all aspects of EU law and the ECHR would benefit the domestic order. For a critical analysis of EU law see, e.g., C Harlow, "European Administrative Law and the Global Challenge" in P Craig and G de Búrca (eds), n. 19 above, p 261. On the ECHR see, e.g., D Oliver, "A Negative Aspect to Legitimate Expectations" [1998] *PL* 558. And see further the "margin of appreciation" in ECHR jurisprudence, considered in ch. 3.

the ECHR,[100] thereby finally bringing to an end the incongruous situation whereby the international standard could not be directly enforced in domestic proceedings. But beyond its obvious impact, it will also be argued that the Act may facilitate a process of increased legal cross-fertilisation in a number of more subtle ways. The courts have, for example, already recognised the proportionality principle as a ground of review in some cases arising under the Human Rights Act,[101] and it will be argued that such recognition of the principle could lead to a much deeper and more general process of adaptation. Likewise, it will be argued that judicial use of the ECHR may also lead the courts to have greater recourse to EU law. This point of argument is based upon an understanding that it will become increasingly difficult, and potentially false, for the courts to differentiate between the respective spheres of influence of domestic law, EU law and the law of the ECHR. It has already been noted above that the ECHR informs the body of EU law which feeds into the UK legal order, and there further exists the possibility that some Human Rights Act cases will raise issues which are governed by common law principle and practice as well as that of the EU legal order.[102] The point which will be argued, therefore, is not just that the Human Rights Act will be seen to be part of a new institutional environment, but also that the new environment could lead the courts to adjudicate beyond dualist divides and in a manner that recognises the interdependent relationship between domestic law, EU law and the law of the ECHR.

In developing this argument, the following chapter of the book considers in greater depth the "internal" dynamics of the UK legal order. It does so by focusing on existing debate about the conceptual foundations of judicial review. The development of a more active review jurisdiction has led to intense debate about whether the legitimacy of the courts' supervisory jurisdiction derives solely from judicial use of the common law or from more orthodox understandings that the purpose of judicial review is to give effect to Parliament's intentions.[103] As such, it will be suggested that there is emerging among the judiciary an increased willingness to emphasise that it is judicial use of the common law that is solely responsible for many developments in judicial review. Judicial recourse to the fluid qualities of the common law is, as will become apparent, central to the book's wider argument, and chapter two examines how emerging approaches afford the courts a greater degree of institutional autonomy than that

[100] See n. 4 above.

[101] See, e.g., *R (on the application of Alconbury Developments Ltd)* v. *Secretary of State for the Environment, Transport and the Regions* [2001] 2 All ER 929, 976 (Lord Slynn) and *R* v. *Secretary of State for the Home Department, ex p Daly*, [2001] 3 All ER 433.

[102] See, e.g., *R* v. *Secretary of State for the Home Department, ex p McQuillan* [1995] 4 All ER 400 and *Gough* v. *Chief Constable of Derbyshire Constabulary* [2001] 4 All ER 289.

[103] C Forsyth (ed.), n. 47 above.

accorded to them by constitutional orthodoxy. Such approaches are then said to provide the more satisfactory means of understanding past developments in judicial review as well as those that may potentially be effected in light of the passage of the Human Rights Act. Highlighting how the Act leaves open, or unresolved, a series of "internal" issues that will only be resolved by recourse to the common law, the chapter argues that orthodox understandings of the institutional balance of the State fail to recognise the true nature of the institutional role performed by the courts. In other words, the chapter suggests that a reliance on orthodoxy has the potential to impose undue constraints on judicial elaboration of the law, with this having an inimical effect on the courts' capacity to engage in lateral debates about the desirability, or otherwise, of borrowing European principle and practice.

Chapter three then considers the dynamics of the wider body of European law which UK courts may wish to borrow principle and practice from. The chapter focuses in the first instance on the dynamics of the body of EU law that feed into the domestic legal order. Here, the chapter introduces several key features of the EU legal order which are central to discussion in later chapters dealing more specifically with the question of legal cross-fertilisation. But beyond providing an overview of some of the core constitutional features of EU law, the chapter also provides a critical analysis of the role of fundamental rights standards in the supranational order. The function of this point of analysis is two-fold. First, it provides an insight into some of the problems that can attend the interaction of different bodies of law.[104] Second, it also serves to introduce the nature of the relationship which EU law has with the ECHR, a point of discussion that likewise lends itself to a more in-depth analysis of the international human rights standard. The chapter concludes by examining more closely some features of ECHR jurisprudence which are likely to be central to the process of change effected by the Human Rights Act.

The argument that the courts' approach to legal borrowing has, in previous years, been limited by orthodox institutional considerations is developed in chapters four to six. Chapter four provides an analysis of the courts' orthodox justification for the discharge of their obligations in the EU law paradigm, while chapter five further develops the argument that the borrowing of principles of judicial review has been inhibited by the existence of the dualist divide. Chapter six thereafter considers the extent

[104] The development by the ECJ of a body of fundamental rights jurisprudence is often said to have been prompted, at least in part, by the German Constitutional Court's refusal in *Internationale Handelsgesellschaft* ([1974] 2 CMLR 540) to recognise the supremacy of EU law. The German Court's refusal was prompted by concerns that EU law was unable to afford fundamental rights a standard of protection comparable to that guaranteed by the German Basic Law. But see also the German Court's judgment in *Re Wünsche Handelsgesellschaft* [1987] 3 CMLR 225.

to which the courts have been willing to develop the domestic law of remedies by reference to EU law. Here, it is argued on the one hand that the courts have tended to permit instances of cross-fertilisation because of UK law's historic emphasis on remedies.[105] On the other hand, however, the chapter also suggests that the adoption of specific forms of remedial relief, while welcome, cannot ensure full and equal remedial protection of the individual. Arguing that the protection of the individual also depends upon the harmonisation of legal principles that determine whether there is entitlement to the remedy, the chapter maintains that harmonisation will only be achieved when the courts view European law and domestic law as equal parts of an interlocking whole. By way of illustrating the point, the chapter concludes by examining the impact that the ECHR has started to have on damages actions against public authorities.[106]

In the final chapters, the book develops more fully the argument that judicial elaboration of the Human Rights Act should be characterised by a deeper process of integration engaging domestic law, EU law and the ECHR. Chapter seven begins by suggesting that the Human Rights Act can best be read as part of an ongoing and wider process of change in which the dynamics of UK public law and European law should only be seen as mutually reinforcing. On this basis the chapter then assesses the prospects for formal recognition of proportionality as a central principle of domestic law, with chapter eight forwarding some more general comments about the likely future dynamics of legal integration.

[105] See, e.g., *Ashby* v. *White* [1703] 2 Ld Raym 938, 953 (Holt CJ); *Abbott* v. *Sullivan* [1952] 1 KB 189, 200 (Denning LJ); and *Kingdom of Spain* v. *Christie, Manson & Woods Ltd* [1986] 1 WLR 1120, 1129 (Browne Wilkinson V-C). The cases where integration has occurred are *Woolwich Building Society* v. *Inland Revenue Commissioners (No 2)* [1992] 3 WLR 366 and *M* v. *Home Office* [1993] 3 WLR 433.

[106] Consideration is given to the importance of the ECtHR's judgment in *Osman* v. *UK* [1999] 1 FLR 193 as considered by the domestic courts in *Barrett* v. *Enfield London* BC [1999] 3 All ER 193 (but see now also the ECtHR judgment in *Z* v. *UK*, judgment of 10 May 2001). It should be noted that some of the remedies examined in chapter 6, namely restitution and damages actions, may more accurately be described as private law rather than public law remedies. Nevertheless, the fact that the cases considered concern actions against public authorities, coupled with the fact that damages actions often raise questions of where to locate the line that divides "public" from "private", is taken to bring the issues generally within the realm of public law.

2

The Dynamics of UK Public Law

1. INTRODUCTION

The internal process that has seen UK courts develop the body of domestic administrative law is often taken to have its origins in a series of cases dating from the 1960s.[1] It is, however, a process that has been at its most active in more recent years. The final two decades of last century were characterised by judicial determination both to expand the reach of judicial review into the realm of non-statutory and private power[2] and to engage more readily in the review of decisions taken by central government ministers.[3] This development of the law, which has not been without difficulty, was prompted by a variety of considerations. The realisation that public power can assume many different forms, for example, quite clearly informed the courts' decision to expand the boundaries of the supervisory jurisdiction.[4] And the perception that judicial review can perform a democratising function underpinned in part the courts' willingness to review the legality of central government decisions.[5] The implementation of Conservative Party policy during 1979–97 was often

[1] Most famously, *Ridge* v. *Baldwin* [1964] AC 40; *Padfield* v. *Minister of Agriculture* [1968] AC 997; and *Anisminic* v. *Foreign Compensation Commission* [1969] 2 AC 147. These cases were described by J F Garner as some of the first moves towards a "coherent system of administrative procedure" in the UK. See, "Administrative Law – A Step Forward?" (1968) 31 *MLR* 446. But note also that Sir Stephen Sedley has suggested that such cases merely saw the reintroduction of principle and practice applied previously by UK courts. See generally, "The Sound of Silence: Constitutional Law without a Constitution" (1994) 110 *LQR* 270.

[2] See, as discussed below, *Council of Civil Service Unions* v. *Minister for the Civil Service* [1985] 1 AC 374 (exercises of the Royal prerogative) and *R* v. *Panel on Take-overs and Mergers, ex p Datafin plc* [1987] QB 815 (decisions taken by non-statutory self-regulating bodies).

[3] See, e.g., *M* v. *Home Office* [1993] 3 WLR 433; *R* v. *Secretary of State for Foreign Affairs, ex p World Development Movement Ltd.* [1995] 1 WLR 386; *R* v. *Secretary of State for the Home Department, ex p Fire Brigade's Union* [1995] 2 WLR 646; and *R* v. *Home Secretary, ex p Venables and Thompson* [1997] 1 All ER 327.

[4] See, e.g., *Re Sherlock and Morris* [1996] NIJB 80.

[5] See Lord Irvine of Lairg, "Judges and Decision-Makers: The Theory and Practice of *Wednesbury* Review" (1996] *PL* 59. It should be noted, however, that Lord Irvine is sceptical of how far judicial review legitimately may be used as a democratising medium. See *ibid*.

associated with the by-passing of Parliament and administrative procedures,[6] and judicial review soon came to be seen as an additional institutional filter that could monitor executive excess.[7] The development of the law, therefore, was to become increasingly politicised as the courts sought to ensure that government decisions did not escape scrutiny for lack of a suitably affected applicant.[8]

The academic and judicial debate that has accompanied the evolution of the domestic order has focused on the relevance to judicial review of the institutional assumptions associated with the ultra vires doctrine. The ultra vires doctrine is, in its traditional form, premised upon an understanding of judicial review as a mechanism for controlling exercises of statutory power. It is, moreover, a doctrine that is born of rigid adherence to orthodox notions of the separation of powers and of the courts as implementers of the sovereign Parliament's intentions.[9] The debate about the doctrine concerns its capacity to accommodate judge-led developments that obviously depart from its statute-centric and restraint-based approach to judicial review. Proponents of constitutional orthodoxy have argued that the doctrine's core assumptions can and, as a matter of constitutional necessity, must be modified by way of justifying the expansion of judicial review.[10] But other commentators equally have suggested that attempts to modify the doctrine obfuscate the true nature of the courts' supervisory

[6] See further P McAuslan and J F McEldowney (eds), *Law, Legitimacy and the Constitution* (Sweet and Maxwell, London, 1985) and C Graham and T Prosser (eds), *Waiving the Rules: The Constitution under Thatcherism* (Open University Press, Milton Keynes, 1988).

[7] H Woolf, "Public Law – Private Law: Why the Divide? A Personal View" [1986] *PL* 220, 221–2. On the "politics" of judicial review see A P Le Sueur, "The Judicial Review Debate: From Partnership to Friction" (1996) 31 *Government and Opposition* 221.

[8] See, e.g., *R* v. *Inland Revenue Commissioners, ex p National Federation of Self-Employed and Small Businesses Ltd* [1982] AC 617, 644 (Lord Diplock); *R* v. *Secretary of State for Foreign Affairs and Commonwealth Affairs, ex p Rees-Mogg* [1994] 1 All ER 457; *Equal Opportunities Commission and Another* v. *Secretary of State for Employment* [1994] 1 All ER 910; *R* v. *Inspectorate of Pollution, ex p Greenpeace Ltd (No 2)* [1994] 4 All ER 328; *R* v. *Secretary of State for Foreign and Commonwealth Affairs, ex p World Development Movement Ltd* [1995] 1 WLR 386; and *R* v. *Secretary of State for the Home Department, ex p Fire Brigade's Union* [1995] 2 WLR 275. See further G Anthony and J Morison, "The Role of Judges in the Formation of Public Law: Activism or Autolimitation?" (1998) 10 *ERPL* 977.

[9] "Having no written constitution on which he can fall back, the judge must in every case be able to demonstrate that he is carrying out the will of Parliament as expressed in the statute conferring the power. He is on safe ground only where he can show that the offending act is outside the power". See H W R Wade and C F Forsyth, *Administrative Law* (Clarendon Press, Oxford, 7th edn, 1994) p 44.

[10] For example, C Forsyth, "Of Fig Leaves and Fairy Tales: The *Ultra Vires* Doctrine, the Sovereignty of Parliament and Judicial Review" (1996) 55 *CLJ* 122 and M Elliott, "The *Ultra Vires* Doctrine in a Constitutional Setting: Still the Central Principle of Administrative Law" (1999) 58 *CLJ* 129.

jurisdiction.[11] More specifically, it has been argued that orthodox understandings of the institutional role of courts not only misrepresent what occurs in practice but also serve, at a conceptual level, to constrain debate about the evolutionary nature of the common law. The result has been for there to emerge an alternative model of review that seeks to identify broader developments in judicial review with more flexible understandings of the courts' knowledge and use of common law principle and practice.[12]

This chapter surveys in greater depth the debate about the relative merits of the modified ultra vires and common law models of review. It suggests that the common law model may increasingly come to dominate thinking in UK public law. Although the models share many features,[13] they are, as implied above, ultimately divided over the nature of the institutional role that should be played by the courts. In short, while the ultra vires model conceives of the courts performing an institutional role that is wholly subordinate to that of the sovereign Parliament, the common law model conceives of the courts working more from a position of institutional partnership with Parliament.[14] In this latter model, the courts are free to develop judicial review (and the law more generally) subject only to the terms of existing statutes and Parliament's final power to override any development of the law through express legislative enactment. Such understandings of the courts discharging a partly autonomous law-making function are central to this book's wider arguments about UK public law's amenability to European legal integration, hence the primary objective of the chapter is to identify those features of the common law model that might be said to lend themselves to an increased process of borrowing. And, while it is true that questions of borrowing also arise in areas of law beyond the context of judicial review,[15] it is intended that the chapter's examination of the ultra vires debate will raise institutional themes that are more generally prescriptive of the courts' capacity to borrow European principle and practice.

[11] For example, H Woolf, "Droit Public – English Style" [1995] *PL* 57 and P Craig, "Ultra Vires and the Foundations of Judicial Review" (1998) 57 *CLJ* 63.

[12] For the strongest statement in this regard see J Laws, "Law and Democracy" [1995] *PL* 72.

[13] T R S Allan, "The Rule of Law as the Foundation of Judicial Review" in C Forsyth (ed.), *Judicial Review and the Constitution* (Hart Publishing, Oxford, 2000), p 413 .

[14] See, e.g., Sir Stephen Sedley's imagery of "bi-polar sovereignty" in "Human Rights: A Twenty-first Century Agenda" [1995] *PL* 386, 389.

[15] See further ch. 6.

2. THE ULTRA VIRES DEBATE AND THE CHANGING NATURE OF JUDICIAL REVIEW

The ways in which the ultra vires doctrine reflects orthodox understandings of the institutional balance of the State are manifold. In its traditional form, the doctrine was predicated on notions of the absolute sovereignty of Parliament and of the need for courts to give effect to specific statutory statements of Parliament's intentions.[16] This emphasis on Parliamentary sovereignty, which was vouchsafed by a judicial refusal to prescribe any limits to Parliament's powers,[17] led the courts to develop a series of juridical techniques that minimised the scope for judicial involvement in the legislative and administrative processes. The courts' approach to the interpretation of legislation, for example, prioritised literal interpretative techniques as a means of ensuring that the courts did not substitute their policy preferences for those of the legislature.[18] Likewise, where Parliament had delegated power to subordinate bodies, the courts emphasised that they would only intervene in the decision-making process when it was self-evident that the recipient of a power had transgressed the boundaries of the power delegated to them.[19] In other words, the institutional role of the courts in review proceedings was limited to implementing the "top-down" preferences of Parliament[20] and characterised by the democratic imperative of judicial self-restraint.[21]

The modified ultra vires model, which exists as an alternative both to the traditional ultra vires and common law models of review, retains many of these points of emphasis, although they have been revised in an attempt

[16] See Wade and Forsyth n. 9 above.

[17] "It is often said that it would be unconstitutional for the UK Parliament to do certain things, meaning that the moral, political and other reasons against doing them are so strong that most people would regard it as highly improper if Parliament did these things. But that does not mean that it is beyond the power of Parliament to do such things. If Parliament chose to do any of them the courts would not hold the Act of Parliament invalid." *Madzimbamuto* v. *Lardner-Burke* [1969] 1 AC 645, 723 (Lord Reid).

[18] See, e.g., *Duport Steels Ltd* v. *Sirs* [1980] 1 WLR 142, 157 (Lord Diplock). The courts' preference for literal interpretative techniques sometimes gave rise to controversial outcomes. See, e.g., *Bromley LBC* v. *Greater London Council* [1983] 1 AC 768 as discussed in J A G Griffith, "Judicial Decision-Making in Public Law" [1985] *PL* 564.

[19] An understanding most famously associated with the standard of *Wednesbury* review. See *Associated Provincial Picture Houses* v. *Wednesbury Corporation* [1948] 1 KB 223, 230 (Lord Greene MR).

[20] See further Roger Cotterrell's *imperium* model of law as developed in *Law's Community: Legal Theory in Sociological Perspective* (Clarendon Press, Oxford, 1995), ch. 11 and "Judicial Review and Legal Theory" in H Genn and G Richardson (eds), *Administrative Law and Government Action* (Clarendon Press, Oxford, 1994), p 13. It should be noted that Cotterrell is sharply critical of the manner in which the *imperium* model of law impacts in practice.

[21] An understanding recently endorsed by Lord Irvine of Lairg in n. 5 above.

to accommodate the emergence of a more searching, and far-reaching, supervisory jurisdiction. The principal revision has seen the doctrine adopt more flexible notions of general legislative intent and incorporate a greater appreciation of the role and relevance of both the common law and the concept of the rule of law. These changes were deemed necessary to ensure that the core constitutional construct of legislative supremacy remained unaffected by the development of a more interventionist judicial role. Accordingly, while the traditional ultra vires model conceives of the relationship between Parliament and the courts in rigid terms, the modified model conceives of the relationship in somewhat more pragmatic terms that, nonetheless, continue to emphasise the role of the courts as implementers of Parliament's intentions: "This . . . has important implications . . . The power of the courts is not unlimited. They do not 'have the power they say they have'. In truth, the courts . . . have the power which the constitutional order says they have".[22]

The suggestion that all judicial development of the law must be traced to Parliament's intentions is rejected in the common law model of review. Indeed, for proponents of the common law model, it is entirely fictitious to argue that each and every legal development could have been foreseen by Parliament. The common law model is, as stated, structured around an understanding that the courts draw on their experience and knowledge of the common law by way of reacting to new legal challenges. This emphasis on the courts performing a reactive role is considered to break the link between parliamentary intent and judicial decision-making precisely because it is unlikely that Parliament could foresee every new legal circumstance that would come before the courts or, more significantly, how the courts would react to those circumstances. The essential logic of this argument has been used by both Lord Woolf and Sir Stephen Sedley by way of justifying the extension of judicial review to include various forms of non-statutory and private power.[23] But the most explicit extra-judicial statement of the common law model's virtues came with the publication of Sir John Laws' article "Law and Democracy".[24] Here, Sir John Laws argued in characteristically forceful manner that it is wholly unrealistic to conceive of the courts as mere implementers of Parliament's intentions. Taking as an example the origins of the principles of administrative law used by the courts in judicial review proceedings, he stated:

> "It cannot be suggested that all these principles, which represent much of the bedrock of modern administrative law, were suddenly interwoven into the

[22] M Elliott (1999) 58 *CLJ* 129, 133. The quotation within this extract paraphrases Sir John Laws' arguments in "Law and Democracy" [1995] *PL* 72.

[23] See respectively, "Droit Public – English Style" [1995] *PL* 57, 65 and "The Sound of Silence: Constitutional Law without a Constitution" (1994) 110 *LQR* 270, 285.

[24] [1995] *PL* 72.

> legislature's intentions in the 1960s and 70s and onwards, in which period they have been articulated and enforced by the courts. They are, categorically, judicial creations. They owe neither their existence nor their acceptance to the will of the legislature. They have nothing to do with the intention of Parliament, save as a fig-leaf to cover their true origins. We do not need the fig-leaf anymore".[25]

The response which proponents of the modified ultra vires model have made to these arguments has been mixed. At one level, they accept Sir John Laws' arguments that the principles of administrative law are common law judicial creations. At another level, however, they equally contend that any suggestion that the creation of the principles was not sanctioned by Parliament amounts to a judicial challenge to the defining democratic value of legislative supremacy. It is at this point, therefore, that the modified ultra vires model invokes notions of general, as opposed to specific, legislative intent informing the development of administrative law. The general legislative intent is said to reside either in Parliament's concern that the rule of law be upheld through the development of principles of administrative law,[26] or in the fact that the sovereign Parliament implicitly has sanctioned such development of the law by virtue of its decision not to legislate in a manner which reverses legal developments.[27] Either way, there remains the democratic imperative of tracing the emergence of the principles to Parliament's intentions.

The notion of general legislative intent also informs the modified model's approach to justifying the expansion of the supervisory jurisdiction to include non-statutory and private power. Mark Elliott, for example, has again sought to rationalise such expansion of the review jurisdiction by reference to Parliament's assumed desire to ensure that all types of power are exercised in accordance with the rule of law.[28] And Christopher Forsyth has suggested that the origins of the extension of the courts' supervisory jurisdiction to private bodies can be found in a line of common law jurisprudence that prohibited the unreasonable exercise of monopolistic power.[29] This line of case law, which is argued to have evolved against a backdrop of parliamentary acquiescence, saw the courts attempt to regulate monopolistic power where it was considered that there existed a public interest in doing so. Thus, while Forsyth emphasises the enduring

[25] *Ibid*, 78–9. On Sir John Laws' approach to the institutional role of the courts see further, e.g., "Is the High Court the Guardian of Fundamental Rights?" [1993] *PL* 59. But see also J A G Griffith, "The Brave New World of Sir John Laws" (2000) 63 *MLR* 159.

[26] See generally M Elliott, "The *Ultra Vires* Doctrine in a Constitutional Setting", n. 10 above.

[27] See C Forsyth, "Of Fig Leaves and Fairy Tales" n. 10 above, 134–5.

[28] See generally n. 26 above.

[29] See n. 27 above, 124–7. Forsyth acknowledges that he borrows this line of argument from P Craig, "Constitutions, Property and Regulation" [1991] *PL* 538.

relevance of the ultra vires doctrine relative to the control of statutory powers, he considers it perfectly acceptable to ground part of the courts' supervisory jurisdiction in the common law.

> ". . .(R)ecognition that the common law provides the basis for judicial review in some circumstances is not an admission of the failure of *ultra vires*. *Ultra vires* retains its central position as far as decisions made under statutory powers are concerned. Moreover, it should be remarked for the avoidance of doubt that recognition of a common law basis for part of judicial review does not challenge legislative supremacy; it is always open to the legislature to intervene to regulate the position".[30]

Forsyth's willingness to situate the courts' supervisory jurisdiction partly within the common law and partly within the ultra vires doctrine has been criticised by Paul Craig.[31] Although Craig welcomes Forsyth's willingness to recognise the role and relevance of the common law, he cautions that the opening up of a split doctrinal justification for the basis of judicial review is conceptually undesirable and practically problematic. For Craig, it is preferable to ground judicial review solely in the evolutionary medium of the common law as regulated by express legislative enactment. This doctrinal basis, Craig argues, has two important features. First, and drawing on the logic of some of Forsyth's comments, Craig argues that the common law model need not necessarily be seen to undermine understandings that final sovereign power rests with the legislature: "If the omnipotent Parliament does not like (a legal development) then it is open to it to make this explicitly clear . . . If it does so the courts will accept this . . . There is therefore nothing in the common law model which involves a strong challenge to sovereignty."[32] The second important feature is then said to lie in the fact that the common law model affords the courts the same degree of latitude for developing judicial review as they enjoy in relation to

[30] Note 27 above, 126–7. Forsyth's most recent contribution is, "Heat and Light: A Plea for Reconciliation" in Forsyth (ed.), n. 13 above, p 393.

[31] "*Ultra Vires* and the Foundations of Judicial Review" (1998) 57 *CLJ* 63, 77–8.

[32] "Competing Models of Judicial Review" [1999] *PL* 428, 437–8. The difference between Craig and Forsyth's positions, while subtle, is of crucial importance. Forsyth considers Parliament's decision not to intervene when it has the power to do so to be indicative of Parliament's implied intentions being upheld. For Craig, by contrast, Parliament's ultimate power of intervention is relevant only insofar as it relates to Parliament's sovereignty, not its intentions. It should further be noted, however, that Craig has conceded that he has doubts about the enduring relevance of traditional notions of the supremacy of the Westminster Parliament. See, "*Ultra Vires* and the Foundations of Judicial Review" 63, 86. And see further the extra-judicial pronouncements of those judges who have stated that they would, under given circumstances, be prepared to frustrate the operation of a statute, e.g., Sir H Woolf, "Droit Public – English Style" [1995] *PL* 57, 69 and Sir J Laws, "Law and Democracy" [1995] *PL* 72, 81.

various areas of private law[33]; as will be argued below, it is this feature of the model that enables the courts more easily to reinvent judicial review in response to changing social, economic and political circumstances.

3. THE ROYAL PREROGATIVE

The expansion of the supervisory jurisdiction to include the review of non-statutory powers first occurred in relation to exercises of the royal prerogative. The Royal prerogative has been described as:

> "a residue of miscellaneous fields of law in which the executive government retains decision-making powers that are not dependent on any statutory authorisation but nevertheless have consequences on the private rights or legitimate expectations of other persons".[34]

The courts' historical approach to reviewing exercises of the royal prerogative denied that they enjoyed any power to do so.[35] In terms of the traditional ultra vires doctrine, of course, this approach could be attributed to the fact that judicial review attended only the exercise of statutory powers. But there were other institutional considerations that also militated against judicial involvement. In particular, the courts' understanding that the prerogative powers were of a political nature meant that the prerogative was, as a minimum understanding, considered ill-suited to judicial control:[36] "The courts will inquire into whether a particular prerogative power exists or not and, if it does exist, into its extent. But once the existence and the extent of a power are established to the satisfaction of the court, the court cannot inquire into the propriety of its exercise".[37]

The case that first heralded the courts' willingness to depart from this position was *Council of Civil Service Unions and Others* v. *Minister for the*

[33] See, "Competing Models of Judicial Review" 432–5. It should be noted that Craig's argument on this point is implied, i.e. it is made by reference to the perceived shortcomings of the modified *ultra vires* model rather than by explicit reference to the advantages of the common law model.

[34] *Council of Civil Service Unions* v. *Minister for the Civil Service* [1985] AC 374, 409–10 (Lord Diplock). *Defining* the Royal prerogative, however, is more problematic. See S Payne, "The Royal Prerogative" in M Sunkin and S Payne (eds.), *The Nature of the Crown: A Legal and Political Analysis* (Oxford University Press, Oxford, 1999) pp 77, 78–87.

[35] *Attorney-General* v. *De Keyser's Royal Hotel Ltd* [1920] AC 508. On the historical position, see further P Craig, "Prerogative, Precedent and Power" in C Forsyth and I Hare (eds), *The Golden Metwand and the Crooked Cord: Essays on Public Law in Honour of Sir William Wade QC* (Clarendon Press, Oxford, 1998), p 65.

[36] See, e.g., *Gouriet* v. *Union of Post Office Workers* [1977] 3 All ER 70.

[37] *Council of Civil Service Unions* v. *Minister for the Civil Service* [1985] 1 AC 374, 398 (Lord Fraser).

Civil Service (the *GCHQ* case).[38] The case arose when the Council of Civil Service Unions sought a judicial review of the Prime Minister's decision to deny trade union membership to civil servants employed at Government Communication Headquarters (GCHQ was responsible for the security of the UK's military and official communications – restrictions on union membership were imposed after various strike actions at GCHQ had caused disruption). The decision in question had been issued as an oral instruction on the basis of the Civil Service Order in Council 1982 and, as the Order in Council had been made under the royal prerogative, the decision had its origins in an indirect exercise of the prerogative powers. The application to the court argued that, irrespective of its origins, the decision should be overturned as it had been made in breach of the applicant's legitimate expectation that they would be consulted about any change in employment conditions.[39] Lawyers representing the Government argued not only that the basis of the decision rendered it immune from review, but also that the sensitive nature of the work carried on at GCHQ allowed national security considerations to trump the applicants' stated interests.

The Government's arguments on the basis of national security were ultimately to prove determinative of the case. However, the Government's related argument that all direct and indirect exercises of the prerogative powers are immune from review was rejected by the House of Lords. While their Lordships recognised that there are some areas of the prerogative powers that are, by virtue of their subject matter, inherently ill-suited to judicial control,[40] they recognised that there are other areas of the prerogative powers that should be regarded as open to review. The concept that their Lordships introduced by way of trying to identify such areas was justiciability. Although the concept of justiciability may be criticised as

[38] [1985] 1 AC 374. But see also *R* v. *Criminal Injuries Compensation Board, ex p Lain* [1967] 3 WLR 348 and *Laker Airways Ltd* v. *Department of Trade* [1977] 2 All ER 182, 192 (Lord Denning).

[39] There was an established practice at GCHQ of consultation between unions and management about important alterations in the terms and conditions of employment of the staff. On this occasion, no consultation took place. On legitimate expectations in UK law see ch. 5.

[40] "Prerogative powers such as those relating to the making of treaties, the defence of the realm, the prerogative of mercy, the grant of honours, the dissolution of Parliament and the appointment of ministers as well as others are not, I think, susceptible to judicial review because their nature and subject matter are such as not to be amenable to the judicial process. The courts are not the place wherein to determine whether a treaty should be concluded or the armed forces disposed in a particular manner or Parliament dissolved on one date rather than another" [1985] 1 AC 374, 418 (Lord Roskill). On the courts' approach the review of the treaty making power, see *Blackburn* v. *Attorney General* [1971] 2 All ER 1380; *ex p Molyneaux* [1986] 1 WLR 331; and *R* v. *Secretary of State for Foreign and Commonwealth Affairs, ex p Rees-Mogg* [1994] 1 All ER 457.

malleable,[41] its use by the House in *GCHQ* enabled their Lordships to shift the focus of review away from narrow "source of power" (i.e. statute) considerations towards more pragmatic considerations of the subject matter of a decision and the manner in which a decision impacts on individual rights. For their Lordships, therefore, the decision at hand would have been reviewed had it not been for the existence of national security concerns:

> "If the executive instead of acting under a statutory power acts under a prerogative power . . . so as to affect the rights of the citizen, I am unable to see, subject to what I shall say later, that there is any logical reason why the fact that the source of the power is the prerogative and not statute should today deprive the citizen of the right to challenge the manner of its exercise which he would possess were the source of the power statutory. In either case the act in question is the act of the executive".[42]

The concept of justiciability was to be quickly and more fully developed by the courts. In *ex p Everett*,[43] Taylor LJ sub-divided prerogative powers into "matters of high policy" and other matters. Matters of high policy were said to include making treaties, making the law, the dissolution of Parliament, and mobilising the armed forces. For his Lordship, "those matters, and no doubt a number of others, are not justiciable".[44] But beyond ring-fencing areas of power ill-suited to judicial control, his Lordship also emphasised that, where an individual's rights are affected by an administrative decision taken on the basis of the prerogative powers (*Everett* concerned a decision not to issue a passport to a suspected criminal living in Spain), the decision at hand should be subject to review. And such concerns for protecting directly affected individual rights were also apparent in the Divisional Court's judgment in *ex p Bentley*,[45] this a case involving the review of exercises of the prerogative of mercy. Here, the court held that, as the prerogative of mercy is an important feature of the

[41] See further A P Le Sueur, "Justifying Judicial Caution: Jurisdiction, Justiciability and Policy" in B Hadfield (ed.), *Judicial Review: A Thematic Approach* (Gill & Macmillan, Dublin, 1995), p 228.

[42] [1985] 1 AC 374, 417 (Lord Roskill). It should be noted that the courts will only review exercises of the royal prerogative by reference to the grounds of illegality and procedural impropriety – irrationality/*Wednesbury* unreasonableness is considered too intrusive: "decisions will generally involve the application of government policy. The reasons for the decision-maker taking one course rather than another do not normally involve questions which, if disputed, the judicial process is adapted to provide the right answer" (*per* Lord Diplock in *GCHQ* [1985] 1 AC 374, 411. See further *R* v. *Ministry of Defence, ex p Smith and others* [1995] 4 All ER 427).

[43] *R* v. *Secretary of State for Foreign and Commonwealth Affairs, ex p Everett* [1989] 1 All ER 655.

[44] [1989] 1 All ER 655, 660.

[45] *R* v. *Secretary of State for the Home Department, ex p Bentley* [1993] 4 All ER 443.

criminal justice system, decisions of the Home Secretary which may be wrong in law should, in principle, be open to review. Indeed, the Court's finding in this regard was highly significant as it made clear that the category of justiciable decisions should not be seen as closed. It had previously been suggested in the *GCHQ* case that the prerogative of mercy fell beyond the scope of judicial review.[46] But the Divisional Court in *Bentley* thought otherwise and, in doing so, it highlighted the fluid and adaptable nature of the supervisory jurisdiction: "We conclude therefore that some aspects of the exercise of the royal prerogative are amenable to the judicial process. We do not think that it is necessary for us to say more than this in the instant case. It will be for other courts to decide on a case-by-case basis whether the matter in question is reviewable or not".[47]

Within this emerging jurisprudence, the most controversial case concerning the review of the prerogative powers was *R* v. *Secretary of State for the Home Department, ex p Fire Brigades Union*.[48] The case arose when the Government sought to revise sections in the Criminal Justice Act 1988 that provided for changes to the structure of the Criminal Injuries Compensation Scheme. The Scheme had first been introduced in the UK under the prerogative powers and it had, until 1988, existed solely on that basis.[49] In 1988, however, the Government decided to place the Scheme on a statutory footing, with the relevant provisions being said to have legal force when the Home Secretary made an order to that effect.[50] Instead of making such order, the Home Secretary indicated in 1993 that the statutory scheme would not be brought into force and, acting on the basis of the prerogative powers, he replaced the existing non-statutory scheme with a less generous tariff scheme that likewise was to be non-statutory. As his decision meant that many individuals would likely receive considerably reduced compensation packages, a number of trade unions applied for judicial review on the ground that the Home Secretary had acted unlawfully by using the prerogative powers to by-pass statutory provisions which were not yet in force and which he was required by statute to activate.

The application was first heard by the Divisional Court which rejected the argument that the Home Secretary's decision to introduce the tariff scheme was unlawful. The Court of Appeal, however, accepted the applicant's arguments, its finding being upheld by the House of Lords. Although the House rejected the applicant's argument that the Home Secretary was

[46] See n. 40 above.

[47] [1993] 4 All ER 442, 453 (Watkins LJ).

[48] [1995] 2 WLR 464.

[49] On the amenability to review of decisions of the Criminal Injuries Compensation Board, see *R* v. *Criminal Injuries Compensation Board, ex p Lain* [1967] 3 WLR 348; *R* v. *Criminal Injuries Compensation Board, ex p Thompson and Crowe* [1984] 1 WLR 1234; and *R* v. *Criminal Injuries Compensation Board, ex P* [1995] 1 All ER 870.

[50] Section 171(1).

under a legally enforceable duty to activate the relevant statutory provisions at any particular time,[51] it decided by a 3 to 2 majority that he was under a continuing duty to consider whether to bring the statutory scheme into force. The lead judgment was delivered by Lord Browne-Wilkinson who, having stated that prerogative powers exist only to the extent that Parliament has not expressly or by implication extinguished them,[52] held that it would be "most surprising if . . . prerogative powers could be validly exercised so as to frustrate the will of Parliament as expressed in statute and, to an extent, to pre-empt the decision of Parliament whether or not to continue with the statutory scheme".[53] His Lordship's findings in this regard were vigorously opposed in the House's dissenting judgments, with Lord Mustill suggesting that "(S)ome of the arguments addressed would have the court push to the very boundaries of the distinction between court and Parliament established in, and recognised ever since, the Bill of Rights 1689".[54] But the majority of the House maintained that there existed the imperative of ensuring that the executive did not use the prerogative powers to usurp law-making functions which properly belong to Parliament. For that reason, "the decision to introduce the tariff scheme at a time when the statutory provisions and his power . . . were on the statutory book was unlawful and an abuse of the prerogative power.[55]

What does the *Fire Brigade's Union* decision reveal about the institutional role of the courts? Certainly there is much within the judgment that can be associated with the language and logic of the modified ultra vires model of review. The House of Lords' apparent desire to ensure that the terms of the Criminal Justice Act were observed was arguably reflective of orthodox understandings of the courts as implementers of the sovereign Parliament's will, with the House's control of the prerogative powers likewise indicating a concern to ensure that executive powers did not subsume powers properly belonging to the legislature. To that extent, the majority of the House may correctly be said to have "applied familiar rules of administrative law, albeit in a highly unusual context".[56]

Yet, beyond orthodox interpretations, *Fire Brigade's Union* might also be rationalised in terms consistent with the notion of institutional partnership that underpins the common law model of review. This is particularly true when the judgment is placed within its wider institutional context. Gabriele Ganz has suggested that the judgment saw the courts intervene

[51] [1995] 2 WLR 464, 472 (Lord Browne-Wilkinson).

[52] His Lordship cited *Attorney-General* v. *De Keyser's Royal Hotel Ltd* [1920] AC 508 on this point.

[53] [1995] 2 WLR 464, 473–4.

[54] [1995] 2 WLR 464, 488.

[55] [1995] 2 WLR 464, 473–6 (Lord Browne-Wilkinson).

[56] E Barendt, "Constitutional Law and the Criminal Injuries Compensation Scheme" [1995] *PL* 357.

"in the legislative process in order to uphold the supremacy of Parliament and (make) good the dysfunctions of the democratic process"[57] and, cast in these terms, *Fire Brigade's Union* arguably becomes less a straightforward case of judicial implementation of Parliament's intentions and more a case of judicial invention to control the executive and resurrect the primacy of statutory provisions. It has often been recognised that there are fundamental shortcomings with the system of parliamentary control of executive action in the Westminster Parliament,[58] and the fact that the House of Lords reacted creatively in *Fire Brigade's Union* might be said to be testimony to the inherent dynamism of the common law model. For some, the manifestation of such dynamism may amount to "an unwarrantable intrusion by the court into the political field and a usurpation of the function of Parliament".[59] For others, however, it may merely be representative of the courts' endeavours to bolster ailing democratic controls[60] and to ensure that the broader interests of legality are not subverted by problematic assumptions about the institutional balance of the State.

4. THE PUBLIC–PRIVATE DIVIDE

The expansion of the review jurisdiction to include the prerogative powers has been accompanied by parallel developments with regard to other areas of non-statutory and private power. Not only had the ultra vires doctrine's historic emphasis on statute created difficulties in relation to controlling the prerogative, it had also given rise to a potential legal shortfall relative to the control of other forms of "public" power. There had long existed many non-statutory self-regulating bodies that enjoyed far-reaching influence in areas of public interest[61] yet it was uncertain how far, if at all, the decision-making processes of such bodies were amenable to review. And the difficulties presented by a statute-centric approach were further highlighted as the policy preferences of the Conservative governments of 1979–97 were implemented.[62] Conservative Party policy was famously associated with the objective of "rolling back the frontiers of the State", and this led to a transfer of public power to the private sector through a legislative programme that, among other things, privatised state-owned industry and contracted-out various government functions.[63] Public power,

[57] "Criminal Injuries Compensation: The Constitutional Issue" (1996) 59 *MLR* 95, 100.

[58] See n. 6 above.

[59] [1995] 2 WLR 464, 468 (Lord Keith).

[60] See R Rawlings, "Courts and Interests" in I Loveland (ed.), *A Special Relationship? American Influences on Public Law in the UK* (Clarendon Press, Oxford, 1995), p 99, 101.

[61] For example, in the financial markets and the sporting worlds. See further below.

[62] M Freedland, "Government by Contract and Public Law" [1994] *PL* 86.

[63] On the reform programme, see J Morison and S Livingstone, *Reshaping Public Power: Northern Ireland and the British Constitutional Crisis* (Sweet & Maxwell, London, 1995),

it had become apparent, could assume many different forms that may not always exist within recognised public law parameters.

The courts' response to the need to control the manifold forms of public power has, at one and the same time, been both inventive and beset by conceptual difficulties. Case law has, for example, seen the introduction of a test that allows a body's decisions to be judicially reviewed when the body is performing a "public function", with the courts using the test to embrace the decision-making processes of some non-statutory self-regulating bodies[64] and privatised utilities.[65] But by developing the reach of judicial review outwards, the courts have also had to consider how far the expansion of the supervisory jurisdiction should be permitted to transcend the public–private divide.[66] The public-private divide, a relatively recent concept in UK law,[67] had previously given rise to a rule of "procedural exclusivity" whereby public law rights were to be protected solely by way of an application for judicial review and private law rights by recourse to private actions.[68] As such, the rule had, on account of the assumed existence of alternative private law remedies, served to exclude applications for judicial review which sought to challenge the legality of decisions taken within the framework of contractual relationships.[69] For some commentators, the increased overlap of public and private, most notably in the context of "government by contract", meant that the rule would render judicial review ill equipped to deal with the demands of

chs 1 and 2. On the legal framework now in place see P P Craig, *Administrative Law* (Sweet & Maxwell, London, 4th edn, 1999) chs 4 and 5.

[64] *R* v. *Panel on Take-overs and Mergers, ex p Datafin plc* [1987] QB 815, as discussed below.

[65] *Re Sherlock and Morris* [1996] NIJB 80.

[66] For a critical account of the origins of the public–private divide see J W F Allison, *A Continental Distinction in the Common Law: A Historical and Comparative Perspective on English Public Law* (Oxford University Press, Oxford, 2nd edn, 2000).

[67] *Ibid*, chs 1 and 2.

[68] *O'Reilly* v. *Mackman* [1983] 2 AC 237. For criticisms of the rule see (among others) S Fredman and G S Morris, "The Costs of Exclusivity: Public and Private Re-examined" [1994] *PL* 69. But see also the relaxation of the rule in *Roy* v. *Kensington and Chelsea and Westminster Family Practitioner Committee* [1992] 2 WLR 239 and *Mercury Ltd* v. *Director General of Telecommunications* [1996] 1 WLR 48. And see now also T Hickman, "*Clark*: The Demise of *O'Reilly* Completed?" (2000) 5 JR 178, considering the impact of the Civil Procedure Rules which came into force in England and Wales in October 2000 (judicial review proceedings in England and Wales are now governed by Part 54 of the Civil Procedure Rules). Note also that the limiting influence of the public–private divide is less pronounced in Scottish law than in English law. See further, e.g., C M G Himsworth, "Judicial Review in Scotland" in B Hadfield (ed.), *Judicial Review: A Thematic Approach* (Gill & Macmillan, Dublin, 1995), p 288, 290 *ff*.

[69] For example, *Law* v. *National Greyhound Racing Club Ltd* [1983] 1 WLR 1302; *R* v. *Lloyds of London, ex p Briggs* [1993] 1 Lloyds Rep 176; and *R* v. *Disciplinary Committee of the Jockey Club, ex p His Highness the Aga Khan* [1993] 2 All ER 853.

modern government.[70] Thus, the challenge for the courts became one of not just expanding the reach of judicial review; it also became one of revisiting conceptual reference points that had only recently come to define the domestic order.

Expanding the reach of judicial review – ex p Datafin

The case that is most readily associated with the expansion of the review jurisdiction to include the decision-making processes of non-statutory self-regulating bodies is *R* v. *Panel on Take-overs and Mergers, ex p Datafin plc*.[71] The case arose when *Datafin plc* made an application to have a decision of the Panel on Take-overs and Mergers, an independent regulatory authority in the City of London, subjected to judicial review.[72] The specific facts of the case concerned a complaint by *Datafin* to the Panel that the Panel had incorrectly applied its own take-over rules, and that the mis-application of the rules had benefited *Datafin's* competitors. *Datafin's* complaint in this regard was unanimously rejected by the Panel, and it was this decision which the court was being asked to quash.

Addressing the question of the Panel's amenability to judicial review directly, Lloyd LJ remarked that, while the courts' supervisory jurisdiction is ordinarily of relevance only to the review of power exercised under statute, it could nevertheless be extended to the review of non-statutory power where the respondent body is "exercising public law functions, or if the exercise of its functions have public law consequences".[73] This reasoning represented an obvious and marked departure from the traditional ultra vires model of judicial review. In short, the Court of Appeal had shown itself willing to forego a test based solely on the "source" of a body's power in favour of a more flexible test which looks also at the kind

[70] Freedland n. 62 above. For practical illustration of some of Freedland's arguments see, e.g., *R* v. *Servite Houses, ex p Goldsmith* [2001] LGR 55.

[71] [1987] QB 815.

[72] Sir John Donaldson MR described the Panel as follows: "The Panel on Take-overs and Mergers is a truly remarkable body. Perched on the 20th floor of the Stock Exchange building in the City of London, both literally and metaphorically it oversees and regulates a very important part of the UK financial market. Yet it performs this function without visible means of legal support. The panel is an unincorporated association without legal personality and, so far as can be seen, has only about twelve members . . . It has no statutory, prerogative or common law powers and it is not in contractual relationship with the financial market or with those who deal in that market". See [1987] QB 815, 824–5.

[73] [1987] 1 QB 815, 847. Sir John Donaldson MR likewise suggested that the courts should enjoy at least the option of reviewing decisions taken by bodies such as that in the instant case: "Possibly the only essential elements are what can be described as a public element, which can take many different forms". See *ibid* 838. It should be noted, however, that the Court of Appeal declined to quash the decision of the Panel, the Court apparently being concerned not to involve itself unnecessarily in the workings of "the markets". *Ibid* 842 (Sir John Donaldson MR).

of "function" performed by a body.[74] A related issue left open by the *Datafin* ruling, however, was the question of how the courts should in future identify "public functions" for purposes of delimiting the reach of judicial review. The Court of Appeal in *Datafin* did not (and could not)[75] formulate a standard test which would apply beyond the circumstances of the instant case, and it has been subsequent judicial attempts to develop the *Datafin* approach that have highlighted the conceptual difficulties associated with judicial review and the public-private divide. One line of case law decided subsequent upon *Datafin*, for example, suggests that non-statutory bodies will be understood to perform public functions where it can be inferred that, if the body in question did not exist, or ceased to exist, Parliament would intervene and create a body to perform like functions.[76] On this understanding, the courts have thought it appropriate to review decisions of the Advertising Standards Authority[77] and of the British Pharmaceutical Industry Association Code of Practice Committee.[78] Decisions of the Chief Rabbi,[79] an Imam[80] and the Football Association,[81] meanwhile, have all been held to lie beyond the reach of judicial review.

A second line of case law decided in light of *Datafin*, however, has seen the courts limit the expansion of the review jurisdiction by emphasising that, when a relationship is governed by contract, the private law nature of the relationship will continue to act as an absolute bar to judicial review.[82] In *R* v. *Disciplinary Committee of the Jockey Club, ex p His Highness the Aga Khan*[83] the Court of Appeal held that the applicant could not seek a judicial review of the Jockey Club's decision to disqualify his filly from the

[74] Or the "nature" of a body's power. See C Forsyth, "The Scope of Judicial Review: 'Public Duty' not 'Source of Power'" [1987] *PL* 356.

[75] On the open-ended nature of the concept of "public functions" see, e.g., De Smith, Woolf and Jowell, *Principles of Judicial Review* (London, Sweet & Maxwell, 6th ed, 1999), pp 65–6.

[76] De Smith, Woolf and Jowell refer to this as the "but for" test. See *ibid*, p 68.

[77] R v. *Advertising Standards Authority, ex p The Insurance Service plc* [1990] 2 Admin LR 77.

[78] R v. *British Pharmaceutical Industry Association Code of Practice Committee, ex p Professional Counselling Aids Ltd* [1991] COD 228.

[79] R v. *Chief Rabbi of the United Hebrew Congregations, ex p Wachmann* [1993] 2 All ER 249.

[80] R v. *Imam of Bury Park James Masjid Luton, ex p Sulaiman Ali* [1992] COD 132.

[81] R v. *Football Association Ltd, ex p the Football League Ltd* [1993] 2 All ER 833.

[82] Indeed, it should be noted that Lloyd LJ stated in *Datafin* that the limits of the CA's approach in that case would be reached when there exists a contractual relationship between two parties: "If . . . the source of power is contractual, as in the case of private arbitration, then clearly the arbitrator is not subject to judicial review". See [1987] QB 815, 847.

[83] [1993] 2 All ER 853. See further N Bamforth, "The Scope of Judicial Review: Still Uncertain" [1993] *PL* 239.

1989 Oaks because the applicant's relationship with the club was governed by contract.[84] The decision was reached despite the fact that many activities and features of the Jockey Club arguably contained "public elements". The Jockey Club had, for example, previously been granted a royal charter, and it was acknowledged by the Court of Appeal in *Aga Khan* as regulating an important national activity.[85] Nevertheless, the existence of a contractual relationship in the instant case trumped any possibility the applicant may have had of succeeding on an application for judicial review.[86] Similar findings were also made in applications challenging the fairness of tendering procedures[87] and disciplinary proceedings in private schools.[88]

The Human Rights Act and judicial review

The courts' reluctance to afford public law any role in the regulation of contractual relations is central to the concerns of those commentators who consider that judicial review is, in its present form, unable to provide effective control of the modern and varied forms of government. At an obvious level, the courts' understanding that contractual relationships exist at the other side of the public–private divide is seen to place various bodies with public powers beyond the reach of public law controls.[89] But there are other difficulties as well. In particular, some commentators have queried whether the current principle and practice of judicial review would, in any event, be suited to the control of private bodies that discharge public functions. The point has been well made by Paul Craig:

[84] The amenability of decisions of the Jockey Club to judicial review had previously been considered in *R* v. *Jockey Club, ex p Massingberd-Mundy* [1990] 2 Admin LR 609 and *R* v. *Jockey Club, ex p RAM Racecourses* [1991] 3 Admin LR 292. In both these cases the Divisional Court held, on the authority provided by the Court of Appeal in *Law* v. *National Greyhound Racing Club* [1983] 1 WLR 1302, that the decisions in question could not be challenged by way of judicial review (in *Law*, the Court of Appeal had held that judicial review was not available because of the existence of a contractual relationship between the applicant and respondent).

[85] It is interesting to note that Neill LJ stated in *R* v. *Jockey Club, ex p Massingberd-Mundy* [1990] that, but for the constraints of precedent, he would have considered decisions of the Jockey Club to be judicially reviewable.

[86] Note that the Court of Appeal in *Aga Khan* was divided over the question of whether, on an application of the "but for" test, the government would intervene and create a body like the Jockey Club in the event that the Club did not, or ceased, to exist. See the contrasting opinions of Sir Thomas Bingham MR (in favour of the idea that the government would intervene) and Farquharson and Hoffmann LLJ (both suggesting that government would not intervene).

[87] *R* v. *The Lord Chancellor, ex p Hibbit & Sanders (a firm)* [1993] COD 326. But see also *R* v. *Legal Aid Board, ex p Donn & Co* [1996] 3 All ER 1.

[88] *R* v. *Fernhill Manor School, ex p Brown* [1993] 5 Admin LR 159 and *R* v. *Muntham House School, ex p R* [2000] LGR 255. But see also *R* v. *Governors of Haberdashers' Aske's Hatcham College Trust, ex p Tyrell* [1995] COD 399.

[89] Freedland n. 62 above, 100.

> "Do we think that the principles concerning the control of discretion (such as impropriety of purpose, relevancy, reasonableness, proportionality, legitimate expectations, and rights-based arguments) can or should be imposed upon (private) institutions . . . Should we apply them all, or with modifications which are suited to the nature of the body under scrutiny?".[90]

Given these criticisms, notably those concerning the still limited reach of judicial review, other commentators have argued that the passage of the Human Rights Act 1998 is potentially of far-reaching significance.[91] Arguments in this regard do, of course, give rise to an interesting problematic in the context of the ultra vires debate. The line of case law initiated by *ex p Datafin* is regarded as central to the common law model of review, and any argument that further expansion may take its lead from the Human Rights Act begs the question of what is the relationship between pre-existing jurisprudence and the Act. It will be recalled that the modified ultra vires model emphasises the imperative of tracing all legal developments to Parliament's intentions, hence it may be argued that the Act is representative of an express statement of Parliament's implied intentions as previously elaborated by the courts. An alternative explanation based on the common law model might argue instead that the Act provides only an additional reference point, rather than *the* starting point, for further elaboration of common law principle and practice.

The provision of the Human Rights Act that is of specific importance is section 6.[92] This section makes it "unlawful for a public authority to act in a way which is incompatible with a Convention right".[93] Although the Act does not provide a set definition of what constitutes a public authority, literature on the Act suggests that public authorities subdivide into two categories. The first category contains those "obvious" public authorities which exist solely for purposes of discharging public functions[94] – central government (including executive agencies); local government; the police; immigration officers; prisons; and courts and tribunals (among others).[95] All actions taken by obvious public authori-

[90] "Public Law and Control over Private Power" in M Taggart (ed.), *The Province of Administrative Law* (Hart Publishing, Oxford, 1997), p 196, 213.

[91] N Bamforth, "The Application of the Human Rights Act 1998 to Public Authorities and Private Bodies" (1999) 58 *CLJ* 159 and A Sherlock, "The Applicability of the UK's Human Rights Bill: Identifying Public Functions" (1998) 4 *EPL* 593.

[92] The broader design and purposes of the Human Rights Act are considered in depth in ch. 7.

[93] Although the provision does not extend to either House of Parliament – s. 6(3). Note also that the actions of public authorities will not be unlawful if they are expressly required by primary legislation – s. 6(2).

[94] The phrase "obvious" public authority is used by the Lord Chancellor. See HL Deb, Nov 16 1997, col 1231.

[95] See *Rights Brought Home: The Human Rights Bill*, Cmnd 3792 (1997) para 2.2.

ties, whether of a public law or private law nature, must be consistent with the ECHR.[96]

The second category of public authorities contains "mixed function" authorities.[97] Mixed function authorities are those which can perform either public or private functions, and it is in an attempt to regulate the discharge of public functions by such bodies that section 6 identifies public authorities as including "any person certain of whose functions are functions of a public nature".[98] This formulation, which evidently incorporates some of the language and logic of the *Datafin* test,[99] has already been said by government to cover the discharge of public functions by privatised utilities, various regulatory bodies and private bodies performing contracted-out public functions.[100] And beyond meeting the challenge of privatisation and contracting-out, it is also apparent that section 6 could be read to include other contractual relationships that were previously considered immune from review. It was noted above that applications challenging the legality of disciplinary proceedings in private schools had, on account of the existence of a contractual relationship, been dismissed by the courts.[101] For Nicholas Bamforth, it is now likely that such applications will be permitted to proceed in cases raising Human Rights Act

[96] An understanding which accords fully with the jurisprudence of the ECtHR. See, e.g., *Swedish Engine Drivers' Union* v. *Sweden* [1979–80] 1 EHRR 617.

[97] This is the term used by G S Morris. See, "The Human Rights Act and the Public/Private Divide in Employment Law" (1998) 27 *ILJ* 297.

[98] Note that s. 6 only applies to such bodies when the nature of the act performed is of a public nature, s. 6(5) stating that "a person is not a public authority . . . if the nature of the act is private". Some commentators have argued that this distinction could give rise to disparities in the field of employee protection, e.g., Morris, *ibid*. But see now also the ascription of horizontal effect to the Act in *Douglas and others* v. *Hello! Ltd* [2001] 2 WLR 992 and *Venables and Thompson* v. *News Group Newspapers and Others* [2001] 2 WLR 1038. On horizontal effect see further M Hunt, "The 'Horizontal Effect' of the Human Rights Act" [1998] *PL* 423 and G Phillipson, "The Human Rights Act, 'Horizontal Effect' and the Common Law: a Bang or a Whimper?" (1999) 62 *MLR* 824.

[99] A comparison might also be made with the formulation of an "emanation of the State" which is used for purposes of identifying those cases in which EU Directives may have direct effect. This formulation, which was first introduced by the ECJ in Case C-188/89, *Foster* v. *British Gas plc* [1990] ECR 1–3313 (see further ch. 3, p 56 *ff*), has since been used by the courts in various cases which parallel some of those discussed above. See, e.g., *Doughty* v. *Rolls Royce plc* [1992] 1 CMLR 1045 (in which Rolls Royce was not considered to be an emanation of the State); *Griffin* v. *South West Water Services Ltd* [1995] IRLR 15 (in which a privatised utility was considered to be an emanation of the State); and *NUT & Others* v. *Governing Body of St Mary's Church of England (Aided) Junior School* [1997] IRLR 242 (in which the board of governors of a voluntary school was considered to be an emanation of the State).

[100] See, e.g., the various statements of the Home Secretary at 314 HC 406–14. For a list of the kinds of bodies embraced by s. 6 see further S Grosz, J Beatson and P Duffy, *Human Rights: The 1998 Act and the European Convention* (Sweet & Maxwell, London, 2000), pp 70–1.

[101] R v. *Fernhill Manor School, ex p Brown* [1993] 5 Admin LR 159.

issues. Citing *Costello-Roberts* v. *UK*,[102] Bamforth notes how the European Court of Human Rights decided in that case that the UK Government could be liable for violations of rights which occur as a result of the administration of discipline in private schools.[103] "The obvious implication of the Convention position on private schools is that they are – contrary to the contract exception in domestic law – sufficiently "public" that their activities are covered by Act".[104] On this basis, therefore, it might be assumed that traditional public–private understandings will no longer automatically apply in Human Rights Act cases or, more importantly, frustrate the full and effective protection of individual rights.[105]

The Human Rights Act and the ultra vires debate

Which institutional model would best explain the further expansion of the review jurisdiction in Human Rights Act cases? In many ways, the answer to this question may not easily be found as there is much in the Human Rights Act that lends support to both modified ultra vires and common law means of reasoning. From the perspective of the modified ultra vires model, the Act can, as is further discussed in chapter seven, be seen to be predicated on orthodox assumptions about the institutional balance of the State.[106] And to the extent that the courts may start to delimit afresh the parameters of judicial review, it may, as has already been suggested above, be argued that such development would accord with Parliament's intentions as now expressed in section 6 of the Act. The modified ultra vires model emphasises notions of general legislative intent informing judge-led development of the law, and, given the overarching nature of the Human Rights Act, section 6 may come to be viewed as a legislative statement of Parliament's long held general intentions. In consequence, the Human Rights Act may, as a result of its inclusion of the language and logic of previous case law, increasingly be argued to provide the required point of democratic legitimation for all past and future development of the principle and practice of judicial review.

[102] [1993] 19 EHHR 112.

[103] See, in particular [1993] 19 EHHR 112, paras 26–8.

[104] Note 91 above, 162.

[105] Whether the courts will similarly revise their approach to judicial review in cases which do not raise Human Rights Act issues remains to be seen. For the argument that the courts should not, in any event, draw rigid distinctions between different categories of cases, see ch. 7. And see now the courts' approach to the reach of section 6 in *Poplar Housing and Regeneration Community Association* v. *Donoghue* [2001] 3 WLR 183 (CA) and *Heather* v. *The Leonard Cheshire Foundation* [2001] EWHC Admin 429.

[106] For example, Parliament retains the sovereign option of legislating contrary to the ECHR, with the courts coming under a corresponding obligation to give effect to such Acts. See discussion of s. 4 of the Human Rights Act (declarations of incompatibility) at p 167. But note also the relationship between ss. 4 and 10 of the Act. For an orthodox account of the Act's importance see M Elliott, "Fundamental Rights as Interpretative Constructs: The Constitutional Logic of the Human Rights Act 1998" in C Forsyth (ed.), n. 13 above, p 269.

Yet, while section 6 may bolster orthodox institutional assumptions, it is also probable that the section will be central to arguments that favour the common law model of review. The open-textured nature of section 6 can easily be conceived of in terms that are consistent with notions of institutional partnership. It was stated above that the common law model incorporates an understanding of the courts deciding individual cases on a "reactive" basis that breaks the link between Parliament's intentions and judge-led elaboration of the law. Such judicial "reaction" is attributed to the fact that legislation cannot accommodate every legal circumstance and, as section 6 is formulated in terms that are open, it is likely that some judges will increasingly justify legal developments by reference to elements of the common law model. For proponents of orthodoxy, such justification would amount to constitutional heresy. But for proponents of the common law model it would merely reflect the reality that when Parliament introduces legislation, whether that be the Human Rights Act or any other Act, it cannot foresee or make provision for every legal eventuality. Under those circumstances, the responsibility for developing the law then befalls the courts. The responsibility is not specifically delegated to the courts by Parliament, but rather is a result of the institutional limitations of legislation and the inherent jurisdiction of the courts. It follows that, while the courts will always take their lead from legislation and defer to the ultimate sovereignty of Parliament,[107] any corresponding development of principle and practice will be structured around knowledge that is almost wholly independent of the intentions of the legislature.

Of course, it may be that the differences between the above models are matters of perception rather than practice. Even active participants in the ultra vires debate have recently conceded that the two models have much in common,[108] and other commentators have suggested that the debate needs to become less normative, more analytical and more concerned with deeper considerations of justice and political morality.[109] It is in the absence of such points of deliberation coming to the fore, however, that the different institutional assumptions underpinning the models remain centrally important in the present context. In short, the fact that the common law model affords the courts a greater degree of institutional autonomy can clearly be seen to infuse domestic public law with an improved capacity to adapt to social, economic and political change. It was highlighted above that some commentators consider the current principles

[107] But see also n. 32 above.

[108] M Elliott, "Legislative Intention Versus Judicial Creativity? Administrative Law as a Co-operative Endeavour" in C Forsyth (ed.), n. 13 above p 341.

[109] N Bamforth, "Ultra Vires and Institutional Interdependence" in C Forsyth (ed.), n. 13 above, p 111. On such themes see further M Loughlin, *Public Law and Political Theory* (Clarendon Press, Oxford, 1992).

of judicial review ill-suited to the control of "private" bodies,[110] and other commentators have suggested that the problem will only be resolved when the courts fashion new principles that by-pass the very concept of a public-private divide.[111] Although proponents of the modified ultra vires model would argue that such reinvention of common law principles would accord with their institutional understandings, it seems that orthodoxy may, on account of its strained points of justification, limit the required judicial creativity. The common law model is, in contrast, much more fluid and accepting of judicial inventiveness. That this is so must surely mean that it is the model best suited to ensuring full and effective development of UK law.[112]

5. CONCLUSION

This chapter has provided an overview of the internal dynamics of UK public law, illustrated by reference to the ultra vires debate. It has argued that the common law model of review best explains previous judge-led endeavours and, moreover, offers the most satisfactory basis for projecting future developments. Drawing on the imagery of an institutional partnership between the legislature and the courts, the chapter has highlighted how the common law model provides the domestic order with an improved capacity to react to new legal challenges. While the chapter has also considered criticisms of the model, it has shown that there is increasing judicial and academic support for its institutional assumptions. Whether dealing with the internal challenge of prerogative power or the public-private divide, therefore, it has been suggested that the common law model of review best enables the courts to effect necessary change.

The institutional assumptions of the model are also of potential relevance beyond the case studies considered in this chapter. This is true not only of existing internal developments in relation to the protection of fundamental rights[113], but it is similarly true of the courts' possible future approach to

[110] Craig n. 90 above.

[111] D Oliver, *Common Values and the Public–Private Divide* (Butterworths, London, 1999). Although see now also existence of "The Administrative Court", established in England Wales pursuant to the recommendations of the *Review of Crown Office List* ("the Bowman Report").

[112] It is interesting to note that the more creative comments re: the public–private divide have come from those judges who endorse the common law model. See, e.g., Lord Woolf, "Droit Public – English Style" [1995] *PL* 57, 63 and Sir Stephen Sedley, *Freedom, Law and Justice* (Sweet & Maxwell, London, 1999), ch. 2.

[113] For example, *R* v. *Secretary of State for the Home Department, ex p Bugdaycay* [1987] AC 514; *R* v. *Home Secretary, ex p Leech* [1994] QB 198; *R* v. *Ministry of Defence, ex p Smith* [1995] 4 All ER 427; *R* v. *Cambridge Health Authority, ex p B* [1995] 23 BMLR 5; *R* v. *Lord Chancellor, ex p Witham* [1997] 2 All ER 778; and *R* v. *Lord Saville, ex p A* [1999] 4 All ER 860. See further chs. 5 and 7.

the more general challenge presented by the constitutional reform package of the New Labour Government.[114] Indeed, while the model's immediate value has been seen to lie in its ability to provide compelling justification for developments at the level of judicial review, its fluid qualities may come to assume a wider significance as the courts seek to fashion public law understandings that embrace emerging constitutional structures. The passage of the Human Rights Act has been accompanied by the devolution of power to Northern Ireland, Scotland and Wales, and it is generally accepted that devolution will strain understandings that sovereign power belongs solely to the Westminster Parliament.[115] This then brings into focus the question of how the courts should resolve disputes between the Westminster Parliament and other elected forums which represent "at (their) lowest, a 'region' and at (their) highest 'a nation'".[116] Although academic proponents of the model have emphasised that it recognises Parliament's final legislative supremacy,[117] they have, in related writings, equally suggested that the wider context that sustained notions of Westminster's absolute sovereign power has altered fundamentally.[118] This understanding has developed most obviously in light of the demands of EU membership and, given that the "external" challenge to sovereignty has now assumed an added "internal" dimension, would the fluidity of the common law model best enable the courts to accommodate the reality of overlapping sovereignties?

The juxtaposition of the common law model of review and the external dynamic of EU law does, of course, then raise afresh the central theme of this book, namely how far UK courts may wish to use European law to inform domestic developments. It was suggested in chapter one that, where a domestic order is internally responsive to change and adaptation, an effective process of legal cross-fertilisation may occur. The fact that the common law model is structured around notions of institutional adaptability would, at an abstract level, thereupon suggest that reliance on the model would allow the courts increasingly to draw upon European

[114] On which see, e.g., R Brazier, "New Labour, New Constitution" (1998) 49 *NILQ* 1 and "The Constitution of the United Kingdom" (1999) 58 *CLJ* 96.

[115] As Lord Cooper famously remarked in *MacCormick* v. *Lord Advocate* [1953] SC 396, 411: "(T)he principle of the unlimited sovereignty of Parliament is a distinctively English principle which has no counterpart in Scottish constitutional law". See further V Bogdanor, "Devolution: The Constitutional Aspects" in J Beatson, C Forsyth and I Hare (eds) *Constitutional Reform in the UK: Practice and Principles* (Hart Publishing, Oxford, 1998), p 9 and A W Bradley, "The Sovereignty of Parliament – Form or Substance?" in J Jowell and D Oliver (eds), *The Changing Constitution* (Oxford University Press, Oxford, 4th edn, 2000), p 23.

[116] B Hadfield, "The Foundations of Review, Devolved Power and Delegated Power" in C Forsyth (ed.), n. 13 above, p 193, 194.

[117] Craig n. 32 above and corresponding text.

[118] See, e.g., P Craig, "Sovereignty of the United Kingdom Parliament after *Factortame*" (1991) 11 *YBEL* 221.

standards as they meet emerging and existing public law challenges.[119] Although it was cautioned that borrowing needs to be controlled with reference to the comparative strengths and weaknesses of the domestic and European orders,[120] the common law model's inherent capacity for invention might be expected to ensure that harmonisation would occur in a manner that is both beneficial and free from unnecessary constraints. Thus, rather that lead to the uncontrolled Europeanisation of domestic standards, reliance on the model would allow the courts to harness the respective strengths of domestic and European law, thereby resolving ongoing internal public law issues as well as those that will assume an added significance in future years.

The abstract expectation that the common law model would facilitate deeper integration should not, however, be taken to mean that borrowing will follow as a matter of course. The courts' existing approach to the challenge of EU membership and legal integration has, as will become apparent in subsequent chapters, largely been structured around orthodox considerations, and the continued co-existence of contrasting judicial approaches to the basis of public law[121] means that uniform and sequential integration is improbable. Nevertheless, the fact that there is an increased emphasis on the common law model in relation to developments in judicial review, coupled with the fact that the courts may increasingly have to reassess the balance of legislative power within the UK, can be taken to mean that the parameters of internal debate about the institutional role of the courts will continue to change. The changing parameters may not always lead to integration,[122] but they should lead to deeper consideration of the possible benefits to be derived from the co-existence and interdependence of legal orders. Even more significantly, the internal debate should allow the courts to react creatively in an evolving institutional environment and to achieve optimum adaptation of domestic standards.

[119] On the possible informative value of European experience relative to devolution see N Burrows, *Devolution* (Sweet & Maxwell, London, 2000).

[120] R Dehousse, "Comparing National and EC Law: The Problem of the Level of Analysis" (1994) 42 *AJCL* 761.

[121] Compare and contrast Irvine n. 5 above with, e.g., Laws n. 24 above.

[122] It might be noted that proponents of the common law model sometimes have divergent views about the desirability of integration. Compare and contrast, *R* v. *Ministry of Agriculture, Fisheries and Food, ex p Hamble Fisheries* [1995] 2 All ER 714 (Sedley J) and *R* v. *Ministry of Agriculture, Fisheries and Food, ex p First City Trading Limited* [1997] 1 CMLR 250 (Laws J).

3

The Dynamics of European Law

1. INTRODUCTION

The suggestion that specific internal institutional understandings would allow UK courts to borrow more actively from European law does, of course, provide only a partial perspective on the dynamics of legal integration. It will be recalled from chapter one that the issue of whether to borrow principle and practice often arises in the first instance from European law's very presence within the domestic order. In this regard, reference was made to the work of those commentators who consider that European law occasions change as a result of the perception that aspects of the supranational order are superior to their domestic equivalents.[1] Although it was noted that such arguments can be criticised for their failure fully to accommodate wider theoretical and functional concerns,[2] it was emphasised that the co-existence of different orders can lead national courts to conduct comparative evaluations with a view to legal harmonisation.[3] It followed that, while the limits to integration are ultimately prescribed by internal institutional considerations, judicial recourse to those considerations is often prompted by the "external" dynamic of European law.

Given this understanding, the present chapter considers more closely those aspects of European law that foster debate about the desirability or otherwise of borrowing. It begins with an examination of various features of the EU legal order that place demands on national courts, and it then examines core doctrines of ECHR jurisprudence. Here, the chapter identifies not only those aspects of ECHR jurisprudence that may be of increasing influence in UK law, it also provides a fuller insight into the nature of the EU legal order. Although the EU institutions have not

[1] For example, J Schwarze, *European Administrative Law* (Sweet & Maxwell, London, 1992).

[2] See, e.g., J W F Allison, "Transplantation and Cross-fertilisation" in J Beatson and T Tridimas (eds), *New Directions in European Public Law* (Hart Publishing, Oxford, 1998), p 169 and R Dehousse, "Comparing National and EC Law: The Problem of the Level of Analysis" (1994) 42 *AJCL* 761.

[3] See, e.g., *Woolwich Building Society* v. *Inland Revenue Commissioners (No 2)* [1992] 3 WLR 366, 395–6 (Lord Goff) and *M* v. *Home Office* [1993] 3 WLR 433 (Lord Woolf), considered in ch. 6.

formally acceded to the ECHR[4] and, indeed, have recently adopted their own Charter of Rights,[5] they have, since the 1970s, used the ECHR as a reference point against which to develop EU law.[6] This recourse to the ECHR was prompted, at least in part, by the threat of constitutional conflict with various national legal orders,[7] and the chapter will suggest that such conflict was one practical manifestation of the abstract difficulties that can be associated with legal integration. But beyond casting the relationship between EU law and the ECHR in conflictual terms, the chapter also suggests that EU institutional recourse to the ECHR has, at least to a limited extent, diminished the sovereign space of individual legal systems. In particular, the chapter notes how the EU's use of the ECHR meant that the latter body of law had the potential to exert some degree of influence on the UK legal order even before the passage of the Human Rights Act.[8] As will become apparent in subsequent chapters, it is such enmeshing of legal orders that is central to the understanding that UK courts may increasingly wish to view domestic law, EU law and the ECHR as equal parts of an interlocking whole.

2. EUROPEAN UNION LAW

It is axiomatic that the body of EU law that feeds into the UK legal order has been constructed around the core doctrines of supremacy and direct effect.[9] These doctrines, which oblige national courts to afford primacy to EU law provisions that confer enforceable rights upon individuals,[10] were developed by the European Court of Justice (ECJ) by way of ensuring that EU law was distinguished from other forms of "international" law and

[4] For the ECJ's view on the prospects of accession see Opinion 2/94 on *Accession by the Community to the ECHR* [1996] ECR I-1759.

[5] OJ 2000 C364/01.

[6] And see also Arts. 6 and 7 (ex F1 & 2) TEU.

[7] See, e.g., the conflict with the German Constitutional Court in Case 11/70, *Internationale Handelsgesellschaft mbH* v. *Einfuhr- und Vorratstelle für Getreide und Futtermittel* [1972] CMLR 255 (ECJ); *Internationale Handelsgesellschaft mbH* v. *Einfuhr und- Vorratstelle für Getreide und Futtermittel* [1974] 2 CMLR 540 (German Constitutional Court); and *Re Wünsche Handelsgesellschaft* [1987] 3 CMLR 225 (German Constitutional Court).

[8] N Grief, "The Domestic Impact of the European Convention on Human Rights as Mediated through Community Law" [1991] *PL* 555. It should be noted, however, that actual influence has been limited. See further ch. 7.

[9] Case 26/62, *Van Gend en Loos* v. *Nederlandse Aministratie der Belastingen* [1963] ECR 1 and Case 6/64, *Costa* v. *ENEL* [1964] ECR 585.

[10] The direct effect of EU law is not automatic. See Case 26/62, *Van Gend en Loos* v. *Nederlandse Aministratie der Belastingen* [1963] ECR 1, 13. But see also Case 2/74, *Reyners* v. *Belgium* [1974] ECR 631 as discussed in P P Craig, "Once Upon a Time in the West: Direct Effect and the Federalization of EEC Law" (1992) 12 *OJLS* 453.

recognised as a body of law *ex proprio vigore*.[11] Although the doctrines have not, as such, enjoyed a universally founded constitutional legitimacy,[12] their introduction was deemed necessary, at least from the perspective of the ECJ, to enable EU law to achieve the objective of European social and economic integration.[13] For the ECJ, the possibility that EU law would only bind Member State governments at the international level would diminish the significance of the project being embarked upon. Thus, there existed almost from the outset of the integration process an understanding that individuals should be able to implement the provisions of "a new legal order" in their domestic courts.[14]

The institutional design of supremacy and direct effect was subsequently augmented by the introduction of related doctrines and standards that impose many more specific obligations on national courts. The understanding that individuals could enforce EU law at the domestic level gave rise to a corresponding concern that EU law interests should be equally protected throughout each of the Member States, and the ECJ gradually developed a series of doctrines that were, and are, intended to harmonise protection in national courts. The elaboration and acceptance of the doctrines has sometimes appeared paradoxical. On the one hand, the fact that the doctrines are entirely judge-made constructs has led commentators to criticise the activism of the ECJ,[15] with some national courts also periodically rejecting the core assumptions of the EU order.[16] But the corresponding fact that the doctrines have been developed within the framework of the Article 234 (ex 177) EC reference procedure has, on the other hand, meant that they have enjoyed the required degree of recognition in practice. Article 234 EC is the mechanism that allows national courts to refer EU law issues to the ECJ and, given that national courts have willingly used the mechanism, it is arguable that they have acted as the ECJ's "interlocutors".[17] The result has been for there to emerge a series

[11] *Costa* v. *ENEL* [1964] ECR 585, 593. See further D Wyatt, "New Legal Order, or Old?" (1982) 7 *ELRev* 147 and T Schilling, "The Autonomy of the Community Legal Order – An Analysis of Possible Foundations" (1996) 37 *Harvard International Law Journal* 389.

[12] See further P Craig and G de Búrca, *EU Law: Text, Cases and Materials* (Oxford University Press, Oxford, 2nd edn, 1998), ch. 6.

[13] *Costa* v. *ENEL* [1964] ECR 585, 593–4.

[14] Case 26/62, *Van Gend en Loos* v. *Nederlandse Aministratie der Belastingen* [1963] ECR 1, 12.

[15] See, e.g., H Rasmussen, *On Law and Policy in the European Court of Justice* (Martinus Nijhoff, Dordrecht, 1986) and T C Hartley, "The European Court, Judicial Objectivity and the Constitution of the European Union" (1996) 112 *LQR* 95. But see also A Arnull, "The European Court and Judicial Objectivity: A Reply to Professor Hartley" (1996) 112 *LQR* 411 and T Tridimas, "The Court of Justice and Judicial Activism" (1996) 21 *ELRev* 199.

[16] See Craig and de Búrca n. 12 above.

[17] J H H Weiler, "A Quiet Revolution: The European Court of Justice and Its Interlocutors" (1994) 26 *CPS* 510. There is wealth of literature on Art 234 EC and national

of interdependent doctrines that now impose, among others things, an overarching duty of "loyalty" to the EU process;[18] an obligation to interpret national legislation in light of EU law (indirect effect);[19] and an obligation to award damages to an individual who has suffered loss as a result of the actions or inactions of a Member State authority (state liability).[20]

The loyalty doctrine and principles of judicial review

The ECJ has developed the loyalty doctrine by reference to Article 10 (ex 5) EC. Article 10 EC states:

> "Member States shall take all appropriate measures, whether general or particular, to ensure fulfilment of the obligations arising out of this Treaty or resulting from action taken by the institutions of the Community. They shall facilitate the Community's tasks. They shall abstain from any measure which would jeopardise the attainment of the objectives of the Treaty".

Although the Article does not make specific reference to national courts, the ECJ's understanding of Member State authority being exercised by each of its legislative, executive and judicial branches[21] has enabled it to use Article 10 EC to justify its description of national courts as "(EU) courts of general jurisdiction".[22] The ascription of this role to national courts is central to the existence of the "EU law paradigm" considered in chapter one,[23] and everything national courts do within the paradigm must

court willingness to invoke it. For a statistical analysis see T L Brunell and A Stone Sweet, "The European Court and the national courts: a statistical analysis of preliminary references, 1961–95" (1998) 5 *JEPP* 66. On reasons for its use see, e.g., M L Volcansek, *Judicial Politics in Europe: An Impact Analysis* (Peter Lang, New York, 1986) and K Alter, "Explaining National Court Acceptance of European Court Jurisprudence: a Critical Evaluation of Theories of Legal Integration" and W Mattli and A M Slaughter, "The Role of National Courts in the Process of European Integration: Accounting for Judicial Preferences and Constraints" in A M Slaughter, A Stone Sweet and J H H Weiler (eds.), *The European Courts and National Courts: Doctrine and Jurisprudence* (Hart Publishing, Oxford, 1998), p 227 and p 253 respectively.

[18] The term is borrowed from K Mortelmans, "The Principle of Loyalty to the Community (Art. 5 EC) and the Obligations of the Community Institutions" (1998) 5 *MJ* 67.

[19] Case 14/83, *Von Colson* v. *Land Nordrhein-Westfalen* [1984] ECR 1891 and Case C-106/89, *Marleasing SA* v. *La Commercial Internacional de Alimentacion SA* [1990] ECR I-4153.

[20] Introduced in a line of case law running from Joined Cases C-6 and 9/90 *Francovich and Bonifaci* v. *Italy* [1991] ECR I-5357 through to Joined Cases C-178–179 and 188–190/94, *Dillenkofer* v. *Germany* [1996] 3 CMLR 469.

[21] See, e.g., Joined Cases C-46 and 48/93, *Brasserie du Pêcheur SA* v. *Germany, R* v. *Secretary of State for Transport, ex p Factortame Ltd* [1996] ECR I 1029, 1145 (para 34).

[22] Case T-51/89, *Tetrapak* [1990] ECR II-309, 361.

[23] M L Fernandez Esteban, "National Judges and EC Law: The Paradox of the Two Paradigms of Law" (1997) 4 *MJ* 143.

be consistent with EU law. This may entail modifying national procedures to protect EU law interests,[24] and it may also entail the modification of domestic juridical technique[25] and the development of new remedies.[26] In any event, the overriding purpose of the duty is to ensure that EU law rights enjoy full and effective protection[27] within a framework of national judicial deference to the jurisdiction of the ECJ.[28]

A further obligation that flows from the loyalty doctrine is the requirement that national courts give effect to the general principles of EU law. This is true both of EU law's fundamental rights standards[29] and of the principles of judicial review that have been identified by the ECJ. These latter principles, which are largely modified versions of administrative law constructs drawn from the French and Germanic legal traditions,[30] typically include proportionality,[31] equality,[32] legal certainty/legitimate expectations[33] and the duty to give reasons.[34] Although there is some national court dispute as to how far the obligation is binding as a matter

[24] Case C-208/90, *Emmott* v. *Minister of Social Welfare* [1991] ECR I-4269. But see Case C-338/91, *Steenhorst-Neerings* v. *Bestuur van de Bedrijfsvereniging voor Detailhandel, Ambachten en Huisvrouwen* [1993] ECR I-5475.

[25] Case 14/83, *Von Colson* v. *Land Nordrhein-Westfalen* [1984] ECR 1891 and Case C-106/89, *Marleasing SA* v. *La Commercial Internacional de Alimentacion SA* [1990] ECR I-4153.

[26] Case C-213/89, *R* v. *Secretary of State for Transport, ex p Factortame* [1990] ECR I-2433 and Joined Cases C-6, 9/90 *Francovich and Bonifaci* v. *Italy* [1991] ECR I-5357.

[27] Case 33/76, *Rewe-Zentralfinanz eG and Rewe-Zentral AG* v. *Landwirtschaftskammer für das Saarland* [1976] ECR 1989; Case 47/76, *Comet* v. *Produktschap voor Siergewassen* [1976] ECR 2043; Case 158/80, *Rewe Handelsgesellschaft Nord mbH* v. *Hauptzollamt Kiel* [1981] ECR 1805; Case 326/88, *Anklagemyndigheden* v. *Hansen & Sons I/S* [1990] ECR I-2911; and Case C-271/91, *Marshall* v. *Southampton and South West Hampshire Area Health Authority (No 2)* [1993] ECR I-4367.

[28] See, e.g., with regard to the ECJ's jurisdiction to determine matters of the legality of EU law in accordance with Art. 234 EC, Case 314/85, *Firma Foto-Frost* v. *Hauptzollamt Lübeck Ost* [1987] ECR 4199. The position with regard to referring matters of EU law for interpretation under Art. 234 EC is less absolute. See further the ECJ's *Guidance on References by National Courts for Preliminary Rulings* [1997] 1 CMLR 78.

[29] Case 5/88, *Wachauf* v. *Germany* [1989] ECR 2609. The significance of this obligation is returned to below.

[30] T Koopmans, "The Birth of European Law at the Cross-roads of Legal Traditions" (1991) 39 *AJCL* 493 and G Nolte, "General Principles of German and European Administrative Law – A Comparison in Historical Perspective" (1994) 57 *MLR* 191. But see also the influence of common law standards with regard to the right to a fair hearing in, e.g., Case 17/74, *Transocean Marine Paint Association* v. *Commission* [1974] ECR 1063.

[31] See, e.g., Case 44/79, *Hauer* v. *Land Rheinland-Pfalz* [1979] ECR 3727.

[32] Or "non-discrimination". See, e.g., Cases 75, 117/82, *Razzouk and Beydoun* v. *Commission* [1984] ECR 1509.

[33] On legal certainty see Case 98/78, *Firma A Racke* v. *Hauptzollamt Mainz* [1979] ECR 69. On (substantive) legitimate expectations see Case 120/86, *Mulder* v. *Minister van Landbouw en Visserij* [1988] ECR 2321.

[34] See, e.g., Case 222/86, *UNECTEF* v. *Heylens* [1987] ECR 4097. And see also Art. 253 (ex 190) EC.

of practice,[35] the ECJ's base understanding is that the principles should be observed in any proceedings which challenge the lawfulness of Member State action relative to the EC Treaty or secondary Acts of the EU institutions. The point was made by Advocate-General Mancini in *Jongeneel Kaas*:

> "(T)he general principles elicited by the Court from the primary and secondary provisions of (EU) law, and in particular those fundamental values which are common to the legal systems of the Member States, form part of the (EU) legal order and may therefore be relied upon by individuals before the national court which, as is well known, is also (an EU) court . . . (T)he general principles of law and, in particular, the principle of proportionality have direct effect. Accordingly they must be applied by national courts if the circumstances in relation to which they are relied upon display a connection with the (EU) system".[36]

Such understandings of the reach of EU law's principles of judicial review are central to the convergence thesis forwarded by Jürgen Schwarze.[37] Schwarze's thesis argues that national court experience of giving effect to the principles within the EU law paradigm subsequently leads to the integration of domestic and European standards in purely domestic cases. This integration, which is driven by national judicial concern to ensure that the domestic order has the full benefit of comparative experience, is argued to be facilitated by the pre-existence of "comparable legal principles" within each of the Member State legal orders.[38] Although these principles "may sometimes be quite differently categorised and defined in doctrinal terms",[39] Schwarze suggests that they are, as a result of having been developed in response to parallel social, economic and political processes, "functionally similar" in nature.[40] For Schwarze, this means that, as the national and supranational orders are now engaged in a joint venture, the co-existing orders may have much to gain from a process of borrowing. The borrowing may take the form of ECJ use of national principle and practice, or it may take the form of national court use of EU law's general principles or of the experience of other national orders. Either way, "it can be stated that the administrative law systems of the (EU), its Member States and the Member States of the Council of

[35] Compare and contrast the approach of UK courts in *R* v. *Ministry of Agriculture, Fisheries and Food, ex p Hamble Fisheries* [1995] 2 All ER 714 and *R* v. *Ministry of Agriculture, Fisheries and Food, ex p First City Trading Limited* [1997] 1 CMLR 250.

[36] Case C-237/82, *Jongeneel Kaas* v. *Netherlands* [1984] ECR 483, 520–2.

[37] See further ch. 1, p 4 *ff*. And see also n. 1 above; "Tendencies towards a Common Administrative Law in Europe" (1991) 16 *ELRev* 3; and "The Convergence of the Administrative Laws of the EU Member States" (1998) 4 *EPL* 191.

[38] Note 1 above, p 1444.

[39] *Ibid*, p 1445.

[40] *Ibid*.

Europe offer . . . a worthwhile and so far wrongly neglected field of research into comparative law".[41]

How far does Schwarze's thesis accurately represent what has happened in practice and, moreover, may occur in future? Certainly, there is, at one level, much to support the argument that borrowing occurs and that the functional overlap of pre-existing national principles enables some domestic orders easily to assimilate domestic and European norms. It was noted in chapter one that some UK judges have long been receptive to the idea of integrating the principles,[42] and Schwarze's argument about functional overlap facilitating integration has been endorsed by academic commentators who consider that EU law has much in common with principle and practice in civil law jurisdictions.[43]

Yet, beyond lending support to the convergence thesis, the fact that EU law's principles of judicial review have been drawn from different legal traditions may, depending on individual judicial preferences, create greater obstacles to assimilation than Schwarze's work presupposes.[44] This may be particularly true of common law courts which are adjudicating on the basis of EU law principles that have been developed by reference to the French and/or Germanic legal traditions. Although Schwarze concedes that the overlap of different legal traditions may give rise to some problems, his consideration of the issue is more cursory than comprehensive.[45] It was highlighted in chapter one that there exists a strong body of academic opinion that argues that the interaction of different legal traditions only causes "irritation"[46], and, although such arguments may in themselves be overstated, they do suggest that integration may sometimes be more problematic than convergence writers assume. Of course, this need not be taken mean that common law courts will not endeavour to give effect to the principles when working within the EU law paradigm, but it does imply that they may not always be able to do so in the manner expected by the ECJ. Perhaps even more significantly, where national courts structure any deeper process of integration, or cross-fertilisation,

[41] *Ibid*, p 1446.

[42] *Council of Civil Service Unions* v. *Minister for the Civil Service* [1985] 1 AC 374, 410 (Lord Diplock). And see further the judgments of Sedley J in *R* v. *Ministry of Agriculture, Fisheries and Food, ex p Hamble Fisheries* [1995] 2 All ER 714 and *R* v. *Secretary of State for the Home Department, ex p McQuillan* [1995] 4 All ER 400.

[43] See E Garcia de Enterria and L Ortega, "Spanish Report" in J Schwarze (ed.), *Administrative Law under European Influence* (Nomos, Baden-Baden and London, 1996), p 731.

[44] On the conceptual underpinnings of EU administrative law see, e.g., C Harlow, "European Administrative Law and the Global Challenge" in P Craig and G de Búrca (eds.), *The Evolution of EU Law* (Oxford University Press, 1999), p 261.

[45] Note 1 above, pp 1443–4

[46] G Teubner, "Legal Irritants: Good Faith in British Law or How Unifying Law Ends Up in New Divergences" (1998) 61 *MLR* 11.

around orthodox internal institutional considerations, discomfort in the EU law paradigm may only militate against final adoption and adaptation of European principle. The extent to which this has previously been true of UK courts is returned to in chapter 5.[47]

Indirect effect

The possibility that EU law obligations may not easily be accommodated within national structures has also been recognised in relation to the indirect effect doctrine. The doctrine, as stated above, imposes an obligation to construe all relevant domestic legislation in light of the terms of EU Directives which should have been implemented in national law.[48] The doctrine has, as such, been criticised for making "unviable" demands upon domestic interpretative techniques and for threatening the cherished value of legal certainty.[49] In other words, the fact that the doctrine demands that national courts develop purposive interpretative techniques is seen to have the potential not only to undermine preferred domestic methods but also, and by so doing, to disrupt "established expectations as to the range of interpretations possible from an instrument".[50] Thus, even though the exacting nature of the doctrine has more recently been modified by the ECJ,[51] its core demand might be argued to be one that may not always be reconciled with domestic institutional models.

The doctrine's introduction into the EU order is often associated with the ECJ's attempts to limit the difficulties created by its judgment in the first *Marshall* case.[52] In the case, the ECJ (in)famously denied that Directives are capable of having horizontal direct effect, i.e. in proceedings between two private parties. Although *Marshall* was ultimately concerned with a question of vertical direct effect,[53] the ECJ was, by analogy,

[47] On Irish court integration of EU administrative law standards see G Hogan, "Irish Report" in J Schwarze (ed.) n. 43 above, p 437. And see also G Hogan, "Ireland" in E Spiliotopolous (ed.), *Towards a Unified Judicial Protection of Citizens in Europe (?)* (Esperia Publications, London, 2000).

[48] Note that, while the obligation applies most readily in relation to Directives, it can also apply to other EU law provisions including Treaty Arts. See, e.g., Case 157/86, *Murphy* v. *An Bord Telecom Eireann* [1988] ECR 673, 690 (para 11) and Case C-165/91, *Van Munster* v. *Rijksdienst voor Pensionen* [1994] ECR I-4661, 4698 (para 34).

[49] D Chalmers, "Judicial Preferences and the Community Legal Order" (1997) 60 *MLR* 164, 189.

[50] *Ibid*, 190. Chalmers references G de Búrca's, "Giving Effect to European Community Directives" (1992) 55 *MLR* 215 on the point about legal certainty.

[51] See further below.

[52] Case 152/84, [1986] ECR 723. Although note that, chronologically, the ECJ had already introduced the interpretative obligation in the years immediately preceding *Marshall* (see Case 14/83, *Von Colson* v. *Land Nordrhein-Westfalen* [1984] ECR 1891).

[53] In the case a female dietician who had been dismissed from her job on the ground that she had passed the normal retirement age for women wished to invoke the terms of the 1976

required to consider how far, if at all, Directives can be invoked horizontally. In finding that Directives can never be used in such manner, the ECJ drew heavily on the text of Article 249 (ex 189) EC, highlighting in particular how the Article refers only to a Directive binding "each Member State to which it is addressed". For the ECJ, this point of emphasis meant that it would be wrong in principle to allow Directives to be used to regulate the actions of private individuals who cannot themselves be bound by the provision in question:

> "(I)t must be emphasised that according to Article (249) . . . the binding nature of a Directive . . . exists only in relation to 'each Member State to which it is addressed'. It follows that a Directive may not of itself impose obligations on an individual and that a provision of a Directive may not be relied upon as such against such a person".[54]

The value of the *Marshall* judgment has often been doubted by commentators who have noted both the juridical inconsistencies in the ECJ's approach and the difficulties that the ruling has created for the equal protection of individual interests. Paul Craig, for example, has stated that the "formalist" approach in *Marshall* did "not sit comfortably with the more purposive approach used by the Court in other areas".[55] The ECJ had, in previous years, adopted a markedly expansive approach to the direct effect of Treaty Articles and secondary Acts,[56] and, viewed from this perspective, *Marshall* clearly departed from the ECJ's integrationist efforts. And the argument that the ruling created difficulties relative to the equal protection of individuals has been made by Jo Shaw. Focusing on the issue of employment protection, Shaw notes how the *Marshall* ruling potentially means that public sector employees will enjoy superior standards of protection to those of their private sector counter-parts: "(T)he potential for injustice is clear. For example, a public sector employee may rely upon

Equal Treatment (Directive 76/207/EEC, OJ 1976 L39/40) in proceedings against her employer (a public authority). Under the employer's retirement policy, women were to retire at 60 while men were to retire at 65. As there was nothing in the relevant national legislation (the Sex Discrimination Act 1975) which dealt with equal retirement ages, she argued that the Directive should have direct effect, despite the fact that it was inconsistent with the domestic legislation. The ECJ, in responding to a reference from the English Court of Appeal, agreed that it should (Directives were first recognised as being able to have vertical direct effect in Case 41/74, *Van Duyn* v. *Home Office* [1974] ECR 1337).

[54] [1986] ECR 723, 749 (para 48).

[55] "Directives: Direct Effect, Indirect Effect and the Construction of National Legislation" (1997) 22 *ELRev* 519, 520.

[56] With regard to the direct effect of EC Treaty Arts. see, e.g., Case 26/62, *Van Gend en Loos* [1963] ECR 1 (vertical direct effect) and Case 127/73, *BRT* v. *SABAM* [1974] ECR 51 (horizontal direct effect). With regard to Regulations see, e.g., Case 34/73, *Variola* v. *Amminstrazione delle Finanze dello Stato* [1973] ECR 981. And with regard to Decisions see, e.g., Case 9/70, *Grad* v. *Finanzamt Traunstein* [1970] ECR 825.

. . . the Equal Treatment Directive in order to challenge alleged sex discrimination on the part of his or her employer, whereas a private sector employee may not".[57] Related arguments have also been made by other commentators.[58]

The ECJ's concern to meet this latter criticism has since prompted partial adaptation of its jurisprudence. In *Foster* v. *British Gas*[59] the ECJ broadened its understanding of what constitutes "the State" by emphasising that Directives can have direct effect in proceedings involving any body which is "an emanation of the State".[60] This concept, which provides a functional test, is clearly intended to assist national courts as they distinguish "public" from "private", and there is ample evidence to suggest that the doctrine has been received uncritically[61] and, moreover, that it has subsequently been used to inform internal legal developments.[62]

The indirect effect doctrine, meanwhile, is designed to be of impact in those proceedings which do not involve the State or one of its emanations. As such, the doctrine's primary purpose is to ensure that, where the *Marshall* ruling applies, its effects will be mediated by national judicial endeavours to interpret existing domestic legislation in light of the terms of any relevant Directives. The obligation, which binds courts "as far as possible", initially applied only to national legislation which was introduced in order to implement a specific Directive in national law.[63] But the ECJ's concern to maximise the reach of EU law later saw the obligation extended to include the interpretation of any legislation, whether passed prior to the Directive, in relation to the Directive, or after the Directive's implementation date had passed:

[57] *Law of the European Union* (Macmillan, London, 2nd edn., 1996), p 269. Note that similar concerns about the equal protection of public sector and private sector employees exist in the UK in relation to the scope of application of the Human Rights Act 1998. See G S Morris, "The Human Rights Act and the Public/Private Divide in Employment Law" (1998) 27 *ILJ* 293. But see now also the ascription of horizontal effect to the Human Rights Act in *Douglas and others* v. *Hello! Ltd* [2001] 2 WLR 992 and *Venables and Thompson* v. *News Group Newspapers and Others* [2001] 2 WLR 1038.

[58] J Coppel, "Rights, Duties and the End of Marshall" (1994) 57 *MLR* 859.

[59] Case C-188/89, *A Foster and Others* v. *British Gas plc* [1990] ECR I-3313.

[60] See further E Szyszczak, "Foster v British Gas" (1990) 27 *CMLRev* 859.

[61] On its application by UK courts see, e.g., *Doughty* v. *Rolls Royce plc* [1992] 1 CMLR 1045 (where Rolls Royce was not found to be an emanation of the State); *Griffin* v. *South West Water Services Ltd* [1995] IRLR 15 (where a privatised utility was found to be an emanation of the State for the purposes of the *Foster* test); and *NUT & Others* v. *Governing Body of St Mary's Church of England (Aided) Junior School* [1997] IRLR 242 (where a board of governors of a voluntary school was found to be an emanation of the State for purposes of EU law).

[62] See, e.g., Kerr J's consideration of *Griffin* v. *South West Water Services Ltd* [1995] IRLR 15 when deciding in *Re Sherlock and Morris* [1996] NIJB 80 that a decision of a privatised utility should, as a matter of domestic law, be subject to judicial review.

[63] Case 14/83, *Von Colson and Kamann* v. *Land Nordrhein Westfalen* [1984] ECR 1891, 1909.

> "(T)he Member States' obligation arising from a Directive to achieve the result envisaged by the Directive and their duty under Article (10) . . . is binding on all the authorities of the Member States including, for matters within their jurisdiction, the courts. It follows that, in applying national law, whether the provisions in question were adopted before or after the Directive, the national court called upon to interpret it is required to do so, as far as possible, in the light of the wording and the purpose of the Directive in order to achieve the result pursued by the latter".[64]

The possibility that the doctrine may frustrate legal certainty and cause national courts to strain unduly the wording of domestic legislation has since been recognised by the ECJ. In *Kolpinghuis Nijmegen*[65] the ECJ stated that the doctrine's operation is to be limited by reference to general principles of EU law such as legal certainty. And in a series of other cases, the ECJ and its Advocates-General have emphasised that the supranational order will defer to national court understandings as to whether a provision of national law can suitably be construed in light of EU law.[66] While the doctrine still pursues the objective of harmonious interpretation, therefore, it does not "go so far as to require a national court to do violence to or expressly contradict the terms of national law"[67] or to require that national courts "undertake an actual redrafting of the provisions of national law".[68]

The fact that the doctrine has been subjected to modification has, however, led commentators to argue that, rather than invent and reinvent new obligations, the ECJ should simply recognise that Directives can have horizontal direct effect. The point has been made both by academic writers[69] and by Advocates-General advising the ECJ. In *Faccini Dori* v. *Recreb Srl*[70] Advocate-General Lenz dismissed the ECJ's previous arguments about why Directives should not be allowed to have horizontal direct effect.[71] Addressing the ECJ's understanding that Directives could

[64] Case C-106/89, *Marleasing SA* v. *La Commercial Internacional de Alimentacion SA* [1990] ECR I-4153, 4159.

[65] Case 80/86, [1987] ECR 3969.

[66] See, e.g., Case C-334/92, *Wagner-Miret* [1993] ECR I-6911; Case C-91/92, *Dori* v. *Recreb Srl* [1994] ECR I-3325; and Case C-192/94, *El Corte Inglés* v. *Cristina Blázques Rivero* [1996] ECR I-1281.

[67] Case C-468/93, *Gemeente Emmen* [1996] ECR I-1721, 1738 (para 34, Advocate-General Fennelly).

[68] Case C-168/95, *Luciano Arcaro* [1996] ECR I-4705, 4715 (para 39, Advocate-General Elmer).

[69] See, e.g., J Coppel n. 58 above.

[70] Case C-91/92, [1994] ECR I-3325.

[71] And see also the opinions of Advocates-General Van Gerven and Jacobs in, respectively, Case C-271/91, *Marshall* v. *Southampton and South West Hampshire Area Health Authority (No 2)* [1993] ECR I-4367 and Case C-316/93, *Vanteeveld* v. *SA Le Foyer* [1994] ECR I-763.

only have direct effect against the State because they were addressed to Member States, he suggested that the wording used in Article 249 EC was intended merely to signify that Member States were under an obligation to introduce implementing legislation.[72] Having further outlined how he perceived the ECJ's approach in *Marshall* to be discriminatory and contrary to the objectives of the internal market and the emerging ideal of European citizenship, he concluded: "(C)onsiderations favouring the horizontal effect of Directives reflect a drive to do justice by the beneficiary of a provision which the (EU) legislator intended to be binding and not to abandon his situation for an indefinite period to the whim of a Member State in default of its obligations".[73]

Despite the persuasive force of Advocate-General Lenz's analysis, the ECJ subsequently used its own judgment in *Faccini Dori* to reaffirm the original *Marshall* ruling.[74] The *Dori* case had arisen when an Italian national sought to avail of a Directive that allows consumers one week to cancel contracts which are entered into at a location other than a business premise.[75] The ECJ, on receipt of the question of whether a Directive can have horizontal effect in the absence of national implementing legislation, again reiterated that Directives cannot have direct effect in proceedings between two private individuals because they can only be addressed to, and bind, Member States. Its decision to do so was criticised as "completely unacceptable in principle and in practice".[76] But for the ECJ, its decision could easily be justified both by reference to the text of Article 249 EC and by reference to the fact that there existed at the time of its judgment two alternative ways in which individuals could benefit from the terms of a Directive. The first of these was through national court observance of the demands of the indirect effect doctrine. The other was through the doctrine of state liability which had recently been introduced in *Francovich and Bonifaci* v. *Italy*.[77]

State liability

The *Francovich* case, like *Faccini Dori*, arose from a failure by the Italian Government to introduce legislation to give effect to a Directive (Directive 80/987/EEC[78] concerning employee rights in the event of employer insol-

[72] On this point see further Craig n. 55 above.

[73] [1994] ECR I-3325, 3339 (para 48).

[74] But see now also Case C-194/94, *CIA Security International SA* v. *Signalson and Securitel SPRL* [1996] ECR I-2201, considered in J Coppel, "Horizontal Effect of Directives" (1997) 26 *ILJ* 69.

[75] Directive 85/577/EEC, OJ 1985 L372/31.

[76] S Turner, "Horizontal Direct Enforcement of Directives Rejected" (1995) 46 *NILQ* 244, 252.

[77] Cases C-6 and 9/90, [1991] ECR I-5357.

[78] OJ 1980 L283/23.

vency). The specific facts of the case involved a claim by Francovich and Bonifaci against the Italian state for wages they had been denied subsequent upon the non-implementation of the Directive (Francovich and Bonifaci had been unable to invoke the terms of the Directive against the State because the terms of the Directive were insufficiently precise to have direct effect).[79] The ECJ, in response to the question of whether a Member State could be liable in EU law for non-implementation of a Directive, referred again to the overriding force of Article 10 EC and held that damages must be awarded when: (1) it can be shown that the purpose of a Directive was to confer rights on an individual; (2) that the content of those rights can be identified on the basis of the Directive's provisions; and (3) there is a direct causal link between the State's failure to implement and the damage suffered by the individual.[80]

What is the significance of the state liability doctrine? In terms of solving the *Marshall* conundrum, *Francovich* might be argued to have succeeded, albeit it in a highly circuitous manner, in achieving the fuller protection of the individual. Although *Faccini Dori* had restated *Marshall's* value to the EU order, *Francovich* equally provided individuals with an additional means of enforcing their rights. In the first instance, of course, the protection of the individual's rights will continue to depend upon national court endeavours to discharge their obligations under the indirect effect doctrine. But where harmonious interpretation cannot be achieved, an individual who suffers loss as a result of the non-implementation of a Directive will subsequently be able to pursue in national courts an action for damages against the defaulting government. Consequently, and despite the practical problems presented by the extra cost of initiating fresh proceedings against the State and of meeting the liability conditions established by the ECJ,[81] there exists, at least as a matter of abstract perfection, the possibility of full protection of each individual's interests.

Beyond its importance in relation to the direct effect of Directives, *Francovich* is also significant insofar as it represented a sea change in the ECJ's wider jurisprudence on the remedial protection of individuals in national courts. The early jurisprudence of the ECJ had not required the creation of new remedies for the protection of an individual's EU law rights,[82] the ECJ emphasising instead that individual rights could best be

[79] On *Francovich* see further G Bebr, "Francovich v Italy, Bonifaci v Italy" (1992) 29 *CMLRev* 559 and E Szyszczak, "European Community Law: New Remedies, New Directions?" (1992) 55 *MLR* 690.

[80] [1991] ECR I-5357, 5414–15.

[81] Craig n. 55 above, 537. And see also C Plaza Martin, "Furthering the Effectiveness of EC Directives and the Judicial Protection of Individual Rights Thereunder" (1994) 43 *ICLQ* 26.

[82] See, e.g., Case 158/80, *Rewe Handelsgesellschaft Nord mbH* v. *Hauptzollamt Kiel* [1981] ECR 1805.

protected through the application of national remedial procedures.[83] The obvious shortcoming with this approach, however, was that it failed to take account of, and equate, systemic variations at the national level in each of the Member States. Although the ECJ was concerned to maximise the strengths of each of the Member State orders, it was also concerned to forge harmonised standards for the protection of EU law interests. The result was that the ECJ began to develop incrementally a series of minimum EU law standards which required national procedures to take account of the EU principles of proportionality,[84] adequacy[85] and effectiveness.[86]

Within the emerging jurisprudence, *Francovich* came to represent the most far-reaching departure from the ECJ's reliance on domestic standards. While the ECJ had previously emphasised the absolute centrality of national procedure and practice, national courts, post-*Francovich*, became obliged for the first time to award "EU law" damages in the event of the breach of an individual's EU law rights. This did not mean that national procedures were to become entirely redundant as any action for "EU damages" in a domestic court would still be determined in accordance with existing domestic models for liability. But the introduction of the doctrine did mean that, irrespective of which domestic model was adopted, it had to be one that would ensure that the individual could enjoy effective protection of their rights.[87] The domestic model could take the form of a "Euro-tort" which replicates the three-stage test elaborated by the ECJ,[88] or it could take the form of an existing tort modified to accommodate the EU standard. Either way, the model chosen must faithfully reflect the EU objective of holding Member States responsible for the breach of EU law interests.

The ECJ's marrying of EU law doctrine to national procedure and practice has been welcomed by commentators who consider that the state

[83] Subject to the requirements of non-discrimination and effectiveness. See Case 33/76, *Rewe-Zentralfinanz eG and Rewe-Zentral AG* v. *Landwirtschaftskammer für das Saarland* [1976] ECR 1989; Case 47/76, *Comet* v. *Produktschap voor Siergewassen* [1976] ECR 2043; and Case 158/80, *Rewe Handelsgesellschaft Nord mbH* v. *Hauptzollamt Kiel* [1981] ECR 1805.

[84] Case 8/77, *Sagulo, Brenca, and Bakhouche* [1977] ECR 1495.

[85] Case 14/83, *Von Colson and Kamann* v. *Land Nordrhein Westfalen* [1984] ECR 1891.

[86] See, e.g., Case 222/84, *Johnson* v. *Chief Constable of the RUC* [1986] ECR 1651; Case C-213/89, *R* v. *Secretary of State for Transport, ex p Factortame Ltd and Others* [1990] ECR I-2433; Case C-377/89, *Cotter and McDermott* v. *Minister for Social Welfare and Attorney General* [1991] ECR I-1155; and Case C-208/90, *Emmott* v. *Minister for Social Welfare* [1991] ECR I-4269.

[87] Cases C-46 & 48/93, *Brasserie du Pêcheur SA* v. *Germany, R* v. *Secretary of State for Transport, ex p Factortame Ltd* [1996] 1 ECR 1029, 1154 (para 73).

[88] The idea of creating new torts in UK law was first forwarded by Lord Denning in *Application des Gaz SA* v. *Falks Veritas Ltd* [1974] 2 CMLR 75. Note that, as Lord Denning's judgment was delivered long before the *Francovich* ruling, his suggestions were made purely from the perspective of domestic law rather than in response to any demand from the EU order.

liability doctrine strikes the correct balance between the respective roles of the ECJ and national courts.[89] The doctrine's emergence has, however, equally been criticised by other scholars who doubt how far it is feasible for supranational liability standards to make demands on national standards which have been developed for entirely different institutional reasons.[90] The doctrine of state liability introduced in *Francovich* has since been greatly expanded, and it now covers any "sufficiently serious" [91] breach of an individual's EU law rights which is caused by the actions or inactions of the legislative, executive or judicial branches of a Member State.[92] For Carol Harlow, the emergence of such a far-reaching supranational standard of government liability will likely only cause "infection" of national liability systems and a corresponding "cross-infection" of EU law's liability system.[93] Although others have argued convincingly that national orders would benefit from integrating the "superior" standards of EU law more fully into domestic law,[94] Harlow is of the opinion that interaction in the EU law paradigm will create difficulties even before the issue of deeper integration is addressed. Cast in terms of the cross-fertilisation problematic, then, the issue again crystallises around the question of how far, or whether, domestic institutions can accommodate external demands and use them informatively. Are domestic institutions and related processes open to deeper and beneficial integration, or are they so inherently different from their supranational equivalents that interaction at any level will only end in institutional displacement and inter-order departures?

[89] Chalmers n. 49 above, 190–2.

[90] C Harlow, "Francovich and the Problem of the Disobedient State" (1996) 2 *ELJ* 199 and Allison n. 2 above. But note that other commentators have criticised the ECJ for not going far enough in its efforts to bring about harmonised protection in the EU. See, e.g., C M G Himsworth, "Things Fall Apart: The Harmonisation of Community Judicial Procedural Protection Revisited" (1997) 22 *ELRev* 291.

[91] Cases C-46 and 48/93, *Brasserie du Pêcheur SA* v. *Germany, R* v. *Secretary of State for Transport, ex p Factortame Ltd* [1996] 1 ECR 1029. On the relationship between the requirement of "sufficient seriousness" and the three-stage test for liability first introduced in *Francovich*, see Joined Cases C-178–179 and 188–190/94, *Dillenkofer* v. *Germany* [1996] 3 CMLR 469.

[92] Cases C-46 and 48/93, *Brasserie du Pêcheur SA* v. *Germany, R* v. *Secretary of State for Transport, ex p Factortame Ltd* [1996] 1 ECR 1029, 1145 (para 34): "(I)n international law a State whose liability for breach of an international commitment is in issue will be viewed as a single entity, irrespective of whether the breach which gave rise to the damage is attributable to the legislature, the judiciary or the executive. This must apply *a fortiori* in the Community legal order". See further with regard to acts of the executive, Case C-5/94, *R* v. *Ministry of Agriculture, Fisheries and Food, ex p Hedley Lomas (Ireland) Ltd* [1996] ECR I-2553. But see also with regard to the legislature, Case C-392/93, *R* v. *HM Treasury, ex p British Telecommunications plc* [1996] ECR I-1631.

[93] Harlow n. 90 above, p 201.

[94] P Craig, "Once More Unto the Breach: The Community, The State and Damages Liability" (1997) 113 *LQR* 67. Craig's arguments are considered in greater depth in ch. 6.

Fundamental rights

The area of law that has illustrated most clearly how the abstract difficulties associated with European legal integration can manifest themselves in practice is fundamental rights. The ECJ's base understanding that EU law constitutes a "new legal order" which should enjoy hegemony over conflicting provisions of national law, while often accepted as a matter of course, has occasionally proven problematic when the ECJ has stated that the supremacy principle should also trump national fundamental rights standards.[95] The point of conflict, simply stated, has arisen from national court refusal to subject domestic constitutional values to the overriding force of a body of law that has a different point of institutional legitimation and, moreover, has been historically conditioned by the constitutional imperative of economic integration.[96] And, although some commentators have queried how far the pursuit of economic integration can truly be said to define EU law,[97] others remain convinced that EU law's historical reference point places it "in a stand-off of constitutional conflict" with national orders that emphasise the primacy of social and civil values.[98]

The potential for conflict first became apparent when the German Constitutional Court refused in *Internationale Handelsgesellschaft*[99] to recognise that the legality of EU measures could only be gauged by reference to EU law's fundamental rights standards.[100] In the case, the ECJ had stated that recourse to national standards was not envisaged because such recourse "would have an adverse effect on the uniformity and efficacy of (EU) law . . . The protection of such rights . . . must be ensured within the framework of the structure and objectives of the (EU)".[101] For the German Constitutional Court, such understandings of the reach of EU law and its

[95] Case 11/70, *Internationale Handelsgesellschaft mbH* v. *Einfur- und Vorratstelle für Getreide und Futtermittel* [1972] CMLR 255, 283 (para 3).

[96] The ECJ has described the four freedoms in the EC Treaty as general principles of law which have constitutional force – see, e.g., Case 240/83, *Procurer de la République* v. *Association de Défense des Brûleurs Usagées* [1985] ECR 520, 531. See further B Hepple, "Social Values and European Law" (1995) 48 *CLP* 39 and P Davies, "Market Integration and Social Policy in the Court of Justice" (1995) 24 *ILJ* 49.

[97] M P Maduro, *We the Court: The European Court of Justice & the European Economic Constitution* (Hart Publishing, Oxford, 1998).

[98] D R Phelan, *Revolt or Revolution? The Constitutional Boundaries of the European Community* (Round Hall/Sweet & Maxwell, Dublin, 1997), p 369.

[99] *Internationale Handelsgesellschaft mbH* v. *Einfuhr und- Vorratstelle für Getreide und Futtermittel* [1974] 2 CMLR 540.

[100] Standards which had only recently been recognised by the ECJ. See the progression from Case 1/58, *Stork* v. *High Authority* [1959] ECR 17 to Case 29/69, *Stauder* v. *City of Ulm* [1969] ECR 419.

[101] Case 11/70, *Internationale Handelsgesellschaft mbH* v. *Einfur- und Vorratstelle für Getreide und Futtermittel* [1972] CMLR 255, 283 (para 3).

general principles were unacceptable. Although the German Court accepted the ECJ's argument that EU law forms a new legal order, it simultaneously denied that EU law's autonomous qualities allowed it to override long-standing domestic constitutional values. Highlighting in particular how the EU process was absent a democratically elected Parliament and a codified catalogue of rights, the German Court concluded that it could not, under such circumstances, accede to the ECJ's claims:

> "(I)n the hypothetical case of a conflict between (EU) law and . . . the guarantees of fundamental rights in the Constitution . . . the guarantee of fundamental rights in the Constitution prevails as long as the competent organs of the (EU) have not removed the conflict of norms in accordance with the Treaty mechanism".[102]

The German Court's judgment is often taken to have prompted the ECJ to adopt a more focused approach to fundamental rights considerations.[103] In *Nold* the ECJ stated clearly its willingness to have recourse to "international treaties for the protection of human rights on which the Member States have collaborated or which they are signatories",[104] with subsequent case law making reference to the European Convention on Human Rights[105] and the International Covenant of Civil and Political Rights.[106] The ECJ's endeavours in this regard, coupled with action taken by the other EU institutions,[107] were soon to satisfy the German Constitutional Court that fundamental rights were suitably protected in EU law. In *Re Wünsche Handelsgesellschaft* the German Constitutional Court retracted its threat to the EU order, finding that recent developments meant that it no longer needed to review the legality of EU measures by reference to standards contained in the German Basic Law.[108] And, while it is true that the German Court's ruling was conditional and predicated on the Court's continuing concern for national constitutional values,[109] it is also true that

[102] *Internationale Handelsgesellschaft mbH* v. *Einfuhr und- Vorratstelle für Getreide und Futtermittel* [1974] 2 CMLR 540, 549–51 (paras 19–24).

[103] But for a more rounded assessment of the emergence of the ECJ's human rights jurisprudence see G de Búrca, "The Language of Rights and European Integration" in J Shaw and G More (eds), *New Legal Dynamics of European Union* (Clarendon Press, Oxford, 1995) pp 29, 39–41.

[104] Case 4/73, *Nold* v. *Commission* [1974] 2 CMLR 338, 354 (para 13).

[105] See, e.g., Case 36/75, *Rutili* v. *Minister for the Interior* [1976] 1 CMLR 140 and Case 222/84, *Johnston* v. *Chief Constable of the RUC* [1986] ECR 1651. See further E Guild and G Lesieur, *The European Court of Justice and the European Convention on Human Rights: Who said what, when?* (Kluwer, The Hague, 1998).

[106] Case 374/87, *Orkem* v. *Commission* [1989] ECR 3283.

[107] See, e.g., the Joint Declaration of the Parliament, Council and Commission, OJ 1977 C 103/1.

[108] [1987] 3 CMLR 225.

[109] A point later confirmed in the Court's judgment in *Brunner* v. *European Union Treaty*

the judgment removed any immediate obstacles to the workings of the EU order. Indeed, it was probably as a result of this that the ECJ subsequently felt able to bind national courts to observe EU law's fundamental rights' standards not only when Member State authorities are enforcing provisions of EU law[110] but also when courts are reviewing the lawfulness of domestic measures which derogate from Treaty obligations.[111]

What, then, does the emergence of EU law's fundamental rights jurisprudence reveal about the dynamics of legal integration? In the first instance, and as stated above, the fact that the jurisprudence was prompted by national court resistance to the demands of the EU order makes clear that the co-existence of contrasting institutional perspectives can lead to actual conflict between European Courts and their national counterparts.[112] The German Court's judgment was to be paralleled in other jurisdictions and, as with the initial threat to the EU order, the latter rulings similarly emphasised that defining domestic values may not always be subjected to the core demands of EU law.[113] In *Society for the Protection of the Unborn Child (Ireland) Ltd* v. *Grogan*[114] the Irish Supreme Court stated definitively that it would not allow national constitutional guarantees of the right to life of the unborn child to be overridden by some "possible or putative right which might exist in European law".[115] Although the threat of conflict was again off set by suitable institutional adaptation and inventive decision-making by the ECJ,[116] the Irish Court's concern that core social values should not be

[1994] 1 CMLR 57. In *Brunner*, a case concerning a challenge to German ratification of the TEU, the German Court ruled that it retained the option of reviewing EU legislation for compatibility with the powers belonging to the institutions under the TEU. For commentary see M Herdegen, "Maastricht and the German Constitutional Court: Constitutional Restraints for an Ever Closer Union" (1994) 31 *CMLRev* 235 and J H H Weiler, "Does Europe Need a Constitution? Reflections on Demos, Telos and the German Maastricht Decision" (1995) 1 *ELJ* 219. But see now also the German Constitutional Court's judgment in *Alcan*, Decision of 17 Feb 2000, annotated by F. Hoffmeister in (2001) 38 *CML Rev* 791.

110 Case 5/88 *Wachauf* v. *Germany* [1989] ECR 2609.

111 Case C-260/89, *Elliniki Radiophonia Tileorassi AE* v. *Dimotiki Etairia Pliroforissis and Sotirios Kouvelas* [1991] ECR I-2925.

112 On the question of how such disputes might be avoided see N Macormack, "Beyond the Sovereign State" (1993) 56 *MLR* 1 and "The Maastricht-Urteil: Sovereignty Now" (1995) 1 *ELJ* 259.

113 See, e.g., *Frontini* v. *Ministero delle Finanze* [1974] 2 CMLR 372 (Italian Constitutional Court).

114 [1990] 1 CMLR 689.

115 *Ibid*, 699 (Finlay C J). The right to life of the unborn is guaranteed by Art. 40.3.3 of the Irish Constitution. *Grogan* arose when the Society for the Protection of the Unborn Child applied for an injunction to prevent students disseminating information about the availability of abortion services in Great Britain. The students argued that, as they were distributing information about services that are lawfully available in other Member States, their actions were vouchsafed by Art. 50 (ex 60) EC (freedom to provide and receive services). The injunction sought was granted.

116 In its ruling on an Art. 234 EC reference from the Irish High Court the ECJ was able

subsumed within more general European economic rights highlighted afresh that there exist limits to the integration of competing standards.[117] In other words, the Irish Court's judgment implied that, where EU law causes irritation to the domestic order, the offending provisions will be rejected in the case at hand. Under such circumstances, legal integration, and, indeed, wider social and economic integration, will clearly be frustrated.

Yet, within the limits to integration established by such cases, the fact that the ECJ's fundamental rights jurisprudence has been developed by reference to the ECHR and national constitutional experience equally indicates that the interaction of European legal orders can be fluid and institutionally far-reaching. The ECJ's use of the ECHR, for example, while criticised by some commentators,[118] has given rise to a striking degree of overlap between supranational, international and national legal standards.[119] Although the EU institutions have not formally acceded to the ECHR and have now adopted their own Charter of Rights,[120] the open recognition of the ECHR's guiding force has meant that it has come to enjoy a prominent position relative to the workings of the EU order.[121]

to distinguish the case on the ground that, while abortion can constitute a service for purposes of EU law, the students could not avail of Art. 50 EC as they were not being paid to disseminate the information by the providers of the service in another Member State. For critical commentary see D Curtin, "Case C-159/90, Society for the Protection of the Unborn Child (Ireland) Ltd v Grogan and others" (1992) 29 *CMLRev* 585. The institutional adaptation effected, meanwhile, took the form of Protocol 17 to the TEU. See further G Hogan, "Protocol 17" in P Keatinge (eds.), *Ireland and Maastricht – What the Treaty Means* (Institute of European Affairs, Dublin, 1992), p 109.

[117] It should be noted, however, that, post-*Grogan*, Irish abortion law has been modified, with some of the reasons for the change being attributable to the impact of EU law and the ECHR (see, in particular, *Open Door Counselling and Dublin Well Woman* v. *Ireland* [1993] 15 EHRR 244). See further J Casey, *Constitutional Law in Ireland* (Round Hall/Sweet & Maxwell, Dublin, 2nd edn, 2000), pp 433–44.

[118] J Coppel and A O'Neill, "The European Court of Justice: Taking Rights Seriously?" (1992) 29 *CMLRev* 669. But see J H H Weiler and N J S Lockhart, "'Taking Rights Seriously' Seriously: The European Court of Justice and Its Fundamental Rights Jurisprudence" (1995) 32 *CMLRev* 51 and 579.

[119] On the manner in which national standards have influenced the ECHR see D A Leonardi, "The Strasbourg System of Human Rights Protection: "Europeanisation" of the Law through the Confluence of the Western Legal Traditions" (1996) 8 *ERPL* 1139.

[120] See nn. 4 and 5 above. Note that Art. 52. 3 of the Charter states: "In so far as this Charter contains rights which correspond to rights guaranteed by the (ECHR) . . . the meaning and scope of those rights shall be the same as those laid down by the (ECHR). This provision shall not prevent Union law providing more extensive protection". Although note also that it is unclear at the time of writing whether the Charter will be legally binding – see the *Declaration on the future of the Union* (para 5) appended to the Treaty of Nice. Although see also the Opinion of Adv-Gen Tizzano in Case C-173/99, *BECTU* v. *Secretary of State for Trade and Industry*, 8 Feb 2001 (para 27).

[121] See Arts. 6 and 7 TEU. Although the overlap between EU law and the ECHR is not without difficulty. See I Canor, "*Primus inter pares*: Who is the ultimate guardian of fundamental rights in Europe?" (2000) 25 *ELRev* 3. For the argument that the EU should, in any

This has had implications not only for the EU institutions, but also for the sovereign space of national legal orders. The understanding that national courts should have regard to EU law's fundamental rights standards has meant that the ECHR has been able to exert an indirect influence in those Member States, like Ireland and the United Kingdom, which had previously declined to incorporate the ECHR in domestic law.[122] While it might be argued that actual impact in those orders has been relatively limited,[123] it can also be argued that EU law has institutionalised legal relationships in a manner that has effectively transcended the legal and political preferences of some Member States. In consequence, it might be expected that the ECHR's recent introduction in UK domestic law will only hasten integration of the kind already facilitated by EU law.

3. THE EUROPEAN CONVENTION ON HUMAN RIGHTS

The body of ECHR jurisprudence, as with that developed by the ECJ, is underpinned by institutional assumptions and characteristics that render the international order different in form from any other system. Although the European Court of Human Rights (ECtHR) has not infused the ECHR with constitutional qualities directly comparable to those which inform EU law, it has, nevertheless, long regarded the ECHR as a living instrument[124] that is "unlike international Treaties of the classic kind".[125] Drawing on teleological interpretative techniques[126] and related understandings that ECHR provisions enjoy autonomous and independent meaning,[127] the ECtHR has been able to expand the reach of the ECHR's guarantees[128]

event, accede to the ECHR, see R Harmsen, "National Responsibility for European Community Acts under the European Convention on Human Rights: Recasting the Accession Debate" (2001) 7 *EPL* 623.

[122] N Grief n. 8 above. For recognition of the point in relation to Irish law see, e.g., *Doyle* v. *Commissioner of An Garda Síochána* [1999] 1 IR 249, 269 (Barrington J). Note that, at the time of writing, the Irish Government has introduced a Bill which will, if passed, afford the ECHR sub-constitutional domestic effect. For details of the Bill see http://www.gov.ie/oirechtas/frame.htm..

[123] See, e.g., in the UK *Allgmeine Gold-und Silberscheideanstalt* v. *Customs and Excise Commissioners* [1978] 2 CMLR 292 and *R* v. *Immigration Appeal Tribunal, ex p Marchon* [1993] Imm AR 98. But see also *R* v. *Secretary of State for the Home Department, ex p McQuillan* [1995] 4 All ER 400, considered in ch. 7.

[124] *Cossey* v. *UK* [1991] 13 EHRR 622, 639 (para 35): "It is true that . . . the (ECtHR) is not bound by its previous judgments . . . the Court (can depart) from an earlier decision . . . in order to ensure that the interpretation of the Convention reflects and remains in line with present day conditions".

[125] *Ireland* v. *United Kingdom* [1979–80] 2 EHRR 25, 103 (para 239).

[126] For example, *Wemhoff* v. *Germany* [1979–80] 1 EHRR 55.

[127] For example, *Engel* v. *Netherlands* [1976] 1 EHRR 647.

[128] The ECHR guarantees, among other things, the right to life (Art. 2); freedom from torture (Art. 3); right to liberty (Art. 5); right to a fair trial (Art. 6); right to respect for

and to emphasise that it represents "a constitutional instrument of European public order".[129] In some areas, development of the law has been far-reaching,[130] while in others, developments have arguably been more limited.[131] Overall, however, it is recognised that the ECtHR has endeavoured both to maximise the strength of existing guarantees and to ensure that they benefit all sections of society.[132]

The ECHR's capacity to prompt change at the level of national courts flows from the principles of effectiveness, legality and proportionality. These principles, which have been developed by reference to the text of the ECHR, are used by the ECtHR when it is deciding whether a contracting party has fallen below the required standard of fundamental rights protection. The ECtHR does not, as such, expressly oblige national courts to give effect to the principles when they are hearing cases raising ECHR issues. The institutional design of the ECHR is markedly different from that of EU law, not least because the ECHR pursues minimum standards of fundamental rights protection rather than absolute standards that govern social, economic and political integration,[133] and this has meant that the ECtHR has not considered it necessary to impose far-reaching procedural and substantive demands on its national counterparts. But it also follows that, when a national court is attempting to protect rights in accordance with the ECHR, their capacity to do so will depend upon their ability to replicate at the domestic level the standards of scrutiny applied by the ECtHR. Ultimately, therefore, principles of ECHR jurisprudence can enjoy the strongest form of indirect influence at the national level, whether that influence is facilitated by EU law or by the terms of any domestic implementing legislation.[134]

private and family life (Art. 8); freedom of thought, conscience and religion (Art. 9); freedom of expression (Art. 10); freedom of association (Art. 11); the prohibition of discrimination (Art. 14 – and see now also Protocol 12); right to peaceful enjoyment of property (Art 1, Prot 1); and the right to education (Art 2, Prot. 1).

[129] *Loizidou* v. *Turkey*, ECHR [1995], Series A Vol 310, 27, para 75.

[130] See, e.g., the ECtHR's understanding of what can constitute civil rights for purposes of Art. 6 ECHR in *Ringeisen* v. *Austria* [1979–80] 1 EHRR 455.

[131] See, e.g., the somewhat inconsistent approach to the rights of transsexuals in *Rees* v. *UK* [1976] 9 EHRR 56; *Cossey* v. *UK* [1981] 13 EHRR 622; *B* v. *France* [1993] 16 EHRR 1; *X, Y, and Z* v. *UK* [1997] 24 EHRR 143; and *Sheffield and Horsham* v. *UK* [1999] 27 EHRR 163.

[132] C Harvey and S Livingstone, "Protecting the Marginalised: The Role of the European Convention on Human Rights" (2000) 51 *NILQ* 445. On the related question of how far the ECtHR's expansion of provisions has amounted to judicial activism see P Mahoney, "Judicial Activism and Judicial Self-Restraint in the European Court of Human Rights: Two Sides of the Same Coin?" (1990) 11 *HRLJ* 57.

[133] Although note that EU Member States can derogate from the "absolute" standards prescribed by EU law under closely defined circumstances. See, e.g., with regard to the free movement of goods, Art. 30 (ex 36) EC.

[134] See, e.g., s. 2 of the Human Rights Act 1998, considered in ch. 7.

Effectiveness, legality, proportionality

The effectiveness principle developed by the ECtHR applies equally to all rights listed in the ECHR and, put simply, requires that those rights enjoy full and meaningful protection in practice.[135] The logic underscoring the principle was identified by the ECtHR in *Airey* v. *Ireland*.[136] Here, the issue was whether the availability of legal aid in civil proceedings (in this case, an application to obtain a decree of judicial separation) was relevant to determining whether the State was in breach of its obligations to observe the right to a fair trial under Article 6 ECHR. While the ECtHR did not go so far as to find that legal aid should be available for all civil proceedings, it did find that, in view of the complexity of the present case, the absence of legal representation may have prejudiced the applicant's interests. Thus, proceeding on the understanding that "the ECHR is intended to guarantee not rights that are theoretical or illusory but rights that are practical and effective"[137] the ECtHR moved towards the imposition of positive obligations under which the State can be required to take active measures (e.g. the provision of legal aid) to ensure the protection of rights.

The principles of legality and proportionality, meanwhile, seek to limit the circumstances under which a state may impose restrictions upon an individual's rights. Both principles find support in the text of the ECHR and seek to ensure that any derogation from ECHR guarantees is regulated by law and implemented in a manner that accounts for the competing demands of the public interest and an individual's interests.[138] The principle of legality, for example, requires not only that any limitation on rights is underpinned by legal authorisation, but also that the source of the authorisation is accessible to those individuals who wish to inquire as to the basis of the State's powers.[139] The principle likewise requires that there

[135] And see also Art. 13 ECHR: "Everyone whose rights and freedoms as set forth in this Convention are violated shall have an effective remedy before a national authority notwithstanding that the violation has been committed by persons acting in an official capacity".

[136] [1979] 2 EHRR 305.

[137] [1979] 2 EHRR 305, 316 (para 26).

[138] The rights contained in the ECHR may be sub-divided into absolute and qualified rights. Absolute rights (e.g. the Art. 3 prohibition on torture) cannot be subject to any limitations. Qualified rights (principally the Art. 8 right to respect for private and family life; the Art. 9 right to freedom of thought, conscience and religion; the Art. 10 right to freedom of expression; and the Art. 11 right to freedom of association and assembly) can be subject to such constraints as are "prescribed by law" (legality) and "necessary in a democratic society" (proportionality). Note also that other ECHR provisions (e.g. the Art. 5 right to liberty and security) can be the subject of limitations but only insofar as those limitations are listed in the ECHR – see, e.g., Art. 5(1)(a)–(e).

[139] See, e.g., *Halford* v. *UK* [1997] 24 EHRR 523. It should be noted that the ECtHR has adopted a flexible approach to the form that a legal framework may take. Thus it has held that the common law and delegated legislation can constitute a sufficient legal basis – see respectively *Sunday Times* v. *UK* [1979–80] 2 EHRR 245 and *Barthold* v. *Germany* [1985] 7 EHRR 383.

exist a degree of certainty in domestic legal structures so that an individual may determine the probable consequences of their actions. And, although the ECtHR recognises that absolute certainty cannot be guaranteed, it has emphasised the need for at least some degree of predictability:

> "(T)he requirement of foreseeability cannot mean that an individual should be enabled to foresee when the authorities are likely to intercept his communications so that he can adapt his conduct accordingly. Nevertheless, the law must be sufficiently clear in its terms to give citizens an adequate indication as to the circumstances in which and the conditions on which public authorities are empowered (to interfere)".[140]

The proportionality principle then seeks to ensure that public authorities which place limitations on an individual's rights do so only insofar as is necessary to achieve a particular objective which will usually be associated with more general notions of the public interest.[141] Jason Coppel, who defines proportionality as requiring "that the restrictive effects of a measure are strictly in proportion to its legitimate aims and objectives",[142] has suggested that there are a series of tests which the ECtHR applies when gauging the proportionality of a measure.[143] The tests include: the "balancing" test (whereby "a measure is disproportionate if it imposes restrictions which are not justified in the light of the objectives which it seeks to achieve");[144] the "relevant and sufficient reasons" test (whereby "a measure will be held disproportionate if it is not supported by relevant and sufficient reasons");[145] the test of "careful design" (whereby a restriction will be disproportionate if it is "over-broad and covers a wider range of situations than is justifiable);[146] the "essence of the right" test (whereby a

[140] *Malone* v. *UK* [1985] 7 EHRR 14, 40 (para 67).

[141] Objectives listed in the text of the ECHR include the protection of "national security, public safety or the economic well-being of the country, for the prevention of disorder or crime, for the protection of health or morals, or the protection of the rights and freedoms of others" – Art. 8(2). And see also Arts. 9(2), 10(2) and 11(2). On proportionality in ECHR jurisprudence see further M A Eissen, "The Principle of Proportionality in the Case-Law of the European Court of Human Rights" in R StJ Macdonald *et al* (eds.), *The European System for the Protection of Human Rights* (Martinus Nijhoff: Dordrecht, 1993), p 125 and J McBride, "Proportionality and the European ECHR on Human Rights" in E Ellis (ed.), *The Principle of Proportionality in the Laws of Europe* (Hart Publishing, Oxford, 1999), p 23.

[142] J Coppel, *The Human Rights Act 1998: Enforcing the European Convention in the Domestic Courts* (Wiley, Chichester, 1998), p 160.

[143] *Ibid*, 161–4.

[144] Coppel cites, e.g., *Young, James and Webster* v. *UK*, A/44 [1982] 4 EHRR 38; *Dudgeon* v. *UK*, A/45 [1982] 4 EHRR 149; *F* v. *Switzerland*, A/128 [1988] 10 EHRR 411; and *Nasri* v. *France*, A/324 [1996] 21 EHRR 458.

[145] Coppel cites, e.g., *Goodwin* v. *UK*, Appl No 17488/90 [1996] 22 EHRR 123 and *Vogt* v. *Germany*, A/323 [1996] 21 EHRR 205. On the ECtHR's understanding of the need for reasons see further *Jordan* v. *UK*, judgment of 4 May 2001.

[146] Coppel cites, e.g., *Open Door Counselling and Dublin Well Woman* v. *Ireland*, A/246 [1993] 15 EHRR 244.

restriction "will always be disproportionate where its impairs the very essence of the right");[147] and the "evidential" test (whereby the State is required "to produce satisfactory evidence of the pressing social need which its restriction seeks to address").[148]

The fact that the proportionality principle has given rise to these tests and requirements, coupled with the overarching requirement that individuals enjoy effective protection of their rights, is of fundamental importance to understanding how and why the ECHR may cause realignment in some national courts. In short, the fact that ECHR jurisprudence is structured around searching methods of enquiry means that national courts may have to substitute ECHR standards for domestic norms when hearing ECHR issues. In some jurisdictions, substitution may not be necessary as domestic standards may already be equivalent to those of the ECHR. But in other jurisdictions, it may be that domestic courts will only be able to afford proper protection to individual rights when they adopt the jurisprudence of the ECtHR. This is particularly true of the UK legal order where the ECHR will increasingly demand that courts become more closely involved in the review of, among other things, administrative decisions. UK administrative law has historically been associated with the standard of *Wednesbury* unreasonableness/review, this being a standard that seeks to keep judges at the outer-reaches of the decision-making process.[149] Although the courts have, consistent with the emergence of a more far-reaching body of judicial review, shown themselves willing to modify the standard whenever fundamental rights are in issue,[150] the ECtHR has made clear that it considers that *Wednesbury*, whether modified or not, cannot guarantee effective protection of individual rights.[151] By choosing to afford the ECHR a central role in domestic law, therefore, the UK legal system may increasingly come to be associated with the more demanding standard of review that underpins the proportionality principle.[152] The significance this point holds for the wider process of legal cross-fertilisation is returned to in chapter seven.

[147] Coppel cites, e.g., *F* v. *Switzerland*, A/128 [1988] 10 EHRR 411.

[148] Coppel cites, e.g., *Kokkinakis* v. *Greece*, A/260-A [1994] 17 EHRR 397.

[149] *Wednesbury*, as originally formulated, permitted the courts to quash a decision only if it was "so unreasonable that no reasonable authority could ever have come to it". See *Associated Provincial Picture Houses* v. *Wednesbury Corporation* [1948] 1 KB 223, 230 (Lord Greene MR). On *Wednesbury* see further Lord Irvine of Lairg, "Judges and Decision-Makers: The Theory and Practice of *Wednesbury* Review" [1996] *PL* 59, considered in ch. 5.

[150] For example, *R* v. *Secretary of State for the Home Department, ex p Bugdaycay* [1987] AC 514, 531 (Lord Bridge); *R* v. *Coventry Airport, ex p Phoenix Aviation* [1995] 3 All ER 37, 62 (Simon Brown LJ); *R* v. *Ministry of Defence, ex p Smith* [1995] 4 All ER 427, 445 (Simon Brown LJ); *R* v. *Cambridge Health Authority, ex p B* [1995] 25 BMLR 5; and *R* v. *Lord Saville, ex p A* [1999] 4 All ER 860 (Lord Woolf).

[151] *Smith and Grady* v. *United Kingdom* [2000] 29 EHRR 493.

[152] A point recently conceded by the HL. See *R* v. *Secretary of State for the Home Department, ex p Daly*, [2001] 3 All ER 433, 447 (Lord Cooke).

The margin of appreciation

One final feature of ECHR jurisprudence that is relevant to any discussion of judicial scrutiny of fundamental rights protection is the margin of appreciation. The doctrine has been defined as meaning "that the (contracting) state is allowed a certain measure of discretion, subject to European supervision, when it takes legislative, administrative or judicial action in the area of a Convention right".[153] The doctrine is, as such, the means through which the ECtHR has sought to reconcile the protection of fundamental rights standards with the concerns and demands of the contracting states. Although the ECHR is premised upon the need to guarantee minimum standards of fundamental rights protection, the ECtHR equally recognises that contracting states are, in view of their particular knowledge of their social, economic and political circumstances, sometimes better placed to determine whether certain individual rights should be limited. While the ECtHR's deference to a contracting party will vary according to the nature of the right in issue,[154] therefore, the core assumption underpinning the margin of appreciation is the need to observe the respective spheres of influence of different institutional forces. The point was made by the ECtHR in *Handyside* v. *UK*:

> "By reason of their direct and continuous contact with the vital forces of their countries, state authorities are in principle in a better position than the international judge to give an opinion on the exact content of those requirements (of morals) as well as on the "necessity" of a "restriction" or "penalty" intended to meet them . . .
>
> Nevertheless (the ECHR) does not give the contracting states an unlimited power of appreciation. The Court, which . . . is responsible for ensuring the observance of those states' engagements, is empowered to give the final ruling on whether a "restriction" or "penalty" is reconcilable with (an ECHR guarantee). The domestic margin of appreciation thus goes hand in hand with a European supervision".[155]

[153] D J Harris, M O'Boyle and C Warbrick, *Law of the European Convention on Human Rights* (Butterworths, London, 1995), p 12. There is an extensive body of literature on the margin of appreciation. See, e.g., T A O'Donnell, "The Margin of Appreciation Doctrine: Standards in the Jurisprudence of the European Court of Human Rights" (1982) 4 *HRQ* 474 and H Yourrow, *The Margin of Appreciation Doctrine in the Dynamics of European Human Rights Jurisprudence* (Kluwer, The Hague, 1996).

[154] The margin operates most obviously in relation to qualified rights such as those contained in Arts. 8–11 ECHR (right to respect for private and family life; freedom of thought conscience and religion; freedom of expression; and freedom of association). See further H Yourrow n. 153 above. And see also J Callewaert, "Is there a Margin of Appreciation in Arts. 2, 3 and 4 of the ECHR?" (1998) 19 *HRLJ*.

[155] [1976] 1 EHRR 737, 753–4 (paras 48–9).

What does the margin of appreciation mean for national courts and for the development of domestic legal orders? Certainly, it would appear, at least at a superficial level, that the margin has much in common with administrative law constructs, like *Wednesbury*, which seek to protect areas of administrative discretion from undue judicial interference. The margin's emphasis on judicial deference under appropriate circumstances clearly reflects domestic legal concerns about the need for courts to observe the parameters associated with traditional separation of powers doctrines. On this basis, therefore, it might be argued that the margin of appreciation could feed almost unnoticed into a domestic order and in a manner that minimises the scope for change to domestic principle and practice.

The problem with an understanding that the margin of appreciation could be transposed into domestic law, however, is that it fails fully to account for the different institutional environments that have given rise to comparable legal constructs. Singh, Hunt and Demetriou have argued forcefully that it is unhelpful to equate the margin of appreciation with the UK standard of *Wednesbury* review because the ECtHR itself "does not equate the concept of the margin of appreciation with what has been called *Wednesbury* unreasonableness in English public law".[156] Although Singh, Hunt and Demetriou note that the purpose of the margin of appreciation and *Wednesbury* review is to ensure due judicial deference to areas of authority that belong to other bodies, they emphasise that domestic court use of the international standard could have a negative impact on the protection of rights. Consequently, and very much in line with the logic of the concept of legal cross-fertilisation, it might be inferred that, while some principles of ECHR jurisprudence (e.g. proportionality) could be of benefit to the domestic order, others (e.g. the margin of appreciation) would not:

> "Instead of resorting to the concept of the margin of appreciation, we suggest that courts should articulate the many different factors which are relevant to the question of the proper level of deference, and provide an indication . . . of the sorts of contexts in which each of those factors has most weight . . . Importation into the domestic sphere of the supranational concept of the margin of appreciation will in our view prevent such an approach emerging and seriously hinder the effective incorporation of the ECHR".[157]

[156] "Is there a Role for the 'Margin of Appreciation' in National Law after the Human Rights Act?" (1999) *EHRLR* 15, 17.

[157] *Ibid*, 21–2. The UK courts have since recognised that the "margin of appreciation" doctrine is not of application at the local level, although they have started to develop a domestic "area of discretion" doctrine. See *R* v. *DPP, ex p Kebeline and others* [2000] 2 AC 326, 379 (Lord Hope). And see further ch. 7.

4. CONCLUSION

This chapter has provided an overview of those aspects of European law that create pressure for adaptation at the national level. It has shown that European law feeds into domestic orders in a manner that has the potential both to demand and foster far-reaching institutional change. Focusing in particular on the range of obligations associated with the workings of the "EU law paradigm", the chapter has highlighted how national courts are required to give effect to the general principles of EU law and to adapt domestic procedure and practice. Consideration in this regard has also been given to the more indirect impact that core features of ECHR jurisprudence may have at the national level.

A further recurrent theme in the chapter has been the fact that national institutional preferences mediate the reception of European law. This point is, of course, central to understanding the fuller dynamics of European legal integration. It was emphasised in chapter one that the process of European legal integration is largely driven by national court willingness to use their experience with European law for purposes of developing more generally the principle and practice of their domestic orders. In its purest form, it was suggested that such borrowing would manifest itself in the direct transplantation of supranational standards into domestic law. But the existence of contrasting institutional perspectives and reference points was also taken to mean that borrowing may not always be sequential or even occur. As considered above, this has then meant that national courts have, in practice, sometimes experienced difficulties discharging their duties within the EU law paradigm, with some courts going so far as to reject the core doctrines of the EU order. Although the difficulties have often been off-set by subsequent institutional adaptation at the supranational level,[158] the existence of difficulties in the EU law paradigm is indicative of the fact that there may be limits to the successful interaction of domestic and European norms. It follows that, while there exists an abstract expectation that national courts will borrow from their experience with European law, the empirical fact may be that deeper integration is constrained by national court prioritisation of defining domestic values.

In the following chapter, the relevance of some of these points is considered with reference to the manner in which UK courts have approached and justified the discharge of their obligations in the EU law paradigm. As will become apparent, the reception of EU law into the domestic order is, from the perspective of academic commentators, widely understood to have undermined the justificatory force of orthodox constitutional values.[159] Yet, for the UK courts, the reception of EU law into the domestic

[158] See, e.g., the above discussion of fundamental rights in EU law.

[159] See, e.g., M Hunt, *Using Human Rights Law in English Courts* (Hart Publishing, Oxford, 1997) chs. 1–3.

order has been taken to be entirely consonant with orthodox institutional understandings.[160] This judicial emphasis on orthodoxy will be seen to have had paradoxical implications for the integration of domestic and European legal standards. In the first instance, and in sharp contrast to the experience of other Member States' legal orders, it will be seen that the UK courts' recourse to orthodoxy within the EU law paradigm has not, to date, prevented them affording practical primacy to EU law.[161] But beyond facilitating apparently harmonious interaction within the EU law paradigm, the UK courts' emphasis on orthodoxy will be seen to have frustrated deeper integration which may occur as a result of borrowing from EU law. Although there have been several significant instances of cross-fertilisation,[162] the pattern of borrowing has been irregular and punctuated by a seeming judicial concern to emphasise how EU law and domestic law occupy essentially different spheres. The pattern and point of emphasis will not only be argued to be attributable to the courts' orthodox justification for their decisions within the EU law paradigm; it will also be argued to have prevented fuller development of the law in the manner associated with the common law model of review considered in chapter two. The related question of why an increased process of borrowing may be expected to occur in future years is returned to in subsequent consideration of the significance of the Human Rights Act 1998.

[160] For the clearest statement in this regard, see *R* v. *Secretary of State for Transport, ex p Factortame (No 2)* [1991] 1 All ER 70, 107–8 (Lord Bridge).

[161] *R* v. *Secretary of State for Transport, ex p Factortame (No 2)* [1991] 1 All ER 70 and *Equal Opportunities Commission and Another* v. *Secretary of State for Employment* [1994] 1 All ER 910.

[162] See, e.g., *Woolwich Building Society* v. *Inland Revenue Commissioners (No 2)* [1992] 3 WLR 366; *M* v. *Home Office* [1993] 3 WLR 433; and *R* v. *North and East Devon Health Authority, ex p Coughlan* [2000] 2 WLR 622.

4

The Reception of EU Law

1. INTRODUCTION

The constitutional conundrum that faced UK courts on accession to the EU was how far, if at all, they could reconcile the competing supremacies of the supranational and domestic legal orders.[1] UK public law orthodoxy is, as has already been discussed in chapter two, predicated on the doctrine of the absolute sovereignty of the Westminster Parliament. The Diceyan conception of the doctrine famously holds that, as each sovereign Parliament enjoys "the right to make or unmake any law whatever",[2] no Parliament can place fetters upon the powers of a later Parliament. Although orthodoxy would, as such, clearly permit one Parliament to subject itself to the overriding force of EU law, any legislation to that effect could not bind the Parliament's successors as the doctrine of implied repeal entails that UK courts give effect to the most recent statement of Parliament's intentions.[3] Thus, even before the UK had acceded to the EU, there already existed debate about whether it was constitutionally possible for the UK to discharge the ongoing obligations of membership.[4] Were the demands of the EU order incompatible with domestic orthodoxy, or was it possible for competing imperatives to co-exist?

The courts' response to the challenge of membership has been one that has prioritised EU law as a matter of practice while maintaining that all corresponding change is consistent with orthodox theory. EU law feeds into the domestic system by virtue of the European Communities Act 1972, and the courts have interpreted the Act to mean that they must modify domestic technique and procedure by way of off-setting confrontation with the EU order. This willingness to adapt technique and procedure has caused alarm among constitutional traditionalists with Sir William Wade arguing that what has happened in domestic law has been nothing less

[1] Historically, of course, it is more accurate to state that the UK acceded to the European Communities.

[2] See *An Introduction to the Study of the Law of the Constitution* (Macmillan, London, 10th ed, 1959), p 40.

[3] See, e.g., *Ellen Street Estates* v. *Minister of Health* [1934] 1 KB 590, 597 (Maugham LJ).

[4] The point had been made by P B Keenan as early as 1962. See "Some Legal Consequences of Britain's Entry into the European Common Market" [1962] *PL* 327, 333.

than "revolutionary".[5] But for the courts, such assessment amounts to hyperbole.[6] Rather than recognise that the reception of EU law has effected a process of institutional change that challenges domestic constitutional assumptions, the courts have preferred to justify their judgments by reference to Parliament's sovereign intentions and to argue that "nothing novel" has occurred.[7] For the courts, therefore, far-reaching practical change has been effected without any need for corresponding conceptual adaptation.

The argument that this approach has limited the potential for the fuller and deeper interaction of domestic and EU law stems from an understanding that references to orthodoxy, whether misplaced or not, preclude domestic orders from evolving in the manner demanded by the process of European integration. Murray Hunt has argued that the courts' failure to elaborate new constitutional understandings leaves the domestic order ill-equipped to react to the wider dynamics of change occurring within and without UK law.[8] Focusing on a series of factors which he says have "undermine(d) both the explanatory and the justificatory power" of orthodoxy,[9] Hunt argues that the courts should emphasise that it is the evolutionary qualities of the common law that enable domestic law to accommodate European norms. His contribution in this regard overlaps in part with arguments made in the context of the ultra vires debate. It will be recalled from chapter two that various judges and commentators have suggested that recent developments in judicial review can better be explained by reference to the inherent qualities of the common law rather than by reference to traditional notions of Parliamentary sovereignty. Although it was seen that the institutional assumptions of the common law model do not enjoy universally founded support, it was suggested that the model's very existence is indicative of a shift within UK public law thinking. Hence, cast in these terms, Hunt's argument might be taken to import an understanding that the common law model's institutional assumptions should be developed far beyond the context of judicial review and, moreover, should become the touchstone of domestic constitutional discourse.

[5] See, "What Has Happened to the Sovereignty of Parliament?" (1991) 107 *LQR* 1 and "Sovereignty – Revolution or Evolution?" (1996) 112 *LQR* 568.

[6] *R* v. *Secretary of State for Transport, ex p Factortame (No 2)* [1991] 1 All ER 70, 107–8 (Lord Bridge).

[7] *Ibid.* And see also *Macarthys Ltd* v. *Smith* [1979] 3 All ER 325, 329 (Lord Denning); *R* v. *Secretary of State for Foreign and Commonwealth Affairs, ex p Rees-Mogg* [1994] 1 All ER 457, 470 (Lloyd, LJ); and *R* v. *Ministry of Agriculture, Fisheries and Food, ex p First City Trading Limited* [1997] 1 CMLR 250, 268–9 (Laws J). There are, of course, some exceptions to the orthodox approach. See in particular Sedley J's judgments in *R* v. *Ministry of Agriculture, Fisheries and Food, ex p Hamble Fisheries* [1995] 2 All ER 714 and *R* v. *Secretary of State for the Home Department, ex p McQuillan* [1995] 4 All ER 400.

[8] *Using Human Rights Law in English Courts* (Hart Publishing, Oxford, 1997), chs. 1–3.

[9] *Ibid*, p 1.

In introducing the argument that orthodoxy precludes deeper integration, therefore, this chapter returns to debate about the institutional role of the courts and suggests that judicial reference to traditional notions has indoctrinated a minimalist approach to the interaction of domestic and European standards. Drawing on Hunt's work, it argues that, as European integration is a process that requires courts to adopt outward looking perspectives,[10] judicial recourse to orthodoxy can only provide the courts with a narrow internal focus. The doctrine of Parliamentary sovereignty has, as will become apparent below, given rise to a rigid form of constitutional dualism in the UK, and the chapter argues that recourse to orthodoxy has created a "dualist divide" which has exaggerated and amplified EU law's understanding that national courts work within two paradigms of law.[11] And, while it is true that the dualist divide does not, of itself, preclude the possibility of deeper integration, it is equally true that it has engendered perceptions of domestic law and European law as separate entities rather than co-equals within a wider community of laws.[12] Within such a framework, it can only be expected that interaction and integration will remain unduly constrained.

2. CONSTITUTIONAL ORTHODOXY AND SUPREMACY

The traditional paradigm which Sir William Wade suggests has been subjected to a revolution in recent years is, as stated above, that which is ordinarily associated with Diceyan constitutionalism. In the paradigm, the role that the courts perform is one of entire subordination to the wishes and dictates of the sovereign Parliament. Many of the features of the subordinate role, which have been developed and enforced by the courts themselves,[13] have already been alluded to in chapter two – the courts have refused to prescribe any limits to Parliament's powers;[14] the courts have historically preferred to interpret legislation literally;[15] and the courts have emphasised that they perform only a limited role relative to the review of powers delegated to other subordinate bodies by the sovereign Parliament.[16]

[10] See also N Macormack, "Beyond the Sovereign State" (1993) 56 *MLR* 1.

[11] M L Fernandez Esteban, "National Judges and EC Law: The Paradox of the Two Paradigms of Law" (1997) 4 *MJ* 143. On the limiting influence of dualist orthodoxy see I Ward, "Dualism and the Limits of European Integration" (1995) *Liverpool LR* 29, 36.

[12] W Van Gerven, "Bridging the Gap Between Community and National Laws: Towards a Principle of Homogeneity in the Field of Legal Remedies" (1995) 32 *CMLRev* 679, 700.

[13] See H W R Wade, "The Basis of Legal Sovereignty" (1955) 13 *CLJ* 172.

[14] *Madzimbamuto* v. *Lardner-Burke* [1969] 1 AC 645, 723 (Lord Reid).

[15] *Duport Steels Ltd* v. *Sirs* [1980] 1 WLR 142, 157 (Lord Diplock).

[16] *Associated Provincial Picture Houses* v. *Wednesbury Corporation* [1948] 1 KB 223, 230 (Lord Greene MR).

The paradigm has likewise given rise to minimalist understandings of what the courts legitimately may do in relation to the interaction of domestic and international law. In the first instance, the courts have adopted a strictly dualist view of the relevance of international law, holding that Treaties can have no impact in domestic law until Parliament passes legislation to that effect.[17] This understanding, which has only occasionally been punctuated by the overlap of the common law and customary international legal standards,[18] has also led the courts to adopt a restrictive approach to the interpretation of legislation which incorporates international norms in the domestic order. In *Ellerman Lines* v. *Murray*[19] the House of Lords refused to interpret the Merchant Shipping (International Labour Conventions) Act 1925 in light of the international instrument it gave effect to, finding that the domestic provision in question was "unambiguous". And a similar understanding of the need for there to exist an ambiguity in domestic enabling legislation before the courts will have recourse to relevant international instruments was later and much more clearly stated by Lord Diplock in *Salomon* v. *Commissioners of Customs and Excise*:

> "If the terms of the legislation are clear and unambiguous, they must be given effect to, whether or not they carry out Her Majesty's Treaty obligations, for the sovereign power of the Queen in Parliament extends to breaking treaties . . . and any remedy for such a breach of an international obligation lies in a forum other than Her Majesty's own courts. But if the terms of the legislation are not clear but are reasonably capable of more than one meaning, the treaty itself becomes relevant, for there is a *prima facie* presumption that Parliament does not intend to act in breach of international law, including therein specific treaty obligations; and if one of the meanings which can reasonably be ascribed to the legislation is consonant with the treaty obligations and another or others are not, the meaning which is consonant is to be preferred. Thus, in case of lack of clarity in the words used in the legislation, the terms of the treaty are relevant to enable the court to make its choice between the possible meanings of these words by applying this presumption."[20]

It was against this backdrop that the European Communities Act 1972 was enacted. The political debate which preceded the passage of the 1972 Act had already provided an indication of the extent to which there existed uncertainty as to how the demands of the EU legal order would interact

[17] See, e.g., *R* v. *Secretary of State for the Home Department, ex p Brind* [1991] 2 WLR 588.

[18] *Chung Chi Cheung* v. *The King* [1939] AC 160, 168 (Lord Atkin).

[19] [1931] AC 126.

[20] [1967] 2 QB 116, 143–4. The treaty obligations at issue in *Salomon* were contained in the Convention on Valuation of Goods for Customs Purposes 1950, as incorporated in the Customs and Excise Act 1952.

with domestic orthodoxy. The official government understanding was that any disruption to the legal system would be minimal, with the pre-accession Command Paper *The United Kingdom and the European Communities* highlighting the government's belief that membership would not cause "any erosion of essential national sovereignty . . . the . . . legal systems will remain intact".[21] Yet, despite the content of such proclamations, the fact that the government ultimately refused to allow a sovereignty clause to be included in the 1972 Act came as a tacit admission that declarations of national sovereignty would be wholly inappropriate given the nature of the integration process the UK was about to join.[22] The consequence was that the European Communities Act 1972 attempted at one and the same time to put in place a legislative framework which would reconcile the seemingly irreconcilable demands of domestic constitutional theory and the foundations of the EU legal order.

Section 2(1) of the 1972 Act makes provision for the direct effect of EU law within the domestic system. It states:

> "All such rights, powers, liabilities, obligations and restrictions from time to time created or arising by or under the Treaties, and all such remedies and procedures from time to time provided for by or under the Treaties, as in accordance with the Treaties are without further enactment to be given legal effect or used in the United Kingdom shall be recognised and available in law, and be enforced, allowed and followed accordingly; and the expression 'enforceable Community right' and similar expression shall be read as referring to one to which this subsection applies."

This section is then augmented by a supremacy clause, section 2(4), which provides that "any enactment passed or to be passed . . . shall be construed and have effect subject to the foregoing provisions of this section" (section 3 further requires that the courts defer to the jurisdiction of the ECJ, both through use of the Article 234 EC reference procedure and through the

[21] Cmnd 4715 (1971) at paras 29 and 31. See also the 1967 White Paper, *Legal and Constitutional Implications of United Kingdom Membership of the European Communities*, Cmnd 3301. For commentary see J D B Mitchell, "'What do you want to be inscrutable for, Marcia?'/The White Paper on the Legal and Constitutional Implications of United Kingdom Membership of the European Communities" (1967) 5 *CMLRev* 112. On the political debate surrounding accession see further J Forman, "The European Communities Act 1972: The Government's Position on the Meaning and Effects of its Constitutional Provisions" (1973) 10 *CMLRev* 39.

[22] It was, for example, decided not to include the following provision in the 1972 Act: "It is hereby declared that nothing in the Treaties or in this Act shall detract from the ultimate sovereignty or supremacy of Parliament or shall prejudice the power and right of Parliament to repeal this Act or to alter any of its provisions or effects; and any determination of the European Court or of any of the Communities or their institutions which is inconsistent herewith shall be null and void". A debate on this clause took place on 5 July 1972. See HC Debates cols 556–644.

resolution of all EU law matters in accordance with the jurisprudence of the ECJ).[23] Section 2(4) has, as such, been central to debate about the constitutional impact of membership as it appears, on its face, to prescribe how the courts should regard the status of subsequent domestic legislation. Joseph Jaconelli has suggested that the section might be viewed from any one of three perspectives.[24] First, it might be seen as an "interpretation" section which lays down "a principle that whatever terms are used in Acts of Parliament their meanings are to be those which avoid clashes with the demands of (EU) law".[25] Second, it might be conceived of as requiring that inconsistent Acts of Parliament be considered "inoperative", that is "debarred . . . from governing the outcome in the instant case".[26] And finally, section 2(4) might be seen as requiring that inconsistent legislation be ignored altogether by the courts: "On this view, English law which is inconsistent with (EU) obligations is, without more, invalid".[27]

The judiciary's approach to the supremacy issue has seemingly drawn upon a variant of Jaconelli's "interpretation" option, with more recent literature referring to the emergence of a "construction" approach.[28] The earliest indication that a construction approach would govern the reception of EU law was given by Lord Denning in *Macarthys Ltd* v. *Smith*.[29] In *Macarthys* the Court of Appeal was asked to interpret the Equal Pay Act 1970 (as amended by the Sex Discrimination Act 1975) in light of Article 141 (ex 119) EC, the case having been brought by a warehouse manageress who was being paid £10.00 a week less than the man previously employed to do the same job.[30] The 1970 Act had introduced an equality clause whereby

[23] "For the purposes of all legal proceedings any question as to the meaning or effect of any of the Treaties . . . or . . . any Community instrument, shall be treated as a question of law (and, if not referred to the European Court, be for determination as such in accordance with the . . . relevant decision of the European Court)".

[24] "Constitutional Review and Section 2(4) of the European Communities Act 1972" (1979) 28 *ICLQ* 65.

[25] *Ibid*, 67.

[26] *Ibid*, 68. On this point he references J D B Mitchell, S A Kuipers and B Gall, "Constitutional Aspects of the Treaty and Legislation Relating to British Membership" (1972) 9 *CMLR* 133.

[27] Note 24 above, 69.

[28] See, e.g., P P Craig, "Sovereignty of the United Kingdom Parliament after *Factortame*" (1991) 11 *YEL* 221. See also Murray Hunt n. 8 above.

[29] [1979] 3 All ER 325. There had been various other rulings on the scope and meaning of the European Communities Act 1972, but these had been largely inconsistent. In *Aero Zipp Fasteners* v. *YKK Fasteners (UK) Ltd* [1973] CMLR 819, Graham J declared himself satisfied that the 1972 Act provided for the supremacy of EU law within the domestic order. This was an opinion which was shared by Lord Denning in *Shields* v. *E Coomes (Holdings) Ltd* [1978] 1 WLR 1408. But see also Lord Denning's judgment in *Felixstowe Dock & Railway Co* v. *British Transport Docks Board* [1976] 2 *Lloyd's Law Reports* 656.

[30] It should be noted that, although the case concerned the interpretation of the Equal Pay Act *1970*, the Act had not, in fact, come into force until 1975, i.e. its coming into force post-dated the European Communities Act 1972.

men and women were to be treated equally "where the woman is employed on like work with a man in the same employment".[31] As such, the Court of Appeal was faced with two possible construction approaches. First, the Court could interpret the domestic legislation in initial isolation, thereby giving full effect to the literal meaning of the words used by Parliament. But the problem with such an approach was that it had the potential to lead the Court to make an initial determination that would conflict with EU law's sex equality regime. The domestic Act, on a literal interpretation, conceived of the equal pay requirement applying only when there was simultaneous employment of the claimant and the "male comparator", and it was argued that this was more restrictive than the position under EU law. Thus, the second possible approach was for the Court to have prior recourse to the existing body of EU jurisprudence, with interpretation of the domestic Act being effected only in light of the supranational standard.

In suggesting that the second option was to be preferred, Lord Denning argued that the Court was, by virtue of sections 2(1) and 2(4) of the European Communities Act, obliged to look to the Treaty not only as an interpretative aid but also as an overriding force. Emphasising how the European Communities Act required the Court to give priority to EU law, he suggested that the best way to achieve harmony was to look first at what EU law required and then to interpret the relevant national provisions in light of the EU standard. Where national legislation did not lend itself to harmonious interpretation, it followed, on the basis of the European Communities Act, that the national standard must give way to the supranational norm. But where national provisions were capable of having more than one meaning, prior recourse to EU law would allow the national court to choose the interpretative outcome best suited to the discharge of the obligations of membership: "By so construing the Treaty and the statutes together we reach this very desirable result: it means that there is no conflict between Article (141) of the Treaty and . . . the Equal Pay Act; and that this country will have fulfilled its obligations under the Treaty".[32]

Lord Denning's suggestion that the Court should look first to EU law and only then to the national legislation quite clearly inverted traditional approaches to the construction of national law in light of international standards. The majority in the Court of Appeal, for example, had approached the issue in the traditional manner, looking first to the national

[31] Art. 141 EC at that time read: "Each Member State shall during the first stage ensure and subsequently maintain the application of the principle that men and women should receive equal pay for equal work". Commentary on *Macarthys* can be found in R C Simpson, "Equal Pay in the Court of Appeal" (1980) 43 *MLR* 209; O Hood Phillips, "High Tide in the Strand? Post-1972 Acts and Community law" (1980) 96 *LQR* 31; E Ellis, "Supremacy of Parliament and European Law" (1980) 96 *LQR* 511; and T R S Allan, "Parliamentary Sovereignty: Lord Denning's Dexterous Revolution" (1983) 3 *OJLS* 22.

[32] [1979] 3 All ER 325, 330.

legislation, which they found to be clear and unambiguous, and only second to Article 141 EC.[33] Lord Denning, however, had shown himself willing to interpret national law purposively in order to achieve harmony with the EU standard, indicating also that he would go so far as to afford precedence to EU law in the event of irreconcilable conflict caused by legislative oversight.[34] The approach and understanding adopted were, of course, institutionally far-reaching, yet they had, for Lord Denning, only been adopted because they had been mandated by Parliament. For his Lordship, the fact that Parliament had enacted the European Communities Act was taken to mean that any change in juridical technique was entirely consonant with Parliament's intentions. Thus, even though Lord Denning modified the doctrine of implied repeal whereby the courts give effect to the latest expression of Parliament's intentions,[35] he repeated the core orthodox understanding that, as EU law feeds into the domestic order only under the terms of the European Communities Act 1972, Parliament retained the authority to override the provisions which had given rise to his revised construction approach:

> "I pause here, however, to make an observation on a constitutional point. Thus far I have assumed that our Parliament, whenever it passes legislation, intends to fulfil its obligations under the Treaty. If the time should come when our Parliament deliberately passes legislation with the intention of repudiating the Treaty or any provision in it or intentionally of acting inconsistently with it and says so in express terms then I should have thought that it would be the duty of our courts to follow the statute of our Parliament . . . Unless there is such an intentional and express repudiation of the Treaty, it is our duty to give priority to the Treaty."[36]

The next significant step in the development of the construction approach came in *Garland* v. *British Rail Engineering*.[37] *Garland*, like *Macarthys*,

[33] See [1979] 3 All ER 325, 333–4 (Lawton J). The majority found themselves uncertain as to the full and proper meaning of Art. 141 EC, so they referred to the ECJ the question of whether the principles inherent in Art. 141 EC applied to the facts of the instant case. The ECJ, in line with Lord Denning's expectations, replied that the equal pay principle in Art. 141 EC did apply to circumstances such as those raised. The CA thereupon found itself obliged to give precedence to Art. 141 EC over the Equal Pay Act 1970 (see Case 129/79, *Macarthys Ltd* v. *Smith* [1981] 1 QB 180). The failure of the majority to follow Lord Denning's lead was subsequently criticised by Hood Phillips for unnecessarily bringing to a head the question of whether EU law should override domestic law in case of conflict. See (1980) 96 *LQR* 31.

[34] The point was also made by the majority in the Court of Appeal. See, e.g., [1979] 3 All ER 325, 335–6 (Cumming-Bruce LJ).

[35] *Ellen Street Estates* v. *Minister of Health* [1934] 1 KB 590, 597 (Maugham LJ). And see now also *Thoburn* v. *Sunderland CC* [2002] EWHC 195 – there can be no implied repeal of the 1972 Act as the courts now recognise it as constitutional in form, i.e. subject to repeal only through express enactment (Laws LJ)

[36] [1979] 3 All ER 325, 329.

[37] [1983] 2 AC 751.

raised questions about the scope of application of Article 141 EC, with the specific facts of the case concerning a scheme organised by British Rail whereby employees enjoyed certain travel concessions for themselves and their families. Although the concessions carried over into retirement, the scheme stipulated that it was only the families of male employees who would continue to benefit at this stage. Mrs Garland claimed that this policy was contrary to section 6(2) of the Sex Discrimination Act 1975, the provision making it unlawful for an employer to discriminate against an employee "in the way he affords her access to opportunities for promotion, transfer or training, or to any other benefits, facilities or services, or by refusing or deliberately omitting to afford her access to them". British Rail, meanwhile, referred to section 6(4) of the 1975 Act, this provision stating that section 6(2) did not apply to benefits in relation to death or retirement. The issue for the court, therefore, was whether the exemption contained in section 6(4) applied to "retirement" benefits of the kind in the instant case and, if it did, whether the exemption was contrary to Article 141 EC.

The question of whether the section 6(4) exemption applied to the facts of the instant case had already elicited conflicting opinions in the lower courts, with an industrial tribunal's initial finding that the concessions fell within the exemption being overturned by an appeal tribunal before being reinstated by the Court of Appeal. When the matter came before the House of Lords, their Lordships, rather than focusing in the first instance on the scope of the 1975 Act, made a preliminary reference to the ECJ, asking whether discriminatory provisions such as those in the present case were contrary to 141 EC.[38] This "EU law first" approach quite clearly approximated the approach urged by Lord Denning in *Macarthys*, and their Lordships in *Garland* pointedly criticised the fact that the rulings in each of the previous hearings in the case had been reached "without any consideration being given to the fact that equal pay without discrimination on the grounds of sex is required by Article (141 EC)".[39] In other words, their Lordships in *Garland* seemingly endorsed Lord Denning's understanding that the courts' primary task in an EU law case is to ascertain the meaning of EU law and then to interpret national law accordingly.

The ECJ, in its response to the reference, stated that the concept of pay contained in Article 141 EC "comprises any other consideration, whether in cash or in kind, whether immediate or future, provided that the worker receives it, albeit indirectly, in respect of his employment from his employer".[40] On this basis, it held that the provision of special travel facilities for male employees after retirement, some of which female employees

[38] In its reference the House of Lords also mentioned Directive 75/117/EEC OJ 1975 L45/19 (the Equal Pay Directive) and Directive 76/207/EEC OJ 1976 L39/40 (the Equal Treatment Directive). The ECJ only addressed the relevance of Art. 141 EC.

[39] [1983] 2 AC 751, 769 (Lord Diplock).

[40] [1983] 2 AC 751, 767.

did not receive, was discriminatory in a manner contrary to Article 141 EC. Lord Diplock, who delivered the subsequent judgment on behalf of the House of Lords, thereupon held that it was incumbent upon UK courts always to endeavour to interpret national legislation in accordance with the UK's treaty obligations:

> "My Lords, even if the obligation to observe the provisions of Article (141) were an obligation assumed by the United Kingdom under an ordinary international treaty or convention and there was no question of the treaty obligation being directly applicable as part of the law to be applied by the courts in this country without need for further enactment, it is a principle of construction of United Kingdom statutes, now too well established to call for citation of authority, that the words of a statute passed after the Treaty has been signed and dealing with the subject matter of the Treaty, are to be construed, if they are reasonably capable of bearing such a meaning, as intended to carry out the obligation, and not to be inconsistent with it. *A fortiori* is this the case where the Treaty obligation arises under one of the Community treaties to which section 2 of the European Communities Act 1972 applies."[41]

Their Lordships' approach in *Garland* was to be warmly endorsed by domestic commentators. Hood Phillips, for example, welcomed their Lordships' decision to make a reference before interpreting the national Act, suggesting that "this is certainly the most satisfactory way of proceeding".[42] For Hood Phillips, the approach adopted by the Lords was both pragmatic and couched in language which ultimately reasserted the enduring value of the doctrine of Parliamentary sovereignty. Although Lord Diplock had used his judgment to highlight the existence of a construction obligation, he simultaneously declined to identify the limits within which the courts should strive to achieve harmonious interpretation, and he also didn't go so far as to endorse Lord Denning's understanding that EU law should override domestic law in the event of irreconcilable conflict.[43] Thus, while the judgment had the effect of ensuring that EU law enjoyed *de facto* primacy in the instant case, Hood Phillips was satisfied that the House had situated its ruling within a framework which deferred to the sovereign

[41] [1983] 2 AC 751, 771.

[42] "A Garland for the Lords: Parliament and the Community Again" (1982) 98 *LQR* 524, 525.

[43] "The instant case does not present an appropriate occasion to consider whether, having regard to the express direction as to the construction of enactments "to be passed" which is contained in section 2(4), anything short of an express positive statement in an Act of Parliament passed after January 1, 1973, that a particular provision is intended to be made in breach of an obligation assumed by the United Kingdom under a Community Treaty, would justify an English court in construing that provision in a manner inconsistent with a Community Treaty obligation of the United Kingdom, however wide a departure from the prima facie meaning of the language of the provision might be needed in order to achieve consistency". [1983] 2 AC 751, 771.

intentions of Parliament: "(T)he Lords founded their jurisdiction specifically on section 2(4) of the European Communities Act. *The Times* report of 26 April 1982, missed this point, but emphasised an irrelevant reference made by Lord Diplock to a judge-made presumption of statutory interpretation in relation to treaties generally".[44]

The "irrelevant reference . . . to a judge-made presumption of statutory interpretation" has, however, been seized upon by Murray Hunt as "both . . . sophisticated and . . . far reaching in its implications".[45] Although Hunt concedes that the *Garland* ruling was on its face more sovereignty friendly than *Macarthys*, he argues that Lord Diplock's statement about the courts' approach to the construction of national legislation in light of treaty obligations is of considerable significance. In the first instance, he notes how *Garland* saw Lord Diplock drop the ambiguity requirement from *Salomon*, and he further notes that his Lordship would seemingly strive to construe *all* national legislation (not just incorporating legislation) in a manner consistent with treaty obligations.[46] And turning to the more specific context of the EU law/domestic law problematic, Hunt ventures behind the substance of Lord Diplock's ruling to emphasise the nature and value of its common law origins. Rejecting Hood Phillips' categorical statement that the House founded its jurisdiction on section 2(4) of the European Communities Act, Hunt argues that the House had used a common law construction approach which potentially affords the courts a greater degree of latitude and institutional flexibility. For Hunt, the latitude and flexibility flows both from the fact that the common law presumption "does not ultimately depend on the notion of the courts as mere implementers of parliamentary will" and also from the related understanding that it faithfully reflects "what judges do when they interpret statutes".[47] Consequently, and despite the paradox that Lord Diplock's judgment was not as institutionally far-reaching as Lord Denning's in *Macarthys*, it is identified by Hunt as having the potential to provide the more appropriate basis for accommodating the demands of integration.

In one sense, of course, the distinction between a statutory justification and a common law justification may appear unremarkable, particularly given that the practical results of both approaches were broadly similar. Nevertheless, as Hunt has skilfully argued, a determination to refer judicial rulings back to Parliamentary intent as encoded in the European Communities Act 1972 serves only to constrain constitutional debate

[44] Note 42 above, 526.

[45] Note 8 above, pp 76–88.

[46] *Ibid*, pp 17–25. The point is central to the broader argument of Hunt's book, namely that the courts should endeavour to interpret national legislation in light of all the UK's international treaty obligations, in particular those concerned with the protection of human rights.

[47] *Ibid*, p 83.

within the boundaries set by traditional public law theory. This approach, Hunt argues, necessarily limits the ability of UK constitutional discourse to develop in response to the broader social, economic and political environment that now surrounds the UK. European integration is seen by Hunt to be a process that has a self-sustaining dynamism, and he argues that, irrespective of whether the UK is an EU Member State, EU law and other institutional forces will still be able to exert some degree of influence on the UK's decision-making processes. Given this understanding, Hunt suggests that the courts' should be more willing to emphasise that it is the evolutionary qualities of the common law that underpin domestic law's interaction with international and supranational standards. Such points of emphasis, he says, would not only allow the courts to elaborate a more coherent "theory of evolutionary constitutional change", they would also allow the courts to forward a more plausible explanation for the manner in which EU law has impacted upon the domestic order.[48] The deeper significance of such arguments is returned to below.

3. CONSTITUTIONAL REVOLUTION AND SUPREMACY

Although *Macarthys* and *Garland* provided early evidence of the extent to which the demands of the EU legal order would challenge traditional public law assumptions, the case which is most readily associated with the argument that EU law has caused a legal "revolution" is *R* v. *Secretary of State for Transport, ex p Factortame (No 2)*.[49] The *Factortame* case concerned an application for judicial review and an action for damages brought by a number of Spanish-owned fishing companies which wished to challenge the legality under EU law of certain provisions of the Merchant Shipping Act 1988. The Merchant Shipping Act had introduced residency and citizenship requirements governing the registration of fishing vessels in the UK. The specific aim of the Act was to counter the practice of "quota-hopping" whereby nationals of one Member State registered their vessels in the territory of another Member State, thereby benefiting from (in this instance) the UK's fishing quota under the Common Fisheries Policy.[50] The applicants argued that these requirements contravened EU provisions on

[48] *Ibid*, p 88.

[49] [1991] 1 All ER 70. See also *R* v. *Secretary of State for Transport, ex p Factortame (No 1)* [1990] 2 AC 85.

[50] The 1988 Act provided that vessels could only be registered as British if they were owned by British citizens domiciled and resident in the United Kingdom or by companies in which 75 per cent of the shareholders were British citizens domiciled and resident in the United Kingdom. The previous legislative regime, the Merchant Shipping Act 1894 had allowed vessels to be registered as British even if owned by persons or companies living/established outside the United Kingdom.

the right to freedom from discrimination on grounds of nationality;[51] freedom of establishment;[52] and the right to participate in the capital of the applicant companies.[53] They further sought an injunction to prevent the Secretary of State for Transport enforcing the terms of the 1988 Act until all the legal issues raised were finally resolved.

The case was first heard before the Divisional Court, which, having recognised that directly effective EU law rights are to enjoy precedence over conflicting national law, acceded to the request for injunctive relief. The award of injunctive relief was subsequently overturned by the Court of Appeal and, when the matter came before the House of Lords, their Lordships likewise denied that they had any jurisdiction to award interim relief against the Crown.[54] The House of Lords did, however, also admit that, in the event of an irreconcilable conflict, EU law should enjoy precedence over national law, with Lord Bridge conceiving of section 2(4) of the European Communities Act 1972 being written into the 1988 Act.[55] Recognising that the UK courts have obligations as EU courts, their Lordships thereupon referred to the ECJ the question of whether they were, as a matter of EU law, obliged to guarantee interim protection to EU law rights pending the resolution of all relevant legal issues, even though national law precluded them from doing so. The ECJ, having stated that national procedures should always operate so as to ensure the effective protection of EU law rights, replied:

> "It must be added that the full effectiveness of (EU) law would be just as much impaired if a rule of national law could prevent a court seised of a dispute governed by (EU) law from granting interim relief in order to ensure the full effectiveness of the judgment to be given on the existence of the rights claimed under (EU) law. It follows that if a court which, in those circumstances would grant interim relief, if it were not for a rule of national law, is obliged to set aside that rule."[56]

When the ECJ's ruling was returned to the House of Lords, their Lordships duly awarded the relief requested. The decision to do so was to prove highly

[51] Ex Art. 7 EC – now repealed.

[52] Arts. 43 and 48 (ex 52 and 58) EC.

[53] Art. 294 (ex 221) EC.

[54] The House considered such award to be precluded by section 21 of the Crown Proceedings Act 1947, the provision prohibiting the grant of injunctions against the Crown in "civil proceedings". The context of this point is developed more fully in ch. 6.

[55] "By virtue of section 2(4) of the Act of 1972 Part II of the Act of 1988 is to be construed and take effect subject to directly enforceable Community rights . . . This has precisely the same effect as if a section were incorporated in Part II of the Act of 1988 which in terms enacted that the provisions with respect to registration of British fishing vessels were to be without prejudice to the directly enforceable Community rights of nationals of any member state of the EEC." See [1990] 2 AC 85, 140.

[56] Case C-213/89, [1990] ECR I-2433, 2465 (para 21).

controversial, with some commentators claiming that the ECJ had effectively "rewritten" the British constitution.[57] Lord Bridge, however, viewed the consequences of the decision in a decidedly less excited manner and intimated that, ultimately, the House of Lords decision only gave effect to the will of Parliament as contained in the European Communities Act 1972:

> "Some public comments on the decision of the Court of Justice, affirming the jurisdiction of the courts of the member states to override national legislation if necessary to enable interim relief to be granted in protection of rights under Community law, have suggested that this was a novel and dangerous invasion by a Community institution of the sovereignty of the United Kingdom Parliament. But such comments are based upon a misconception. If the supremacy within the European Community of Community law over the national law of the member states was not always inherent in the EEC Treaty it was certainly well established in the jurisprudence of the Court of Justice long before the United Kingdom joined the Community. Thus, whatever limitation of its sovereignty Parliament accepted when it enacted the European Communities Act 1972 it has always been clear that it was the duty of a United Kingdom court, when delivering final judgment, to override any rule of national law found to be in conflict with any directly enforceable rule of Community law. Similarly, when decisions of the Court of Justice have exposed areas of United Kingdom statute law which failed to implement Council directives, Parliament has always loyally accepted the obligation to make appropriate and prompt amendments. Thus there is nothing in any way novel in according supremacy to rules of Community law in areas to which they apply and to insist that, in the protection of rights under Community law, national courts must not be prohibited by rules of national law from granting interim relief in appropriate cases is no more than a logical recognition of that supremacy."[58]

This line of reasoning clearly built upon Lord Denning's "EU law first" approach in *Macarthys*, with the point of progression in the instant case being that the domestic Act was suspended prior to any attempt to reconcile conflicting norms.[59] For Sir William Wade, however, the approach in

[57] The *Independent* newspaper greeted the ECJ ruling with the headline "EC 'rewrites' British Constitution".

[58] [1991] 1 All ER 70, 107–8. The judicial view that European integration does not limit national sovereignty beyond that which is authorised by Parliament was also evident in parts of the judgment in *R* v. *Secretary State for Foreign and Commonwealth Affairs, ex p Rees-Mogg* [1994] 1 All ER 457, 470 (Lloyd LJ, concerning the legality of the government's decision to ratify the TEU): "In the last resort, as was pointed out in argument, though not pursued, it would presumably be open to the government to denounce the Union Treaty, or at least to fail to comply with its international obligations under Title V" (Title V of the Treaty on European Union established a common foreign and security policy among the Member States). And see now also *Thoburn* v. *Sunderland CC* [2002] EWHC 195 – EU law enjoys supremacy only because the courts, as a matter of *domestic* law, recognise the 1972 Act as a constitutional Act (which can, in the last resort, still be expressly repealed by Parliament).

[59] In the event the ECJ subsequently made clear that it considered that the 1988 Act was contrary to EU law (Case C-221/89, *R* v. *Secretary of State for Transport, ex p Factortame II*

Factortame went far beyond any logical progression of pre-existing case law, representing instead a change in the "rule of recognition" which underpins the Diceyan conception of Parliamentary sovereignty.[60] Wade's starting point in this regard can be traced to his seminal article on sovereignty first published in 1955.[61] In the article, Wade outlined his understanding that the continuing sovereignty of Parliament is a judge-made construct[62] and that, accordingly, the rule of recognition which underpins the sovereignty of Parliament is historical, rather than legal, in nature.[63] "The point is simply that the rule of recognition is itself a political fact which the judges themselves are able to change when they are confronted with a new situation which so demands".[64] In light of this, Wade suggests that *Factortame* departs from the UK's traditional constitutional paradigm because the House effectively recognised that the Parliament of 1972 had bound the Parliament of 1988: "While Britain remains in the (EU) we are in a regime in which Parliament has bound its successors successfully, and which is nothing if not revolutionary".[65]

A corresponding issue left open by Wade is the question of what now constitutes the doctrinal basis of the domestic order. Wade chose to leave the issue open because the House of Lords itself had declined to address the doctrinal conundrum: "Lord Bridge held that the situation was "in no way novel", and since he did not appear to recognise that there was any

[1991] ECR I-3905) and the offending provisions were repealed by the Merchant Shipping (Registration, etc.) Act 1993, Sch 5 (although note that the application of the relevant sections of the Act had, in light of ongoing proceedings brought against the UK by the European Commission, already been suspended by virtue of the Merchant Shipping Act 1988 (Amendment) Order 1989, SI 1989/2006). Note also that the applicants' claim for damages arising from the operation of the Act led to further references to the ECJ on the question of state liability. See Joined Cases C-46 and 48/93, *Brasserie du Pêcheur SA* v. *Germany, R* v. *Secretary of State for Transport, ex p Factortame Ltd* [1996] 1 ECR 1029. And see further ch. 6.

60 Note 5 above.

61 Note 13 above.

62 He discussed three cases to illustrate the point: *Vauxhall Estates Ltd.* v. *Liverpool Corporation* [1932] 1 KB 733; *Ellen Street Estates Ltd* v *Minister of Health* [1934] 1 KB 590; and *British Steel Corporation* v. *The King* [1935] AC 500.

63 "Once this truth is grasped, the dilemma is solved. For if no statute can establish the rule that the courts obey Acts of Parliament, similarly no statute can alter or abolish that rule. The rule is above and beyond the reach of statute . . . because it is itself the source of the authority of statute. This puts it into a class by itself among the rules of common law, and the apparent paradox that it is unalterable by Parliament turns out to be a truism. The rule of judicial obedience is in one sense a rule of the common law, but in another sense – which applies to no other rule of the common law - it is the ultimate political fact upon which the whole system of legislation hangs. Legislation owes its authority to the rule: the rule does not owe its authority to legislation". Note 13 above 187–8.

64 See Wade (1996) 112 *LQR* 568, 574.

65 *Ibid*, 571.

problem of a constitutional kind, it is hazardous to draw conclusions".[66] This willingness to leave the issue unresolved has, however, been criticised by T R S Allan.[67] In the first instance, Allan argues that the doctrinal vacuum identified by Wade need not be seen to exist because the *Factortame* ruling should not be seen as "revolutionary". Criticising Wade's understanding of the rule of recognition as political in origin and associable with only one form of judicial reasoning, Allan argues that the categorisation of the rule as a matter of political fact does not properly account for the existence of compelling legal reasons for deciding cases in light of changing circumstances. In an approach which is similar to that adopted by Murray Hunt, Allan suggests that there is within the common law rule of obedience to statutes a degree of flexibility which should allow the courts to modify their understanding of what the constitutional order requires on a case-by-case basis: "(T)reatment of the rule of recognition as a matter merely of political fact leaves no room for an adequate account of what qualify as good reasons – good *legal* reasons – for resolving doubts about the rule in one way or another".[68]

Allan's arguments in this regard are clearly predicated on an understanding that it is imperative for constitutional discourse to distinguish between the parameters of legal reasoning and political decision-making. Indeed, in making his argument, Allan suggests that, for so long as the courts fail to elaborate a more coherent legal philosophy, their role will continue to be seen as one which is designed "merely to accept, on grounds of expediency, what ever the politicians decide".[69] Such understandings of the institutional role of the courts, he suggests, make it possible to talk of "revolution" because it denies that the courts enjoy the legal powers that inhere within them. Arguments of this kind do, of course, reflect elements of the ultra vires debate. The argument that the courts enjoy a greater degree of institutional autonomy is central to the common law model of judicial review, with the value of the model being that it allows the courts to develop the law reactively and in the manner best suited to changing social,

[66] *Ibid.*, 574–5. One possible point of doctrinal justification, eschewed by Wade but considered by Craig, is that Parliamentary sovereignty in the UK should be seen as "self-embracing". Self-embracing sovereignty theories hold that Parliament's power extends to the ability to adopt "self-limiting" legislation, i.e. legislation which places limitations on the manner and form in which Parliament exercises power. For the classic statement of the self-embracing paradigm see R F V Heuston, *Essays in Constitutional Law* (Stevens and Sons, London, 1964). On Wade's dismissal of the paradigm's applicability in the context of EU law see (1996) 112 LQR 568, 571 (n. 13). For Craig's analysis see "Sovereignty of the United Kingdom Parliament after *Factortame*" (1991) 11 *YEL* 221, 251–3. For further rejection of its explanatory force see T R S Allan n. 31 above, 27–8.

[67] See, "Parliamentary Sovereignty: Law, Politics and Revolution" (1997) 113 *LQR* 443.

[68] *Ibid*, 444.

[69] *Ibid*, 451.

economic and political circumstances.[70] Compared with debates about the basis of judicial review, therefore, Allan's work might be seen to demand that the courts' role be presented in terms of an institutional partnership with Parliament rather than in terms of a relationship of absolute subservience to the legislature. This need not mean that the courts are seen to be challenging the democratic legitimacy of Parliament when it passes legislation, but it does mean that they will approach the interpretation of that legislation in the manner best suited to a changing institutional climate: "The existence of good legal reasons for the *Factortame* decisions shows that, far from any dramatic, let alone unauthorised, change in the 'rule of recognition', the House of Lords merely determined what the existing constitutional order required in novel circumstances".[71]

The need for the courts to forward the revised common law explanation for the prioritisation of EU law was to become even more compelling as a result of *Equal Opportunities Commission* v. *Secretary of State for Employment*.[72] In the case, the EOC sought to challenge the validity of certain provisions of the Employment Protection (Consolidation) Act 1978 relative to Article 141 EC and corresponding secondary legislation[73] (the EOC argued that the Act discriminated indirectly against women by granting preferential employment protection rights to full-time workers, a majority of whom were men, as opposed to part-time workers, a majority of whom were women). The Chief Executive of the EOC wrote to the Secretary of State for Employment in the Spring of 1990, detailing the EOC's concerns about the Act and asking whether the government was prepared to introduce legislation with a view to removing the relevant provisions. The Secretary of State's reply, in the form of a letter, stated that the government considered the provisions of the 1978 Act to be "entirely justifiable" and that there were no plans to legislate in the manner suggested. The EOC thereupon applied for a judicial review of the Secretary of State's statement in the letter, seeking a declaration that the UK was in breach of its treaty obligations. After being dismissed by the Divisional Court[74] and by the Court of Appeal,[75] the application was heard by the House of Lords.

[70] See, e.g., P Craig, "Competing Models of Judicial Review" [1999] *PL* 428. Although see also Allan's endorsement of aspects of the modified ultra vires model of review in "The Rule of Law as the Foundation of Judicial Review" in C Forsyth (ed.), *Judicial Review and the Constitution* (Hart Publishing, Oxford, 2000), p 413.

[71] Note 67 above, 445.

[72] [1994] 1 All ER 910.

[73] Directives 75/117/EEC OJ 1975 L45/19 and 76/207/EEC OJ 1976 L39/40. On *EOC* see further S Moore, "Sex Discrimination and Judicial Review" (1994) 19 *ELRev* 425; H McClean, "In Europe Part-Time Workers Have Rights Too" (1994) 53 *CLJ* 210; and P Maxwell, "The House of Lords as a Constitutional Court: The Implications of *Ex p EOC*" in P Carmichael and B Dickson (eds.), *The House of Lords: Its Parliamentary and Judicial Roles* (Hart Publishing, Oxford, 1999), p 197.

[74] [1992] ICR 341.

[75] [1993] WLR 872.

The Secretary of State's arguments before the House were to centre on the point that the declaration requested could not be made because the "decision" contained in the letter was not a decision for purposes of judicial review.[76] Lord Keith, delivering the lead judgment of the House, agreed in the first instance that the statement was not a decision, but rather that it constituted only a statement of opinion. However, turning to the wider context of the EOC's application, his Lordship ultimately rejected the Secretary of State's contentions, stating that they misunderstood the true nature of the application. Finding that the Secretary of State's arguments were premised upon "too narrow an interpretation of the court's powers", Lord Keith stated that the real issue for the court was "whether judicial review is available for the purpose of securing a declaration that certain United Kingdom primary legislation is incompatible with (EU) law".[77] Deciding that *Factortame* had established that judicial review should be available, his Lordship then turned to the question of whether the 1978 Act was, in fact, contrary to Article 141 EC and related Acts. In finding that it was, Lord Keith had recourse not only to the jurisprudence of the ECJ but also to various social studies presented to the House, with his approach in this regard going beyond the approach of the House in *Factortame*. As seen above, the House of Lords in *Factortame* resolved the question of the availability of injunctive relief by referring the matter to the ECJ and then justifying the subsequent decision to grant the remedy with close reference to the European Communities Act 1972. But in *EOC* no attempt was made to engage the ECJ directly, with the declaration instead being made entirely under the authority of the *Factortame* precedent and existing EU jurisprudence. For that reason, *EOC* may rightly be seen as another case that took the courts beyond orthodoxy without apparent judicial recognition of the fact.[78]

4. ORTHODOXY, INDIRECT EFFECT AND THE DUALIST PARAMETERS OF INTEGRATION

The consequences of the courts' failure to elaborate revised constitutional understandings were, at least insofar as relates to the deeper interaction of domestic and EU law, ultimately to become apparent in relation to the indirect effect doctrine. The doctrine, considered in the previous chapter, sought to circumvent the difficulties created by the rule that Directives

[76] More specfically, it was argued that the House could not make the declaration requested as declarations could only be made if one of the prerogative orders was also available: prerogative orders, in turn, were argued to be available only in respect of a "decision".

[77] [1994] 1 All ER 910, 919.

[78] Harlow and Szyszczak described that judgment as "a landmark decision and turning point in the public law arena". See, "Case Law: *R* v. *Secretary of State for Employment, ex p Equal Opportunities Commission and Another*" (1995) 32 *CMLRev* 641, 650.

cannot have horizontal direct effect by requiring national courts to interpret domestic legislation in light of relevant EU law provisions.[79] The original formulation of the doctrine, elaborated in *Von Colson*,[80] imposed an obligation only in respect of domestic legislation passed in order to implement a specific EU Directive. But the ECJ's concern to improve the protection of individual rights led the Court, six years later, to introduce the extended *Marleasing* obligation under which national courts are required to interpret all national legislation, irrespective of its date of passage, in light of the terms of relevant Directives.[81]

The limited value of orthodoxy was in evidence during the six-year period that separated the *Von Colson* and *Marleasing* judgments. Although UK courts showed themselves willing to discharge the *Von Colson* obligation,[82] they refused to accept that the obligation could extend to the interpretation of legislation that had not been passed in order to give effect to a Directive. At one level, of course, the restrictive approach could simply be attributed to the fact that the ECJ itself had not yet bound over national courts to adopt the expansive approach, with the institutional assumptions of the doctrine also being potentially problematic.[83] But the courts' refusal might, at another level, also be attributed to their failure to elaborate new understandings of the relationship between the EU and domestic legal orders. The line of domestic jurisprudence that achieved the reception of EU law, while clearly effecting far-reaching institutional change, was, as discussed above, justified by reference to the fact that the European

[79] The rule against horizontal direct effect for Directives was introduced by the ECJ in Case 152/84, *Marshall* v. *Southampton and South West Area Health Authority* [1986] ECR 723. For application of the *Marshall* principle by UK courts see, e.g., *R* v. *Secretary of State for Employment ex p Seymour Smith* [1997] 2 All ER 273. But see also, e.g., *R* v. *Durham CC, ex p Huddlestone* [2000] 1 WLR 1484.

[80] Case 14/83, *Von Colson and Kamann* v. *Land Nordrhein-Westfalen* [1984] ECR 1891.

[81] Case 106/89, *Marleasing SA* v. *La Comercial Internacional de Alimentación SA* [1990] ECR I-4135: "It follows that, in applying national law, whether the provisions in question were adopted before or after the directive, the national court called upon to interpret it is required to do so, as far as possible, in the light of the wording and the purpose of the directive". [1990] ECR I-4135, 4159 (para 8).

[82] See, e.g., *Pickstone* v. *Freemans plc* [1989] AC 66 and *Litster* v. *Forth Dry Dock & Engineering Co* [1990] 1 AC 546. In *Pickstone*, the House of Lords was asked to interpret the Equal Pay Act 1970 (as amended by the Sex Discrimination Act 1975 and the Equal Pay (Amendment) Regulations 1983 (SI 1983/1794)) in light of Art. 141 EC and the Equal Pay Directive (Directive 75/117/EEC OJ 1975 L45/19) as interpreted by the ECJ. The case turned in particular on the meaning to be attributed to the Regulations of 1983 as these has been introduced in response to a finding of the ECJ that the UK's equal pay provisions as they then stood were contrary to EU equal pay law (see Case 61/81, *Commission* v. *UK* [1982] ECR 2601). *Litster*, meanwhile, concerned the interpretation to be given to the Transfer of Undertakings (Protection of Employment) Regulations 1981 (the Regulations sought to implement the Acquired Rights Directive (Directive 77/187/EEC, OJ 1977 L61/27)).

[83] D Chalmers, "Judicial Preferences and the Community Legal Order" (1997) 60 *MLR* 164, 189–90. And see further ch. 3, p 54 *ff*.

Communities Act obliged the courts to give effect to the jurisprudence of the ECJ.[84] Where a case was taken to raise issues that fell squarely within the realm of EU law and ECJ jurisprudence, as in *Macarthys*, *Garland*, *Factortame* and *EOC*, the courts could, consistent with the "intentions of Parliament", adapt domestic procedure to give prior effect to EU law. However, where a case raised arguments which were not taken to have a firm basis in ECJ jurisprudence, orthodoxy seemingly did not require that the courts take into account the wider possible context of a case, but rather that they determine the case solely in accordance with domestic principle and practice.[85] In other words, the courts' recognised a sharp "dualist divide" between cases that fell within and without the range of outcomes prescribed by the ECJ, with the distinction being maintained even where it was clear that there was overlap between the substantive content of supra-national and pre-existing domestic legislative standards.

The limited approach

The case which illustrated most clearly the courts' reluctance to adopt an expansive approach to the indirect effect doctrine was *Duke* v. *GEC Reliance Ltd*.[86] *Duke* concerned an action brought by a female employee who had been forced to retire at the age of sixty. Mrs Duke claimed that, as the obligatory age requirement only applied to women (men did not have to retire until the age of sixty-five), it constituted discrimination which was contrary to EU law. On this point, the ECJ had already ruled in *Marshall*[87] that the UK legislation in question was inconsistent with the 1976 Equal Treatment Directive,[88] and the decision had subsequently prompted the enactment of the Sex Discrimination Act 1986. However, as the 1986 Act had been passed after the initiation of the action in the instant case, Mrs Duke was unable to invoke its provisions, and she was further precluded from relying directly on the terms of the Equal Treatment Directive because GEC was a private respondent. Part of Mrs Duke's argument before the House of Lords, therefore, centred on the suggestion that the House was, on the basis of the *Von Colson* ruling, obliged to interpret the Equal Pay Act of 1970 (as amended by the Sex Discrimination Act, 1975) in accordance with the relevant EU Directive.

[84] Section 3.

[85] And see by analogy, *R* v. *Ministry of Agriculture, Fisheries and Food, ex p First City Trading Limited* [1997] 1 CMLR 250, 268–9 (Laws J).

[86] [1988] 1 All ER 626. See further A Arnull, "The Duke Case: An Unreliable Precedent" [1988] *PL* 313; E Ellis, "EEC Law and the Interpretation of Statutes" (1988) 104 *LQR* 379; and E Szyszczak, "Sovereignty: Crisis, Compliance, Confusion, Complacency" (1990) 15 *ELRev* 480.

[87] Case 152/84, *Marshall* v. *Southampton and South West Area Health Authority* [1986] ECR 723.

[88] Directive 76/207/EEC, OJ 1976 L39/40.

In refusing to accede to Mrs Duke's request, the House stressed that the national legislation governing the present case had not been passed with a view to implementing the terms of the Equal Treatment Directive, but rather, and as a matter of historical fact, it had the intention of preserving the application of discriminatory retirement ages.[89] Given this, their Lordships held that they could not distort the meaning of the UK statute in order to remove inconsistencies with EU law, stating further that the *Von Colson* ruling was:

> "no authority for the proposition that a court of a member state must distort the meaning of a domestic statute so as to conform with EU law which is not directly applicable . . . The EEC Treaty does not interfere and the European Court of Justice in the *Von Colson* case did not assert power to interfere with the method or result of the interpretation of national legislation by national courts."[90]

The House of Lords reiterated this understanding two years later in *Finnegan* v. *Clowney Youth Training Ltd.*[91] Here, the plaintiff again brought an action against a private employer, seeking redress for the application of differential retirement ages. Although the case raised substantially the same issues as *Duke*, it differed in one important respect, namely that the domestic legislation in question post-dated the adoption of the Equal Treatment Directive. In the case, the relevant legislation was the Sex Discrimination (Northern Ireland) Order 1976[92] and it was argued that, departing from *Duke*, the domestic legislation could and should be given an interpretation consistent with EU law. Their Lordships, however, rejected the argument, noting that the Order had been intended merely to extend the application of the Sex Discrimination Act 1975 to Northern Ireland. On this basis, their Lordships held that it could not reasonably be argued that Parliament had, through the adoption of the Order, sought to implement the EU Directive in Northern Ireland when the corresponding legislation in the rest of the UK had a different historical purpose. The Order had thus to be given the same meaning as that which had been given to the earlier Act. *Duke* was thereupon directly reaffirmed, with the House confirming again its belief that pre-existing national legislation that overlapped with EU law should be interpreted solely in accordance with domestic expectations.

[89] Lord Templeman referred to the 1974 White Paper *Equality for Women* and said: "If the government had intended to sweep away the widespread practice of differential retirement ages, the 1974 White Paper would not have given a contrary assurance and if Parliament had intended to outlaw differential retirement ages, s. 6(4) of the Sex Discrimination Act 1975 would have been very differently worded in order to make clear the profound change which Parliament contemplated". See [1988] 1 All ER 626, 634.

[90] [1988] 1 All ER 626, 641 (Lord Templeman).

[91] [1990] 2 AC 407.

[92] SI 1976/1042.

The revised approach

Within the same year as *Finnegan*, however, the future validity of the House of Lords' approach was called into question by the *Marleasing* decision of the ECJ.[93] *Marleasing*, as stated above, saw the ECJ greatly expand the reach of the indirect effect doctrine. Although the ECJ has since modified its understanding of how exacting the interpretative obligation is,[94] the significance of the expanded obligation for present purposes lay in the fact that it brought into sharp relief the difficulties that could arise from the UK courts' use of orthodoxy as the basis for justifying the reception of EU law. Although orthodoxy had not presented difficulties when a case fell squarely within the framework of EU law, it had prevented the courts conceiving of EU law as a body of law which could be of deeper relevance to the outcome of domestic proceedings. *Duke* and *Finnegan* had, in effect, seen the courts identify national sex discrimination legislation which existed in apparent isolation from EU law, this being so despite the fact that EU law had a rich and highly developed body of tangential jurisprudence. The result was that individual litigants had been denied the possible benefit of EU law on account of an orthodox judicial distinction that seemed increasingly anamolous in a climate of overlapping standards.

The test case which set the UK courts' previous approach against the rule in *Marleasing* was *Webb* v. *EMO Air Cargo (UK) Ltd.*[95] *Webb* again centred on a possible inconsistency between the Sex Discrimination Act 1975 and the Equal Treatment Directive. The plaintiff had initially been employed in order to replace an employee due to take maternity leave. Shortly after being hired, she found herself to be pregnant and, when she informed her employer of this, she was dismissed. The plaintiff argued that her dismissal was discriminatory and contrary to the terms of the relevant national legislation[96] and the terms of the Equal Treatment Directive as read in conjunction with related ECJ jurisprudence.[97] The claim was

[93] Case 106/89, *Marleasing SA* v. *La Comercial Internacional de Alimentación SA* [1990] ECR I-4135.

[94] See, e.g., Case C-468/93, *Gemeente Emmen* [1996] ECR I-1721, 1738 (Advocate-General Fennelly) and Case C-168/95, *Luciano Arcaro* [1996] ECR I-4705, 4715 (Advocate-General Elmer).

[95] [1992] 2 All ER 43.

[96] Section 1(1) of the Sex Discrimination Act 1975 prohibits direct discrimination (whereby a woman, by virtue of her sex, is treated less favourably than a man) and indirect discrimination (whereby certain requirements/conditions, while theoretically of equal application to men and women, nevertheless act effectively to the detriment of women).

[97] In particular, Case C-177/88, *Dekker* v. *Stichting Vormingscentrum voor Jonge Volwassenen (VJV-Centrum) Plus* [1990] 1 ECR 3941 and Case 179/88, *Handels-og Kontorfunktionaerenes Forbund i Danmark* v. *Arbejdsgiverforening* [1990] ECR I-1979. In these cases the ECJ had developed a principle in EU law that, because only women can be refused employment on the grounds of pregnancy, such a refusal of employment is directly discriminatory and thereupon contrary to the terms of the Equal Treatment Directive. The

rejected by an industrial tribunal, an employment appeal tribunal and by the Court of Appeal, with each of the decisions holding that there had not been any discrimination for purposes of the national legislation as Ms Webb had not been dismissed because she was pregnant, but rather because she would be unable physically to perform the task for which she had been hired. This, the Court of Appeal held, was a fate which could on the face of the legislation equally befall a man with a condititon comparable to pregnancy.[98] Thus, while the Court of Appeal recognised that the *Marleasing* case now required it to interpret the Sex Discrimination Act 1975 in light of the EU authorities cited by the plaintiff, it held that harmonious interpretation would only be achieved if the Court distorted the ordinary meaning of the national provisions. That approach, the Court reasoned, was not required even by the more expansive obligation introduced in *Marleasing*.

When the case was appealed to the House of Lords their Lordships modified the approach previously taken in *Duke*.[99] In the first instance, their Lordships continued to hold that the meaning of a domestic statute could not be distorted so as to conform with non-directly effective EU law. But beyond this understanding, and reflecting *Marleasing*, their Lordships did accept that legislation should, irrespective of its date of passage, be construed in conformity with EU standards. Turning to the substantive question of whether there had been discrimination in the instant case, and having endorsed the Court of Appeal's finding that the domestic legislation was on its face non-discriminatory, the House thereupon referred to the ECJ the question of whether Ms Webb's dismissal was contrary to EU law. The ECJ, in turn, made clear that it considered there had been unlawful discrimination in the instant case, finding that EU law precluded "dismissal of an employee who is recruited for an unlimited term with a view, initially, to replacing another employee during the latter's maternity leave and who cannot do so because, shortly after recruitment, she is herself found to be pregnant".[100] Having received the ECJ's judgment, the House of Lords then duly "interpreted" the national legislation to conform with the EU

ECJ also established in these cases that financial loss suffered by an employer as a result of pregnancy may not justify dismissal and that it is not necessary for purposes of EU law to make a comparison between men and women for the purpose of showing that there has been discrimination on the grounds of pregnancy.

[98] "To postulate a pregnant man is an absurdity, but I see no difficulty in comparing a pregnant woman with a man who has a medical condition which will require him to be absent for the same period of time and at the same time as does the woman's pregnancy . . . Obviously one can think of others which might be more appropriate in the circumstances of this particular case. Suppose that a man is suffering from an arthritic hip condition . . . ". See [1992] 2 All ER 43, 52 (Glidewell LJ). See further A Arnull, "When is pregnancy like an arthritic hip?" (1992) 17 *ELRev* 265.

[99] *Webb* v. *EMO Air Cargo (UK) Ltd* [1992] 4 All ER 929.

[100] Case 32/93, *Webb* v. *EMO Air Cargo (UK) Ltd* [1994] ECR 1–3567, 3588 (para 29).

standard, with Lord Keith suggesting that the best way to achieve harmony was to treat pregnancy as a condition without comparison for purposes of the domestic instrument.[101]

What did *Webb* reveal about the interaction of UK public law and EU law? Certainly, the judgment illustrated again how the courts are willing to react creatively when expressly required to do so by the ECJ. The House of Lords' previously narrow approach to the indirect effect doctrine, while partly attributable to the ECJ's failure to identify more clearly the boundaries of the interpretative obligation, was quickly revised to ensure that the emerging duties of membership were discharged. For Murray Hunt, this accommodation of *Marleasing* was significant not only because it achieved the result prescribed by the ECJ but also because of the judicial understandings he suggests underpinned the House of Lords' judgment. Noting how the modification of *Duke* had occurred without any reference to the European Communities Act, Hunt commented:

> "(I)t is surely not without significance that the courts themselves have not sought to justify their acceptance of the interpretative obligation in terms of the (European Communities Act) at all . . . The better explanation of the judicial acceptance of the ECJ's interpretative obligation is that it represents a further stage in the evolution of Lord Diplock's common law principle of construction in *Garland*".[102]

Hunt's situation of *Webb* within the common law principle, whether reflective of judicial understandings in the case or not, raises again the issue of why a common law institutional role for the courts better equips the domestic order to deal with the demands of integration. The line of domestic jurisprudence that preceded *Webb* provided evidence of the potentially limiting influence of orthodoxy, and Hunt's approach clearly implies that domestic law will only become more amenable to integration when it increasingly emphasises the role and relevance of the fluid qualities of the common law. Of course, this is not to suggest that judicial reliance on orthodoxy in the context of the indirect effect doctrine had precluded all and any possibility of deeper integration. The courts had, when discharging the *Von Colson* obligation,[103] previously consulted *Hansard* as an aid to interpreting the relevant legislation, and in *Pepper* v. *Hart* the House of Lords allowed this method to spill over into a purely domestic case.[104] The House's decision to do so was highly significant as it ran contrary to the long-standing "exclusionary rule" whereby courts did not,

[101] See *Webb* v. *EMO Air Cargo (UK) Ltd (No 2)* [1995] 4 All ER 577.

[102] See M Hunt n. 8 above, p 122.

[103] Note 82 above.

[104] [1993] AC 593. See in particular Lord Browne-Wilkinson's reference to *Pickstone* v. *Freeman's plc* [1989] AC 66 – [1993] AC 593, 633.

both as a matter of practice[105] and as a matter of constitutional propriety,[106] consider oral ministerial statements when interpreting legislation. Thus, even within the context of the indirect effect doctrine, the courts' emphasis on orthodoxy did not preclude them subsequently using their experience with EU law to effect domestic changes which departed from traditional techniques of literal statutory interpretation.[107]

The relative value of the common law approach, therefore, lies not in the fact that it allows the courts to achieve outcomes which are unattainable within the framework of orthodoxy, but rather that it equips the domestic order with a more immediate appreciation of the benefits of institutional adaptation. Although orthodoxy has not prevented the courts guaranteeing the supremacy of EU law as a matter of practice, it has hindered a constitutional analysis of the EU and domestic legal orders as co-equals within a wider community of laws. In essence, the courts' reliance on orthdoxy has perpetuated the perception that EU law and national law are wholly separate bodies of law, with EU law occupying only those areas of the domestic order identified by the ECJ and validated by the European Communities Act. That this is so was clearly evidenced by the difficulties the courts had with the indirect effect doctrine, and it has also been true in other contexts.[108] In consequence, Hunt's argument that it was the fluidity of the common law which facilitated the reception of *Marleasing* assumes a much wider significance. Not only would a judicial emphasis on the

[105] As Lord Reid noted in *Beswick* v. *Beswick* [1968] AC 58, 74: "For purely practical reasons we do not permit debates in either House to be cited: it would add greatly to the time and expense involved in preparing cases involving the construction of a statute if counsel were expected to read all the debates in Hansard, and it would often be impracticable for counsel to get access to at least the older reports of debates in Select Committees of the House of Commons; moreover, in a very large proportion of cases such a search, even if practicable, would throw no light on the questions before the court".

[106] "From the constitutional viewpoint, I do not think it appropriate with a view to the comity between the different branches of Government, and their independence of each from the other, that the actual proceedings in Parliament should be the subject of discussion (and thereby inevitably criticism) in the courts both from the Bench and by counsel . . . It would be constitutionally most undesirable". See Lord Hailsham, *Hamlyn Revisited: The British Legal System Today* (Stevens and Sons, London, 1983), p 69.

[107] For commentary on the institutional significance of *Pepper* v. *Hart* see S C Styles, "The Rule of Parliament: Statutory Interpretation after *Pepper* v. *Hart*" (1994) 14 *OJLS* 151; D Oliver, "*Pepper* v. *Hart*: A Suitable Case for Reference to Hansard?" [1993] *PL* 5; N Lyell, "*Pepper* v. *Hart*: The Government Perspective" (1994) 15 *Statute LRev* 1; A Lester, "*Pepper* v. *Hart* Revisited" (1994) 15 *Statute LRev* 10; and K Mullan, "The Impact of *Pepper* v. *Hart*" in P Carmichael and B Dickson (eds.) n. 73 above, p 213.

[108] See, e.g., Laws LJ dissenting judgment in *R* v. *Secretary of State for Health, ex p Imperial Tobacco Ltd* [2000] 1 All ER 572, 594 *ff* (addressing the question of which standard – national or supranational – should govern the award of interim relief when a challenge is made to the legality of domestic regulations that give effect to an EU Directive *before* the required implementation date has passed). And see also Lord Hoffmann's judgment on appeal at [2001] 1 All ER 850, 856 *ff* (HL).

common law provide compelling jusitification for the decisions in *Factortame*, *EOC* and *Webb*, it would also enable the courts to view EU law and domestic law as equal parts of an interlocking whole. This may, depending on the nature of the principle and practice at issue, then lead the courts to engage in a deeper process of legal cross-fertilisation and borrowing. In any event, it should have the minimum effect of redrawing the parameters of debate about the desireability of inter-order assimilation.

5. CONCLUSION

This chapter has considered the manner in which UK courts have received EU law into the domestic order. It has focused primarily on the question of how the courts have accommodated the doctrine of the supremacy of EU law and it has argued that, while the courts have afforded EU law *de facto* supremacy, they have failed to address the corresponding constitutional dilemma, preferring instead to state that orthodoxy remains unaffected by EU membership. This failure has not undermined the courts' ability to discharge their EU law obligations, but it has given rise to strained lines of reasoning, and it has also prompted an active debate about what alternative doctrinal justification should be offered for the reception of EU law. On this latter point, the chapter has considered the relative merits of increased judicial recourse to the common law, suggesting that such endeavour would better equip domestic law to meet the challenge of integration.

The chapter has also highlighted how the courts' reception of EU law has created a sharp divide between those cases that are governed by EU law and those that are not. Although the ECJ itself conceives of domestic courts existing both as "national courts" and "EU courts",[109] the divide identified in the chapter has been seen to be a by-product of dualist understandings of domestic and international law as independent rather than interdependent bodies of law. The existence of the "dualist divide" is, as will become apparent in subsequent chapters, central to the argument that the courts' use of orthodoxy has prevented the deeper integration of domestic and European standards. It was stated in chapter one that European legal integration depends upon national courts using their experience with European law to develop domestic principle and practice, and it will be argued that the manner and form of the dualist divide has imposed additional constraints on the UK courts' capacity to borrow from EU law. In short, the orthodox dualist divide will be argued not only to have led the courts to over-emphasise functional and institutional differences between EU and domestic law, but also, and by so doing, to have

[109] See further M L Fernandez Esteban n. 11 above.

frustrated the potential for legal development which inheres within the internal dynamics of UK public law. Consistent with foregoing argument, therefore, it will be suggested that integration beyond the dualist divide will only occur when the courts emphasise the institutional assumptions of the common law model discussed in chapter two and alluded to above.

5

EU Law and Principles of Judicial Review

1. INTRODUCTION

The area in which the limiting influence of the dualist divide has been most pervasive is principles of judicial review. Principles of judicial review are used by courts to gauge the lawfulness of administrative decisions and they are, as such, reflective of wider institutional assumptions about the nature of public law and the corresponding role of the judiciary. The principles may, for example, import an understanding that the primary function of courts is to control exercises of administrative power and to offset arbitrary infringement of an individual's interests. Such understandings, which have dominated thinking in UK public law orthodoxy, see the courts as separate from the administration and charge them with ensuring that recipients of statutory powers observe the parameters of the power delegated to them.[1] Alternative conceptions of the role of the courts then move beyond "control theories",[2] suggesting that the courts and the administration are engaged in a collective endeavour to guarantee effective and efficient provision of public services. This understanding, which is typically associated with the French legal tradition, emphasises the instrumental nature of the law and the need for courts to strike the correct balance between the pursuit of a public good and the protection of private interests.[3] In other words, "instrumentalist theories" involve courts more intimately in the workings of the administration, requiring that they closely scrutinise decisions relative to the objective pursued and the impact expected.[4]

[1] See further the imagery of *imperium* considered critically in R Cotterrell, "Judicial Review and Legal Theory" in H Genn and G Richardson (eds.), *Administrative Law and Government Action* (Clarendon Press, Oxford, 1994) p 13 and *Law's Community: Legal Theory in Sociological Perspective* (Clarendon Press, Oxford, 1995), ch. 11.

[2] The term "control theories" is used by Carol Harlow. See "European Administrative Law and the Global Challenge" in P Craig and G de Búrca (eds.), *The Evolution of EU Law* (Oxford University Press, Oxford, 1999), p 261, 263.

[3] R Thomas, *Legitimate Expectations and Proportionality in Administrative Law* (Hart Publishing, Oxford, 2000), ch. 1.

[4] The term "instrumentalist theories" is again borrowed from Carol Harlow n. 2 above. See further the distinction between red and green light theories of administrative law used

The UK courts' willingness to use EU law as a reference point against which to develop domestic principles of review has, on account of the manner of the reception of EU law, tended to depend on how far the supranational standards accord with orthodoxy. Although EU law incorporates elements of both control and instrumentalist theories of administrative law,[5] its longer-term interaction with the French and German legal systems[6] has led to a presumption that its principles involve courts more closely in the review of administrative decisions than do UK principles of review. This is particularly true of the proportionality principle, with comparable institutional assumptions also being taken to characterise EU law's approach to the protection of legitimate expectations. For UK courts, the understanding that they need only give effect to the principles when working on the "EU law side" of the dualist divide has allowed them to discharge their obligations without demanding a deeper recasting of the institutional assumptions of the domestic order.[7] This has, of course, contradicted the "internal" process of change and realignment ongoing within UK law. The process of change has, as considered in chapter two, emanated in part from a debate about the constitutional nature and origins of domestic principles of review.[8] Within the debate, some judges have argued not only that the principles owe their existence solely to judicial use of the common law,[9] but also that the principles can, and should, be revised to allow closer scrutiny of administrative decisions which impact on an individual's fundamental rights.[10] Several commentators have thereupon argued that UK law would benefit from the spill-over of corresponding principles of European law, primarily because European standards offer more structured and transparent means of review.[11] But the

by C Harlow and R Rawlings in *Law and Administration* (Butterworths, London, 2nd edn, 1997) chs. 2 and 3.

[5] Harlow n. 2 above, p 265. Note that Harlow acknowledges these are not the only possible models for understanding EU – or any other body of – administrative law.

[6] T Koopmans, "The Birth of European Law at the Cross-roads of Legal Traditions" (1991), 39 *AJCL* 493, 500 and G Nolte, "General Principles of German and European Administrative Law – A Comparison in Historical Perspective" (1994) 57 *MLR* 191.

[7] Although this is not to suggest that the UK courts have not had some difficulty discharging the obligation. See, e.g., *Stoke-On-Trent CC and Norwich CC* v. *B & Q plc* [1991] Ch. 48, considered below.

[8] See generally C Forsyth (ed.), *Judicial Review and the Constitution* (Hart Publishing, Oxford, 2000).

[9] Sir John Laws, "Law and Democracy" [1995] *PL* 72.

[10] For example, *R* v. *Secretary of State for the Home Department, ex p Bugdaycay* [1987] AC 514 (Lord Bridge); *R* v. *Ministry of Defence, ex p Smith* [1995] 4 All ER 427 (Simon-Brown LJ); *R* v. *Cambridge Health Authority, ex p Child B* [1995] 25 BMLR 5 (Laws J); and *R* v. *Lord Saville, ex p A* [1999] 4 All ER 860 (Lord Woolf MR).

[11] J Jowell and A Lester, "Beyond *Wednesbury*: Substantive Principles of Administrative Law" [1987] *PL* 368 and "Proportionality: Neither Novel Nor Dangerous" in J Jowell and D Oliver (eds), *New Directions in Judicial Review* (Stevens, London, 1988), p 51; and M Hunt, *Using Human Rights Law in English Courts* (Hart Publishing, Oxford, 1997) ch. 6.

orthodox understanding that EU principles exist separately from national law has seemingly created a barrier between the orders, heightening the impression that EU principles can be of only limited use beyond the outcomes prescribed by the ECJ. The consequence has been for legal cross-fertilisation to be structured around domestic assumptions that, while not precluding integration, frequently cause the process of borrowing to be limited by the increasingly strained language of orthodoxy.[12]

2. THE DUALIST DIVIDE

The core principle of judicial review in UK law has historically been *Wednesbury* unreasonableness.[13] *Wednesbury* unreasonableness, or review, is, by definition, a standard that incorporates orthodox understandings of the courts as the implementers of Parliament's intentions. The principle's core assumption is that the courts control exercises of administrative discretion to ensure that the decision-maker has faithfully observed the parameters of power delegated to it by Parliament. The notion of control within the standard does not, as such, allow the courts to examine the merits of a decision as judicial review is concerned not with questions of substance but only with questions of legality.[14] *Wednesbury* is, therefore, inextricably linked to an institutional understanding that, where Parliament has delegated discretionary powers to a subordinate body, it is for that body, not the courts, to exercise the power received. Lord Diplock, in his seminal judgment in the *GCHQ* case, famously characterised *Wednesbury* as enabling the courts to impugn an administrative decision only where that decision is ". . . so outrageous in its defiance of logic or of accepted moral standards that no sensible person who had applied his mind to the question could have arrived at it".[15] And the principle's constitutional properties have likewise, and more recently, been identified by Lord Irvine of Lairg:

[12] For example, Sir J Laws, "Wednesbury" in C Forsyth and I Hare (eds.), *The Golden Metwand and the Crooked Cord* (Clarendon Press, Oxford, 1998), p 185.

[13] *Associated Provincial Picture Houses* v. *Wednesbury Corporation* [1948] 1 KB 223. The other established headings of domestic review are illegality and procedural impropriety. See further *Council of Civil Service Unions* v. *Minister for the Civil Service* [1985] AC 374, 410–11 (Lord Diplock). But see also the following discussion of proportionality below and in ch. 7.

[14] As Lord Brightman stated in *Chief Constable of the North Wales Police* v. *Evans* [1982] 3 All ER 141, 154: "Judicial review is concerned, not with the decision, but with the decision-making process". And see further Lord Hoffmann's judgment in *Tesco Stores Ltd* v. *Secretary of State for the Environment* [1995] 1 WLR 759, 771 *ff*.

[15] *Council of Civil Service Unions* v. *Minister for the Civil Service* [1985] AC 374, 410–11. The original formulation was cast as follows: "It is true to say that, if a decision on a competent matter is so unreasonable that no reasonable authority could ever have come to it, then the courts can interfere." See [1948] 1 KB 223, 230 (Lord Greene MR).

> "(P)ublic authorities receive their powers from Parliament . . . Parliament . . . entrust(s) that authority with decision-making power . . . it follows that the courts are, in relative terms, ill-equipped to take decisions in place of the designated authority . . . What this reduces to is a doctrine of judicial self-restraint in deference to the sovereignty of Parliament".[16]

EU administrative law, in contrast to UK law, is less readily associated with one defining institutional principle of review. The body of EU administrative law which has been developed by the ECJ has instead given rise to a series of general judicial review principles which enjoy equal prominence and importance within the EU order.[17] The principles, which include proportionality,[18] equality,[19] legitimate expectation[20] and related standards such as the duty to give reasons,[21] are used by the ECJ to "fill gaps and as aids to interpretation",[22] and they may, depending on the nature of the case at hand,[23] operate as independent,[24] interacting[25] or interchangeable[26]

[16] See, "Judges and Decision-Makers: The Theory and Practice of *Wednesbury* Review" [1996] *PL* 59, 60–1. Note that within the general framework of *Wednesbury* there operate a series of other standards which are supposed to reflect the logic of *Wednesbury*. These standards include the obligation to take into account all relevant considerations and not to act for improper purposes.

[17] On the principles see further ch. 3, p 50 *ff*.

[18] See, e.g., Case 44/79, *Hauer* v. *Land Rheinland-Pfalz* [1979] ECR 3727.

[19] Or "non-discrimination". See, e.g., Cases 75, 117/82, *Razzouk and Beydoun* v. *Commission* [1984] ECR 1509. Note also that the principle of equality/non-discrimination is expressly provided for in various provisions in the EC Treaty, e.g., Art. 12 (ex 6) EC (prohibiting discrimination on the grounds of nationality); Art. 13 (ex 6a) EC (a provision enabling the EU to adopt general anti-discrimination measures); and Art. 141 (ex 119) EC (prohibiting discrimination on the grounds of sex).

[20] Case 120/86, *Mulder* v. *Minister van Landbouw en Visserij* [1988] ECR 2321.

[21] Case 222/86, *UNECTEF* v. *Heylens* [1987] ECR 4097. See also Art. 253 (ex 190) EC.

[22] J Schwarze, *European Administrative Law* (Sweet & Maxwell, London, 1992), p 65. Note that use of the principles also has a Treaty basis, e.g., Art. 230 (ex 173) EC states that an act of the EU institutions can be annulled on the grounds that it amounts to "an infringement of this Treaty or of any *rule of law relating to its application*". Emphasis added.

[23] On the variable proportionality standard used to review exercises of Commission and Member State discretion see, e.g., T Tridimas, "Proportionality in European Community Law: Searching for the Appropriate Standard of Scrutiny" in E Ellis (ed.), *The Principle of Proportionality in the Laws of Europe* (Hart Publishing, Oxford, 1999), p 65.

[24] The best example in this regard is the principle of proportionality. Thus, where a Member State wishes to derogate from its Treaty obligations, any measures adopted for this purpose must, firstly, fit within the recognised grounds for derogation provided for by EU law, and, secondly, be objectively justified, i.e. be proportionate.

[25] The ECJ has, e.g., sought to protect substantive legitimate expectations through what amounts to an application of a proportionality test. See Case 120/86, *Mulder* v. *Minister van Landbouw en Visserij* [1988] ECR 2321.

[26] For example, the ECJ occasionally appears reluctant to review exercises of Commission discretion by reference to the proportionality principle, preferring instead to review the legality of a Decision by reference to the adequacy of reasons given by the Commission. See Case 259/85, *France* v. *Commission* [1987] ECR 4393, 4440 wherein A-G

grounds of review. Sometimes, the principles may even come into conflict with one another.[27]

The key difference between *Wednesbury* and EU law's principles of review is, as stated above, often taken to lie in the fact that the EU standards involve courts more closely in the review of administrative decisions. Although it has been suggested that such perceptions are overstated,[28] the presumed difference has had a marked effect on UK judicial attitudes to the integration of domestic and supranational standards. Indeed, the perception that EU and UK principles of review perform functionally different roles has been added to by the fact that the respective principles have been developed in considerably different institutional environments.[29] EU law and UK law have different historical starting points; different points of emphasis; and different end objectives, and each of these factors has seemingly copperfastened judicial understandings of the two bodies of law as separate. EU law can, for example, be primarily associated with the operation of an internal economic market,[30] with the corresponding body of administrative law being seen to control exercises of discretion which impact upon the market.[31] UK administrative law, on the other hand, may be seen as less concerned with economic regulation and the protection of market rights,[32] impacting

Mancini stated that, "provided that they are supported by a logical and adequate statement of reasons, Decisions taken by the Commission cannot be challenged from the point of view of expediency".

[27] For example, legal certainty and equality in Case 2/70, *Riva* v. *Commission* [1971] ECR 97 (note that equality trumped legal certainty).

[28] As Lord Slynn, a former A-G at the ECJ stated in *R* v. *Chief Constable of Sussex, ex p International Trader's Ferry Ltd* [1998] 3 WLR 1260, 1277 (HL): "In *Reg.* v. *Secretary of State for the Home Department, Ex p Brind* . . . the House treated Wednesbury unreasonableness and proportionality as being different. So in some ways they are though the distinction between the two tests in practice is in any event much less than is sometimes suggested. The cautious way in which the European Court usually applies the test, recognising the importance of respecting the national authority's margin of appreciation, may mean that whichever test is adopted, and even allowing for a difference in onus, the result is the same". And see now also Lord Slynn's judgment in *R (on the application of Alconbury Developments Ltd)* v. *Secretary of State for the Environment, Transport and the Regions* [2001] 2 All ER 929, considered in ch. 7.

[29] R Dehousse, "Comparing National and EC Law: The Problem of the Level of Analysis" (1994) 42 *AJCL* 761.

[30] As Jürgen Schwarze has written: "(EU) law itself is primarily made up of rules of administrative law, drawn in particular from the area of law governing the management of the economy". See n. 22 above, p 4.

[31] On the problem of devising a model of administrative law suited to the task of balancing the competing interests in the EU market see M Everson, "Administering Europe" (1998) 36 *JCMS* 195.

[32] Indeed, the UK courts have proven reluctant to involve themselves in the review of economic policy decisions. See, e.g., *R* v. *Secretary of State for the Environment, ex p Nottinghamshire CC* [1986] 1 AC 240. But see also *R* v. *Secretary of State for Foreign and Commonwealth Affairs, ex p World Development Movement Ltd* [1995] 1 WLR 386.

instead in other areas which include the provision of housing,[33] immigration and asylum,[34] and the administration of criminal justice[35] and prisons.[36]

The understanding that EU law and UK law occupy functionally different spheres was particularly evident in *R* v. *Ministry of Agriculture, Fisheries and Food, ex p First City Trading Limited*.[37] Here, a challenge was made to the legality of the Beef Stocks Transfer Scheme, the scheme having been introduced in an attempt to alleviate the financial difficulties befalling the British beef industry as a result of the BSE crisis. The BSE crisis had prompted the European Commission to introduce a worldwide ban on the export of beef from the United Kingdom, with the result that the domestic beef industry and related sectors were thrown into financial turmoil. The Beef Stocks Transfer Scheme thereupon provided that aid be given to some, but not all, sectors of the British beef industry. The applicants, who were not eligible for aid,[38] challenged the government scheme as contrary to the EU principle of equal treatment, with the central issue for the court being whether the EU principle of equal treatment applied at all as regards the scheme adopted.[39] The applicant argued that, where a national measure operated in a broader EU context, as this one did, the measure's legality was subject to the general and fundamental principles of EU law. The respondents, in turn, argued that EU law's general and fundamental principles are of relevance only where the act in question was performed in direct response to an obligation imposed by the EU order.

Judgment in the High Court was delivered by Laws J. In finding for the respondents, the judge adopted a rigid and minimal approach to the reach of the fundamental and general principles of EU law, holding in the first instance that those principles "are not provided for on the face of the Treaty of Rome. They have been developed by the Court of Justice".[40] Laws J further found that any requirement that the courts observe the general principles of EU law just because a domestic measure was broadly within an area associated with EU competence "would condition or moderate the internal law of the Member State without that being authorised by the

[33] *Wandsworth London Borough Council* v. *Winder* [1985] AC 461.

[34] *R* v. *Secretary of State for Social Security, ex p the Joint Council for the Welfare of Immigrants* [1997] 1 WLR 275.

[35] *R* v. *Horseferry Road Magistrates Court, ex p Bennett* [1993] 3 All ER 138.

[36] *R* v. *Secretary of State for the Home Department, ex p Doody* [1994] 1 AC 531.

[37] [1997] 1 CMLR 250.

[38] Aid was to be paid to the slaughtering and cutting sector of the beef industry, but not the export sector (although exporters who also operated slaughter houses were eligible for aid). The applicants in the instant case were exporters only.

[39] The Scheme adopted by the Government was one which had implications for domestic agriculture: agriculture is, of course, the policy area which EU law most closely regulates. See Arts. 32–8 (ex 38–47) EC.

[40] [1997] 1 CMLR 250, 267.

Treaty".[41] In essence, Laws J drew a distinction between domestic measures which incidentally affect the operation of the Common Market, thereby falling "within the scope of the Treaty" ("the first situation"), and Member State measures which are adopted directly pursuant to the demands of the EU process ("the second situation"):

> "There are here, as it seems to me, two fundamentally different kinds of legal obligation. The first is the duty to obey the Treaty, a duty plainly imposed upon the Member State in the first situation where its measure is within the Treaty's scope. Like any statute law containing orders or prohibitions, the Treaty is *dirigiste*: it is law in the shape of command. Law of this kind may intrude into areas previously altogether free of any legal controls, because of the sovereign force of the legislation . . . But it is to be sharply distinguished from law which is made by a court of limited jurisdiction . . . the Court of Justice has no inherent jurisdiction. Its authority is derived solely from the Treaties. Although (by virtue, ultimately, of the European Communities Act 1972) its decisions are as a matter of English law supreme, it supremacy runs only within appointed limits . . .
>
> Where action is taken, albeit under domestic law, which falls within the scope of the Treaty's application, then of course the Court has the power and duty to require that the Treaty be adhered to. But no more: precisely because the fundamental principles elaborated by the Court of Justice have not been vouchsafed by the Treaty, there is no legal space for their application to any measure or decision taken otherwise than in pursuance of Treaty rights and obligations . . .
>
> The position is altogether different where a measure is adopted *pursuant* to Community law . . . Then, the internal law of the Court of Justice applies . . . This must be so, since in all such instances the Member State's domestic law is no more than the vehicle for a measure whose validity falls to be tested according to the law of the Community. If the Member States were in such cases permitted to legislate or take other action purely according to its own rules, free from the constraints and disciplines of the Community's internal law, the legal regime of the Community would plainly lack harmony and uniformity."[42]

The foregoing dicta highlight clearly how the dualist divide has the potential to cause a "drifting apart from within" of domestic and EU administrative law standards.[43] There are within the abstract framework of UK dualism two relatively unproblematic scenarios, and there is the more difficult scenario that arose in *First City Trading*. Unproblematic dualism would arise where there is a purely domestic administrative decision which is in no way related to the EU process, for example a

[41] *Ibid*, 268.

[42] *Ibid*, 268–9. Note, however, that Laws J's understanding of the ECJ as a "court of limited jurisdiction" is not necessarily one which is shared by the ECJ itself. See A Arnull, "Does the Court of Justice Have Inherent Jurisdiction?" (1990) 27 *CMLRev* 683.

[43] The phrase is borrowed from W Van Gerven, "Bridging the Gap Between Community and National Laws: Towards a Principle of Homogeneity in the Field of Legal Remedies" (1995) 32 *CMLRev* 679, 700.

decision with regard to the allocation of housing. Under such circumstances, it is axiomatic, albeit from the perspective of domestic orthodoxy, that *Wednesbury* applies. The other unproblematic dualist scenario is that sketched by Laws J, namely where an EU measure is being implemented by a national authority. Under these circumstances, it follows, as Laws J accepted, that any review of the implementation process must be conducted with full reference to the terms of the EC Treaty and the jurisprudence of the ECJ as the case falls squarely within the ambit of the EU process.[44]

The facts of *First City Trading*, however, fell somewhere between these straightforward scenarios. In essence, the case involved a domestic decision which had quite obviously been introduced in response to, but was not directly demanded by, developments in the EU process. In other words, the facts straddled the dualist divide and forced the court to address the question of how far it wanted to engage in a European based jurisprudence. In the event, Laws J focused narrowly on the wording of the Treaty and the principles expressed therein rather than on the more general principles contained in the jurisprudence of the ECJ. His determination to do so prevented the deeper integration of domestic and EU standards, highlighting instead the existence of presumed and actual differences between the respective bodies of law. Of course, the question of whether the EU equality principle might have been used to develop domestic understandings would have raised related themes about how far it is viable to transplant the legal principle of one jurisdiction into the institutional circumstances of another.[45] But by drawing such a sharp distinction between the respective spheres of influence of EU and domestic law, Laws J effectively precluded any consideration of the value or otherwise of some form of integration. Thus the question raised by *First City Trading* is how far judicial attitudes of the kind displayed have frustrated the fuller evolution of the domestic order?

3. PROPORTIONALITY

The EU law principle which has met with most resistance in UK courts is, as noted above, proportionality. Proportionality has been defined by the Council of Europe Committee of Ministers as requiring public bodies to "maintain a proper balance between any adverse effects which its decision may have on the rights, liberties or interests of persons and the purpose it

[44] Although see also Laws LJ dissenting judgment in *R* v. *Secretary of State for Health, ex p Imperial Tobacco Ltd* [2000] 1 All ER 572, 594 *ff*.

[45] See further ch. 1. On equality in EU and domestic law see respectively J Schwarze n. 22 above, ch. 4 and A Lester, "Equality and United Kingdom Law: Past, Present and Future" [2001] *PL* 77.

pursues".[46] The principle is, as a national construct, most readily associated with German administrative law,[47] although it is also recognised in other Member State legal orders.[48] In EU law, proportionality is centrally concerned to ensure that there is some degree of balance between the means used to achieve a particular end, with the principle further requiring that all relevant competing interests are taken into account.[49] The ECJ's application of the principle has been varied, " . . . ranging from a very deferential approach, to quite a rigorous and searching examination of the justification for a measure . . . a distinction is often drawn between 'political' issues . . . and 'legal' issues on which a court is competent to adjudicate".[50] Thus, where a measure being challenged is one in which the decision-maker has enjoyed a wide discretion as to how to attain a particular EU policy objective, the ECJ has sometimes required that the measure adopted be "manifestly inappropriate" before it will be considered disproportionate.[51] In instances where Member States have sought to derogate from EU provisions governing freedom of movement, by contrast, the ECJ has been more demanding of the rationale underlying any relevant measure, the purpose being to ensure that the measure adopted is no more " . . . than is necessary for the protection of those interests which it is intended to serve".[52]

The difficulties which the UK courts have had with the proportionality principle have been evident in both "EU law cases" and in "domestic cases" where questions of legal cross-fertilisation have arisen.[53] In EU law cases the approach of the courts has ranged from apparent resistance to the principle through to a more inconsistent understanding of what a proportionality inquiry requires of them. The best example of judicial resistance

[46] R(80)2, II 4.

[47] G Nolte n. 6 above.

[48] See Schwarze n. 22 above, ch. 5. See further the national reports in J Schwarze (ed.), *Administrative Law under European Influence* (Nomos, Baden Baden and London, 1996).

[49] Craig and de Búrca have identified the following stages as inherent in any proportionality inquiry: "(i) The relevant interests must be identified; (ii) There must be some ascription of weight or value to those interests, since this is a necessary condition precedent to any balancing operation; (iii) Some view must be taken about whether certain interests can be traded off to achieve other goals at all; (iv) A decision must be made on whether the public body's decision was indeed proportionate . . . for example . . . is the measure the least restrictive which could be adopted in the circumstances? (v) The court (has) to decide how intensively it is going to (review the relevant decision)". See *EU Law: Text, Cases and Materials* (Oxford University Press, Oxford, 2nd edn, 1998) pp 350–1.

[50] G de Búrca, "Proportionality in EC Law" (1993) 13 *YEL* 105, 110.

[51] Case C-331/88, *R* v. *The Ministry of Agriculture, Fisheries and Food and the Secretary of State for Health, ex p Fedesa* [1990] ECR I-4023, 4063 (para 14).

[52] Case 12/78, *Eggers* v. *Freie Hansestadt Bremen* [1978] ECR 1935, 1956 (para. 30).

[53] On the courts' treatment of the proportionality principle in both EU and domestic cases see further G de Búrca, "Proportionality and *Wednesbury* Unreasonableness: The Influence of European Legal Concepts on UK Law" (1997) 3 *EPL* 561.

to the principle came with Hoffmann J's ruling in *Stoke-On-Trent CC and Norwich CC* v. *B & Q plc*.[54] *Stoke-On-Trent* was one in a long line of cases questioning the legality under EU law of section 47 of the Shops Act 1950. The provision prohibited Sunday trading, and B & Q, among others, argued that their inability to sell imports on a Sunday amounted to a quantitative restriction on imports contrary to Article 28 (ex 30) EC.[55] The issue was to become highly politicised, attracting the interests not only of retail companies and local authorities, but also of church groups, trade unions and backbench MPs. Although required to examine the issues on the basis of EU law principle and practice, Hoffmann J declared himself unwilling to balance competing interests in the manner required by the proportionality principle:

> "In my judgment it is not my function to carry out the balancing exercise or to form my own view on whether the legislative objective could be achieved by other means. These questions involve compromises between competing interests which in a democratic society must be resolved by the legislature. The duty of the court is only to inquire whether the compromise adopted by the UK Parliament, insofar as it affects Community trade, is one which a reasonable legislature could have reached. The function of the court is to review the acts of the legislature but not to substitute its own policies or values . . . The primacy of the democratic process is far more important than the question of whether our Sunday trading laws could or could not be improved."[56]

The line of case law that demonstrates how different judges have different understandings of what the proportionality principle requires them to do can best be illustrated by reference to *R* v. *Chief Constable of Sussex, ex p International Trader's Ferry Ltd (ITF)*.[57] In the case, an application was made for judicial review of a decision of the chief constable to reduce the number of days per week on which the police would oversee the export of live animals to the Continent (there were ongoing public protests at the ports through which the animals were being exported). The chief constable stated that he had taken the decision due to resource considerations which were making it increasingly difficult for him to discharge his policing obligations to the wider population. In the Divisional Court, his

[54] [1991] Ch. 48.

[55] For an analysis of the litigation surrounding the Shops Act 1950, see R Rawlings, "The Eurolaw Game: Some Deductions from a Saga" (1993) 20 *JLS* 309.

[56] [1991] Ch. 48, 69. See further Lord Hoffmann, "The Influence of the European Principle of Proportionality Upon UK Law" in E Ellis (ed) n. 23 above, p 107.

[57] [1997] 2 All ER 65. For contrasting understandings see further the judgments of Steyn LJ in *R* v. *Secretary of State for the Home Department, ex p Adams* [1995] All ER (EC) 177 and Sedley J in *R* v. *Secretary of State for the Home Department, ex p McQuillan* [1995] 4 All ER 400 (both cases concerning the legality under EU law of "exclusion orders" whereby persons associated with certain political organisations, most notably Irish Republican groupings, were prevented from travelling to, or residing in, Great Britain).

decision was found to constitute a disproportionate restriction on the free movement of livestock contrary to Article 29 (ex 34) EC. While the Court accepted that the decision had been taken on grounds of public policy (which, under Article 30 [ex 36] EC, can provide a basis for derogating from EU obligations), the chief constable's failure to request additional funding from the Home Office nevertheless meant that he could not argue that there existed no less restrictive means of achieving his objective as he had not fully sought to find one. The Divisional Court's finding was thereupon "... consistent with the approach of the Court of Justice that derogations to fundamental provisions must be narrowly construed".[58]

The chief constable's failure to request additional resources from the Home Office was, however, to be viewed much more sympathetically in the Court of Appeal. Having stated that the chief constable's decision could not " . . . possibly be regarded as so unreasonable as to enable a court to interfere",[59] Kennedy LJ proceeded to consider whether the same decision could be reviewed on grounds of proportionality. Given the plurality of interests involved in the litigation,[60] Kennedy LJ stated that the application of a test of proportionality in such circumstances should afford the chief constable "a margin of appreciation" in the decision-making process. He then noted that, once the necessary margin of appreciation is given to the decision-maker in circumstances such as those of the instant case, the result is for the test of proportionality to become something akin to *Wednesbury* unreasonableness: "I accept that . . . proportionality and *Wednesbury* irrationality cannot be regarded as simply co-terminous . . . and I accept, that in the context of this case and allowing for differences in terminology, each test will in practice yield the same result".[61] On this basis, Kennedy LJ dismissed ITF's application.[62]

Kennedy LJ's link between proportionality and *Wednesbury* raises the question of what status proportionality enjoys in the domestic order in cases that do not contain an EU law element. The debate about proportionality has typically concerned how the proportionality principle can be reconciled with *Wednesbury's* pivotal role in domestic law.[63] It has already

[58] C Barnard and I Hare, "The Right to Protest and the Right to Export: Police Discretion and the Free Movement of Goods" (1997) 60 *MLR* 394, 403.

[59] [1997] 2 All ER 65, 78.

[60] The court identified three competing interests: (1) ITF's right to protection for its lawful economic activity; (2) the right of the residents of Sussex to protection from crime and disorder; and (3) the right of animal rights protesters to protest peacefully. See [1997] 2 All ER 65, 80.

[61] [1997] 2 All ER 65, 78.

[62] The CA ruling was upheld by the HL. See [1998] 3 WLR 1260.

[63] Note that it has been argued that proportionality has long functioned in domestic law but that the courts have preferred to use the language of *Wednesbury* as it preserves the pretence that they remain at the outer limits of the decision-making process. For a criticism of such use of *Wednesbury* see n. 11 above. But see also S Boyron, "Proportionality in English Administrative Law: A Faulty Translation?" (1992) 12 *OJLS* 237.

been stated several times above that *Wednesbury* review is a standard which, by its nature, seeks to minimise court involvement in the process of administrative decision-making. Proportionality, then, which requires courts to balance and evaluate competing interests, is ordinarily conceived of in terms of lessening the threshold point at which the courts' supervisory jurisdiction can be invoked to a level set below that of *Wednesbury* review.[64] Thus, the core issue with proportionality is whether it would, if recognised as a ground of review, supersede the standard of *Wednesbury* review, thereby fundamentally redefining the institutional role of the courts.[65]

The possibility that proportionality may be recognised as a free-standing ground of review in domestic law was first, and famously, suggested by Lord Diplock in *Council of the Civil Service Unions* v. *Minister for the Civil Service*.[66] Despite his Lordship's expectation, however, formal recognition of the principle had not, until very recently, been forthcoming.[67] The most authoritative statement to the effect that proportionality was not a ground of review was given by the House of Lords in *R* v. *Secretary of State for the Home Department, ex p Brind and Others*.[68] *Brind* concerned an application for judicial review made by several journalists who wished to challenge the validity of the Home Secretary's decision to ban the BBC and IBA from broadcasting directly statements made by representatives of certain groups and political parties in Northern Ireland (the Home Secretary had made his decision pursuant to discretion belonging to him under the Broadcasting Act 1981).[69] The applicants challenged the decision on several grounds, included among which was the argument that the directives issued were disproportionate to the end to be achieved. The applicants also argued that the Home Secretary's decision was contrary to Article 10.[70]

[64] But see Lord Slynn at n. 28 above.

[65] It has previously been suggested that proportionality could be seen to operate as a subtheme of *Wednesbury* unreasonableness. *Wednesbury* unreasonableness/irrationality, as discussed above, allows domestic courts to review the decision of a public authority when a decision is so unreasonable or irrational that no reasonable public authority could have made it. In *R* v. *Secretary of State for Health, ex p US Tobacco International Inc* [1992] 1 All ER 212, 221 proportionality was seen by Taylor LJ as one possible way of gauging irrationality: "Was the decision . . . so disproportionate to the risk as to be irrational?" And see also Sir John Laws at n. 12 above.

[66] [1985] AC 374, 410.

[67] See *R (on the application of Alconbury Developments Ltd)* v. *Secretary of State for the Environment, Transport and the Regions* [2001] 2 All ER 929, 976 (Lord Slynn) and *R* v. *Secretary of State for the Home Department, ex p Daly*, [2001] 3 All ER 433, considered in ch. 7.

[68] [1991] 2 WLR 588. Commentary on *Brind* can be found in B Thompson, "Broadcasting and Terrorism in the House of Lords" [1991] *PL* 346 and M Halliwell, "Judicial Review and Broadcasting Freedom: The Route to Europe" (1991) 42 *NILQ* 246.

[69] Section 29(3). And see also clause 13 of the licence and agreement governing the broadcasting activities of the BBC.

[70] Counsel for the applicants argued on the latter point that, as the domestic courts seek to interpret national legislation in a manner which is not contrary to the ECHR, they should

The House of Lords unanimously dismissed the application, rejecting the argument that the proportionality principle had any role to play in the instant case. Their Lordships did, however, forward different reasons why this was so. Lord Lowry aligned himself to more orthodox understandings of the institutional role of the courts, finding that the adoption of proportionality as a ground of review would move the courts unacceptably away from the standard of *Wednesbury* review.[71] Lord Roskill, by contrast, delivered a judgment reflective of Lord Diplock's expectation in the *GCHQ* case, suggesting that the facts of the instant case were not the appropriate ones on which to develop the law in the manner proposed.[72] Lord Ackner's judgment then fell somewhere between those of Lords Lowry and Roskill, finding that the incorporation of the ECHR might provide the most appropriate legal basis for the importation of the principle.[73]

Post-*Brind*, and prior to the passage of the Human Rights Act, the closest the courts came to recognising proportionality was in the context of proceedings that challenged the lawfulness of administrative decisions which impacted upon fundamental rights. The origins of the line of jurisprudence can be traced to before *Brind*,[74] but it was in the years immediately after *Brind* that the revised approach was most apparent. Although the courts remained cautious not to use the term proportionality, they nevertheless emphasised that they were willing to lower the threshold of *Wednesbury* review whenever fundamental rights were in issue.[75] The revised approach was evident in cases dealing with the rights of asylum seekers,[76] issues of sexual orientation[77], and in cases dealing with the allocation of medical resources. In *R* v. *Cambridge Health Authority, ex p B*[78] the father of a 10-year-old cancer patient applied for judicial review of a decision of Cambridge Health Authority that further treatment would not be in his child's best interests. The application was heard in the High

similarly seek to interpret the exercise of ministerial discretion under national legislation. The argument failed.

[71] See [1991] 2 WLR 588, 606–10. See, in particular, 609–10.

[72] *Ibid*, 593–4.

[73] *Ibid*, 595–606. See, in particular, 605–6. And see further ch. 7 below.

[74] *R* v. *Secretary of State for the Home Department, ex p Bugdaycay* [1987] AC 514, 531 (Lord Bridge). Note further that Lord Bridge stated in *Brind* that, when the exercise of ministerial discretion impacts on fundamental rights, the courts are " . . . perfectly entitled to start from the premise that any restriction . . . requires to be justified and nothing less than an important competing public interest will be sufficient to justify it". See [1991] 2 WLR 588, 592–3.

[75] See further M Fordham and T de la Mare, "Anxious Scrutiny, the Principle of Legality and the Human Rights Act" (2000) 5 *JR* 40.

[76] *R* v. *Secretary of State for the Home Department, ex p Bugdaycay* [1987] AC 514.

[77] *R* v. *Ministry of Defence, ex p Smith* [1995] 4 All ER 427, 445 (Simon Brown LJ. But see also *Smith and Grady* v. *UK* [2000] 29 EHHR 493).

[78] [1995] 25 BMLR 5 (High Court). See further R James and D Longley, "Judicial review and tragic choices: *Ex p B*" [1995] *PL* 367.

Court by Laws J who considered that the health authority's decision interfered with child B's fundamental right to life.[79] Given this, Laws J stated that it was incumbent upon the health authority to provide a sufficient public interest justification for its decision. The health authority had, as such, been arguing that the heavy expense of the proposed treatment had to be balanced against the interests of other patients, particularly in light of child B's marginal chances of recovery. Laws J, however, was unimpressed: "(W)here the question (is) whether the life of a girl aged 10 might be saved by however slim a chance the responsible authority (has) to do more than toll the bell of tight resources". Laws J accordingly granted *certiorari*, requiring that the health authority re-take its decision.

Laws J's ruling was subsequently overturned by the Court of Appeal.[80] In short, the Court of Appeal considered that Laws J had gone too far in requiring the health authority to justify its use of resources. Finding that it would be "totally unrealistic" to expect health authorities to come "to court with its accounts", the Court of Appeal held that judicial intervention of the kind preferred by Laws J would prevent authorities from discharging their obligations properly.[81] Sir Thomas Bingham MR, who delivered the lead judgment in the Court, restated the orthodox understanding that the courts in a review case are concerned only with the legality of a decision and not its merits. Thus, while he emphasised how he sympathised with the plight of child B and her father, Sir Thomas Bingham MR nevertheless considered himself unable to intervene: "While I have . . . every possible sympathy with B, I feel bound to regard this as an attempt, wholly understandable but none the less misguided, to involve the court in a field of activity where it is not fitted to make any decision favourable to the patient".[82]

What did the judgments in *ex p B* reveal about the *Wednesbury v* proportionality debate? Certainly, the Court of Appeal's ruling encapsulated all the misgivings which UK orthodoxy has about lowering the threshold of *Wednesbury* review to something approximating proportionality. The Court's consideration that it should not constrain unduly the exercise of discretionary powers accorded fully with *Wednesbury* understandings of the courts remaining at the outer-reach of the decision-making process, and the judgment clearly incorporated the traditional distinction between judicial review and appeal.[83]

The more revealing judgment, however, was Laws J's. The approach adopted in the judgment, as in others before it, represented such an

[79] On Laws J's wider approach to the role of courts protecting fundamental rights see "Is the High Court the Guardian of Fundamental Rights?" [1993] *PL* 59.

[80] [1995] 2 All ER 129.

[81] [1995] 2 All ER 129, 137 (Sir Thomas Bingham MR).

[82] *Ibid*, 138.

[83] Note 14 above.

obvious departure from *Wednesbury* orthodoxy that some commentators have suggested it represented an application of the proportionality principle "in all but name".[84] This then begs the question why, if the High Court was effectively applying the proportionality principle, did it not formally recognise the fact? For Laws J, the reason may simply have been that, in his opinion, the principle wasn't actually being used. Writing extra-curially, Laws J has argued that *Wednesbury*, suitably modified, is easily capable of performing the role ascribed to the proportionality principle.[85] Such understandings of the domestic order being equipped to perform tasks without the assistance of European standards are, of course, consonant with Laws J's strictly dualist judgment in *First City Trading*. But the corresponding problem with such understandings is that they deny that proportionality requires courts to conduct an essentially different form of review from that associated with *Wednesbury*.[86] Jowell and Lester have long argued that "intellectual honesty" requires the courts to move beyond the vague language of orthodoxy and to embrace instead the more transparent and structured method of the proportionality principle. This, they imply, would not only allow the courts to bring to the fore latent common law principle, but it would also allow the domestic order to draw upon the comparative experience of other European orders.[87] The extent to which such development of the law may now be said to be occurring within the framework of the Human Rights Act is returned to in chapter seven.

4. SUBSTANTIVE LEGITIMATE EXPECTATIONS

The courts' preference for the institutional logic of *Wednesbury* has also been apparent in relation to substantive legitimate expectations.[88] Here, the preference has manifested itself in two ways. First, there has been a judicial debate about whether domestic law actually recognises a free-standing doctrine of substantive legitimate expectations (the debate has now been resolved in favour of the doctrine's existence).[89] Second, there has been dispute about how substantive legitimate expectations may best be protected in domestic law, and it is on this point that the

[84] M Hunt n. 11 above pp 216–21. Note that Hunt does not discuss *B* on this point, but rather refers to related case law on the modification of *Wednesbury*, e.g., *R* v. *Secretary of State for the Home Department, ex p Bugdaycay* [1987] AC 514.

[85] Note 12 above, p 201.

[86] D Feldman, "Proportionality and the Human Rights Act" in E Ellis (ed) n. 23 above, pp 117, 127–8.

[87] See generally the references at n. 11 above.

[88] For a summary of the different ways in which the term legitimate expectations may be used in UK law see *R* v. *Devon CC, ex p Baker* [1995] 1 All ER 73, 88–9 (Simon Brown LJ).

[89] See, e.g., *R* v. *Inland Revenue Commissioners, ex p Unilever and Related Application* [1996] STC 681.

proportionality–*Wednesbury* divide has again become apparent. It was noted previously how the general principles of EU administrative law interact, and this is particularly true of substantive legitimate expectations and the notions of balance associated with the proportionality principle. The ECJ, when deciding whether an individual's substantive legitimate expectations should trump a particular policy preference, often determines the matter only after it has carefully considered and balanced relevant and competing interests. It is the institutional validity of this approach that has dominated debate in UK courts.

Issues of substantive legitimate expectations typically arise when a public authority, having led an individual to expect certain consequences, either through the formulation of a particular policy or through sustained practice, subsequently frustrates those "expectations" by changing its policy or practice.[90] Under such circumstances, an individual's expectation that a particular policy direction will be maintained may be enough to override the desired administrative change. The leading EU law case on substantive legitimate expectations, thus stated, is *Mulder* v. *Minister van Landbouw en Visserij*.[91] In *Mulder* a farmer undertook to cease producing milk for five years in return for a premium. When he subsequently sought to resume production on the expiry of the 5-year period, he was refused a quota on the grounds that he had to have produced milk the preceding year in order to be eligible for a quota for the forthcoming year. This provision had, however, been introduced during the said 5-year period, and Mulder argued that it frustrated his expectation of re-entering the milk market. Given this, the ECJ proceeded to balance the general policy objective the EU was pursuing against Mulder's stated interests.[92] While noting that Mulder could not expect to re-enter the market under exactly the same conditions as he "left" it, the ECJ nevertheless concluded that Mulder " . . . may legitimately expect not to be subject, upon the expiry of his undertaking, to restrictions which specifically affect him precisely because he availed himself of the possibilities offered by the (EU) provisions".[93] Furthermore, when the EU institutions subsequently revised their position to allow Mulder to resume production with a quota of 60 per cent of his previous production, the ECJ again intervened, finding that the 60 per cent quota was too low and requiring that the position be reconsidered.[94]

[90] For comparative and much more detailed analysis see S Schonberg, *Legitimate Expectations in Administrative Law* (Oxford University Press, Oxford, 2000).

[91] Case 120/86, [1988] ECR 2321. See further, e.g., Case C-152/88, *Sofrimport Sarl* v. *Commission* [1990] ECR I-2477.

[92] Note that, while the ECJ did not expressly state in *Mulder* that it was applying the proportionality principle, the balancing exercise undertaken was clearly reflective of a proportionality test (argument on the basis of proportionality was also presented to the ECJ).

[93] [1988] ECR 2321, 2352 (para 24).

[94] Cases C-104/89 and 37–190, *Mulder* v. *Council and Commission* [1992] ECR I-3061.

In UK law, legitimate expectations have historically been associated with notions of procedural propriety rather than substance.[95] The distinction between procedure and substance is, of course, crucial as an emphasis on procedural propriety is wholly consonant with *Wednesbury* notions of a body of administrative law built around legality rather than appeal. Within the procedural paradigm, an individual may have a substantive legitimate expectation that something may be done. The courts, however, will only overturn a "contrary" administrative decision on review where it can be shown that the decision maker failed to allow the individual concerned to make representations *vis-à-vis* their respective interests. On this basis, the courts can, in a manner consistent with domestic orthodoxy, maintain that they have been concerned only with the legality of the decision-making process rather than with the substance of any decision reached.

The understanding that substantive legitimate expectations can be protected procedurally was apparent *Schmidt* v. *Secretary of State for Home Affairs*.[96] In *Schmidt*, the plaintiffs had been admitted to study at the Hubbard College of Scientology and, in accordance with the government policy operative at that time, were granted residence permits. The permits had been granted pursuant to the Aliens Order 1953[97] whereby the government granted residency to individuals studying at "recognised educational establishments". While the plaintiffs were studying at Hubbard, however, the Home Secretary, in response to growing concerns about the practice of Scientology, announced that the college in question would no longer be accorded the status of a "recognised educational establishment". When the plaintiffs applied to have their residence permits renewed, their applications were thereupon refused. The plaintiffs alleged that this refusal amounted to a denial of natural justice as they had not been given a hearing before the said decision was reached. Lord Denning rejected the plaintiffs' immediate arguments, finding that there were no legitimate expectations in the instant case because the original permits were for a limited time which had since expired. But beyond the initial finding, Lord Denning stated that, had the plaintiffs' residence permits been revoked *before* they had expired, the court's approach would have been different. Under those latter circumstances, he said, the plaintiffs ". . . ought . . . to be given an opportunity of making representations: for (they) would have a legitimate expectation of being allowed to stay for the permitted time".[98] For Christopher Forsyth, this would have provided a clear example of "a *substantive* expectation . . . being *procedurally* protected".[99]

[95] See C Forsyth, "The Provenance and Protection of Legitimate Expectations" (1988) 47 *CLJ* 238.

[96] [1969] 2 Ch. 149.

[97] See SI 1953/1671.

[98] [1969] 2 Ch. 149, 171.

[99] See, "Wednesbury protection of substantive legitimate expectations" [1997] *PL* 375, 377. Emphasis in the original.

The related question of whether domestic law recognises a doctrine of substantive legitimate expectations which exists independent of issues of procedural propriety was raised in *R* v. *Secretary of State for Transport, ex p Richmond upon Thames LBC*.[100] In *Richmond*, the government had revised its policy with regard to the reduction of noise levels in and around Heathrow, Gatwick and Stanstead airports. As the change in policy had been introduced in accordance with required procedures, the applicants argued that the revision frustrated their substantive expectation that noise levels would be reduced to below a certain level. The issue for the court, therefore, was whether domestic law accepted that free-standing substantive legitimate expectations could, by themselves, override a change in policy. Laws J began by stating that domestic administrative law recognises and protects procedural legitimate expectations. Thereafter, however, he denied that UK law recognises free-standing substantive legitimate expectations, indicating further that he would consider it undesirable for such recognition to be given by the domestic order: "(S)uch a doctrine would impose an obvious and unacceptable fetter upon the power, and duty, of a responsible public authority to change its policy when it considered that that was required in fulfilment of its public responsibilities".[101]

Laws J's concern to ensure that administrative discretion should not become subject to unnecessary fetters was undoubtedly designed with *Wednesbury* in mind. His corresponding suggestion that there did not exist in domestic law an independent doctrine of substantive legitimate expectations has, however, been criticised by academic commentators. Paul Craig, for example, has suggested that there exists a body of direct and indirect authority for the proposition that the doctrine of substantive legitimate expectations already existed in the domestic order.[102] And beyond academic commentary, there has also emerged in recent years a line of jurisprudence which has explicitly recognised free-standing substantive legitimate expectations in the context of changes to agricultural and fisheries policy;[103] changes in the long-established practices of the Inland Revenue *vis-à-vis* the

[100] [1994] 1 WLR 74. And see also *R* v. *Secretary of State for Health, ex p US Tobacco International Inc* [1992] 1 All ER 212.

[101] [1994] 1 WLR 74, 93.

[102] See P Craig, "Substantive Legitimate Expectations in Domestic and Community Law" (1996) 55 *CLJ* 289. Craig finds "direct authority" for the existence of substantive legitimate expectations in *R* v. *Secretary of State for the Home Department, ex p Ruddock* [1987] 1 WLR 1482 and "indirect authority" in *R* v. *Secretary of State for the Home Department, ex p Khan* [1985] 1 All ER 40 and *R* v. *Liverpool Corporation, ex p Liverpool Taxi Fleet Operators' Association* [1972] 2 QB 299. See also *Schmidt* as discussed above.

[103] *R* v. *Ministry of Agriculture, Fisheries and Food, ex p Hamble (Off-shore) Fisheries Limited* [1995] 2 All ER 714.

tax affairs of a large corporation;[104] and changes with regard to prisoner release dates:[105]

> ". . . the real question is one of fairness in public administration. It is difficult to see why it is any less unfair to frustrate a legitimate expectation that something will or will not be done by the decision-maker than it is to frustrate a legitimate expectation that the applicant will be listened to before the decision-maker decides whether to take a particular step. Such a doctrine does not risk fettering a public body in the discharge of public duties because no individual can legitimately expect the discharge of public duties to stand still or be distorted because of that individual's peculiar position."[106]

Beyond the emerging judicial consensus about the existence of free-standing substantive legitimate expectations, however, familiar tensions have arisen around the question of how expectations should be protected by domestic law. The issue in these cases, it should be emphasised, has not just been about the relationship between procedure and substance, but also about how free-standing substantive legitimate expectations may be protected *in the absence* of any suggestion of procedural impropriety. In *Hamble Fisheries*, Sedley J's approach was to encourage the adoption of a variant of the EU law model.[107] In essence, Sedley J suggested that substantive legitimate expectations can best be protected by balancing asserted individual expectations against the public interest in seeing any revised policy implemented. In the first instance, as Sedley J acknowledged, this was a matter for the decision-maker. But:

> ". . . if the outcome is challenged by way of judicial review, I do not consider that the court's criterion is the bare rationality of the policy-maker's conclusion. While policy is for the policy-maker alone, the fairness of his or her decision not to accommodate reasonable expectations which the policy will thus thwart remains the court's concern . . . To postulate this is not to place the judge in the seat of the minister . . . It is the court's task to recognise the constitutional importance of ministerial freedom to formulate and to reformulate policy; but it is equally the court's duty to protect the interests of those individuals whose expectation of different treatment has a legitimacy which in fairness outtops the policy choice which threatens it."[108]

[104] *R* v. *Inland Revenue Commissioners, ex p Unilever* [1996] STC 681. See further N Bamforth, "Fairness and Legitimate Expectation in Judicial Review" [1997] 56 *CLJ* 1.

[105] *R* v. *Secretary of State for the Home Department, ex p Hargreaves* [1997] 1 All ER 397. The point can only be inferred from this judgment as it was held that there was no legitimate expectation on the facts of the case.

[106] *R* v. *Ministry of Agriculture, Fisheries and Food, ex p Hamble Fisheries (Off-shore) Limited* [1995] 2 All ER 714, 724.

[107] *Ibid*. See further Forsyth n. 99 above and C M G Himsworth, "Legitimately expecting proportionality?" [1996] *PL* 46.

[108] [1995] 2 All ER 714, 731. Note that there is some debate about when the legitimacy of an expectation will be established. For Sedley J in *Hamble*, an expectation need only be

Sedley J's attempt to protect substantive legitimate expectations within a framework that balances competing interests was roundly rejected by the Court of Appeal in *R* v. *Secretary of State for the Home Department and Another, ex p Hargreaves*.[109] *Hargreaves* concerned an application for judicial review made by a prisoner who wished to overturn a decision of the Home Secretary to revise the criteria governing home release. The applicant argued that a compact he had made previously with the Prison Service gave him a legitimate expectation that he would be released on a certain date (that date had since changed under the revised guidelines). The applicant further argued on the basis of *Hamble Fisheries* that the test which the court was to apply when determining whether his legitimate expectation of release should trump the change in prison policy was that of balancing the respective interests involved. The Court of Appeal, however, was not persuaded by the applicant's reliance on *Hamble Fisheries*, describing Sedley J's approach as "heresy": "(O)n matters of substance . . . *Wednesbury* provides the correct test".[110] The application was thereupon dismissed.

The "progression" from *Richmond* through *Hamble Fisheries*, back to the Court of Appeal's judgment in *Hargreaves*, illustrates clearly the extent to which EU law can act as a catalyst for debate within domestic orders. The contrasting judicial approaches in *Hamble Fisheries* and *Hargreaves* brought into sharp focus the question of how far, or whether, it is desirable to retain contrasting standards of judicial review in EU law and domestic law.[111] Sedley J's attempt in *Hamble Fisheries* to import the EU standard was clearly informed by a concern for harmonisation of legal standards

reasonable in the first instance, with the question of whether it has sufficient legitimacy to allow it to trump the policy change in question being answered only after all competing interests have been balanced ("a legitimacy which in fairness outtops the policy choice which threatens it"). Paul Craig, however, questions the logic of Sedley J's approach, arguing that the expectation needs to be legitimate before it can be taken to have the potential to trump an administrative decision: "If the applicant can establish, from a governmental promise or from its past practice, the requisite objective, reasonable expectation then this should suffice to establish its legitimacy. A separate issue would then be whether the public interest was such as to allow the public body to resile from the expectation . . . (this approach) . . . comports better with reality . . . (and) . . . it is conceptually clearer". See n. 102 above, 301–3.

[109] [1997] 1 All ER 397. See further Forsyth n. 99 above and S Foster, "Legitimate Expectations and Prisoners' Rights: The Right to Get What You are Given" (1997) 60 *MLR* 727.

[110] [1997] 1 All ER 397, 412 (Hirst LJ). See also the earlier case *Re Findlay* [1985] AC 318.

[111] The point has been made by Christopher Forsyth: "Can it be the law that the courts will balance the broader public interest against the protection of legitimate expectations in cases arising under EU law, but in purely domestic cases they will only be able to intervene on a *Wednesbury* basis? This surely will not prove a tenable position in the medium to long term. Why should domestic legitimate expectations be less well protected than European expectations?". See n. 99 above, 381.

within the broader process of European integration,[112] yet his preferred approach was rejected unequivocally by the Court of Appeal in *Hargreaves*. Of course, it may be that the point of functional overlap between EU law and domestic law in *Hamble Fisheries* lent itself much more readily to a process of legal cross-fertilisation,[113] whereas the issues in *Hargreaves* highlighted the extent to which the spheres of influence of EU law and domestic law are, on occasion, fundamentally different. In any event, the fact remained that, post-*Hargreaves*, there was an obvious difference between the approaches of EU law and domestic law, with domestic interests seemingly being afforded lesser protection than comparable EU law interests.

It is perhaps in light of this that the Court of Appeal has recently revisited the question of which standard governs the protection of substantive legitimate expectations. In *R* v. *North and East Devon Health Authority, ex p Coughlan*[114] the Court accepted that the *Hargreaves* and *Hamble Fisheries* standards could, depending on the facts of a case, each be of application in purely domestic cases. *Hargreaves*, the Court reasoned, would continue to govern those cases in which the individual may legitimately expect that the decision-making body will "bear in mind its previous policy . . . before deciding whether to change course . . . the court is restricted to reviewing the decision on conventional grounds".[115] The *Hamble Fisheries* approach, meanwhile, would apply in those cases, like the instant one, where the individual may legitimately expect to receive a benefit which is substantive in nature.[116] Under such circumstances, the

[112] Sedley J's entire ruling apparently was driven by an integrationist perspective: "Mr Paines . . . submits that the present question is in law an entirely domestic one. This seems to me to be unreal. It may no doubt be said that the immediate case is the formulation of policy within a discretion conferred entirely by domestic legislation. But the purpose of the legislation and policy alike is to permit the respondent, under the principle of subsidiarity, to exercise its powers for the purposes of implementing the common agricultural policy of the European Community. If each member state were to be governed in carrying out its part of this joint exercise by no jurisprudence but its own domestic law, a major objective of the policy would be frustrated. The availability of eventual recourse to the Court of Justice from and against all member states in relation to the carrying out of the common agricultural policy must require domestic courts to have full regard to the jurisprudence of the Court of Justice". See [1995] 2 All ER 714, 724–5.

[113] The facts of this case concerned a change in policy regarding the transfer and aggregation of certain types of fishing licences. In other words, the decision overlapped in part with the EU's common agriculture policy.

[114] [2000] 2 WLR 622. For commentary see M Elliott, "*Coughlan*: Substantive Protection of Legitimate Expectations Revisited" (2000) 5 *JR* 27 and P Craig and S Schonberg, "Substantive Legitimate Expectations after *Coughlan*" [2000] *PL* 684.

[115] [2000] 2 WLR 622, 645.

[116] In *Coughlan* the applicant was moved into a residential nursing home which, the local health authority had assured her, would be her home for life. The local authority subsequently decided to close the home. It was this decision which was argued to frustrate the applicant's legitimate expectations.

courts should only accept administrative change where they are satisfied that there is an overriding public interest which justifies denial of the benefit:

> "Where the court considers that a lawful promise or practice has induced a legitimate expectation of a *benefit which is substantive* . . . authority now establishes that here too the court will in a proper case decide whether to frustrate the expectation is so unfair that to take a new and different course will amount to an abuse of power. Here, once the legitimacy of the expectation is established, the court will have the task of weighing the requirements of fairness against any overriding interest relied upon for the change of policy."[117]

The distinction between cases in which *Hargreaves* and *Hamble Fisheries* will apply might be criticised on the ground that it may not always easily be made in practice.[118] Nevertheless, the fact that the Court of Appeal was willing to modify its previously rigid approach provides further evidence of the manner in which the courts' institutional role is evolving. Some judges may, as considered above in the context of the *Wednesbury v* proportionality debate, choose to situate the dynamic of change solely within internal processes ongoing in UK public law. Other judges, however, may equally wish to attribute the evolution to a wider process of change involving the fusion of domestic and European standards. It is surely not without significance that Sedley LJ (as he now is) sat on the bench in both the *Hamble Fisheries* and the *Coughlan* cases. Sedley LJ, perhaps more than any of his peers, has been a strong advocate of both the common law model of review considered in chapter two and of the need to conceive of domestic and European legal standards as co-equivalent rather than separate.[119] That is not to say, of course, that *Coughlan* was representative of a straightforward process of legal osmosis as the judgment also attempted to preserve some role for traditional notions of *Wednesbury* review. But the corresponding fact the Court distinguished the reach of *Wednesbury* clearly implies that, where there is a willingness to use the common law and European law together, the domestic order can extricate itself from the increasingly strained language and logic of orthodoxy. The evolution may take the form of direct "spill-over",[120] or it may take the form of more incremental change of the kind seen in *Hamble Fisheries* through *Coughlan*. Either way, the process of

[117] [2000] 2 WLR 622, 645.

[118] Elliott n. 114 above, 29 (footnote 14). But see also the CA's consideration of the distinction in *R* v. *Secretary of State for Education and Employment, ex p Begbie* [2000] 1 WLR 1115. For subsequent application of *Hamble*, as mediated by *Coughlan* and *Begbie* see, e.g., *R* v. *Barking and Dagenham LBC, ex p Lloyd* [2001] LGR 86.

[119] See further *R* v. *Secretary of State for the Home Department, ex p McQuillan* [1995] 4 All ER 400, considered in ch. 7.

[120] See, e.g., *M* v. *Home Office* [1993] 3 WLR 433, considered in ch. 6.

fusion provides clear evidence that there is the potential for beneficial integration.

5. THE DUTY TO GIVE REASONS

The suggestion that judicial use of the common law would benefit from increased recourse to European principle and practice can also be made in relation to the duty to give reasons for administrative decisions. In domestic law, the question of whether a decision-maker is bound to give reasons is answered by reference to notions of natural justice and fairness, these notions again complementing *Wednesbury* understandings of judicial review as concerned solely with matters of procedure and legality rather than substance.[121] The historical position in UK law has been that the common law does not, in absence of any statutory obligation, impose a general duty to give reasons.[122] Although the courts have, consistent with developments in other areas of judicial review, modified the common law understanding,[123] the changes effected have been incremental and have not, as yet, gone so far as to create a base assumption that reasons should be given subject to competing considerations.[124] This position may be contrasted with EU law where it is arguable that there exists a more far-reaching obligation to inform individuals of the reasons for a particular outcome. In short, EU law proceeds from an understanding that effective judicial protection of an individual's interests can only be guaranteed when the individual is given reasons for a decision that affects him or her.[125] Consequently, it may be said that, while there may often be little practical difference between the common law and EU law approaches, the supranational standard proceeds from a position which is, at least at an abstract level, more inclined to prioritise the interests of the individual.

Arguments which favour the imposition of a general duty to give reasons typically pertain to deeper understandings of public authority propriety and openness in government. The requirement that a decision-maker give reasons for his decisions may, for example, serve to focus the

[121] Note 14 above.

[122] See, e.g., *Minister of National Revenue* v. *Wrights' Canadian Ropes Ltd* [1947] AC 109, 123 (Lord Greene MR); *McInness* v. *Onslow-Fane* [1978] 1 WLR 1520, 1532 (Megarry VC); and *R* v. *Home Secretary, ex p Duggan* [1994] 3 All ER 277, 287 (Rose LJ).

[123] See, e.g., *R* v. *Civil Service Appeal Board, ex p Cunningham* [1991] 4 All ER 310; *R* v. *Home Secretary, ex p Doody* [1994] 1 AC 531; *R* v. *City of London Corporation, ex p Matson* [1997] 1 WLR 765; *R* v. *Secretary of State for the Home Department, ex p Fayed* [1997] 1 All ER 228 and *R* v. *Ministry of Defence, ex p Murray* [1998] COD 134.

[124] See further P Craig, "The Common Law, Reasons and Administrative Justice" (1994) 53 *CLJ* 282 and Sir Patrick Neill, "The Duty to Give Reasons: the Openness of Decision-making" in C Forsyth and I Hare (eds) n. 12 above, p 161.

[125] For example, Case 222/86, *UNECTEF* v. *Heylens* [1987] ECR 4097, considered below.

decision-maker's mind on the right questions. The giving of reasons may also demonstrate that all relevant factors have been taken into consideration, and it may likewise demonstrate that such factors have been fully and properly addressed.[126] Ranged against such "positive" considerations, then, are familiar concerns that a requirement to give reasons may place extra and unnecessary burdens on administrators; require a decision-making authority to deliver an apparently unanimous decision when the deliberations leading to the decision were characterised by close debate and division; and task administrators with articulating inexpressible value judgments, thereby facilitating additional legal challenges.[127]

In the EU legal order, considerations of propriety and openness have apparently long overtaken concerns for administrative convenience.[128] Article 253 (ex 190) EC requires that the relevant EU institutions provide reasons for the adoption of Regulations, Directives and Decisions.[129] Indeed, the EU's concern for transparency was further illustrated by the adoption of Declaration No 17 in the Final Act of the Treaty on European Union. The Declaration sought to guarantee a right of public access to information on the EU process, and it subsequently led the Council and Commission to adopt individual Decisions to that effect.[130] The Decisions contain Codes of Conduct governing rights of access to EU documents and require that reasons be given when access is refused. Furthermore, and to the extent that the Codes contain a list of grounds upon which access to documentation may be refused, the Court of First Instance has shown itself determined to ensure that the grounds are not invoked lightly and that their use should be fully and explicitly justified in line with Article 253 EC.[131]

It is the EU law requirement that a national authority provide reasons for any action which derogates from its EU law obligations, however, which is of immediate relevance in the present context. Here, the nature and origins of the reason giving obligation are different from those underlying the EU institutions' obligation. Whereas the institutions' obligation is

[126] See *R* v. *Higher Education Funding Council, ex p Institute of Dental Surgery* [1994] 1 All ER 651, 665 (Sedley J).

[127] *Ibid.*

[128] It might be argued, however, that the EU's concern to ensure greater openness and transparency has arisen precisely because, for many years, the EU process was characterised by elitism and a much discussed democratic deficit. See G de Búrca, "The Quest for Legitimacy in the European Union" (1996) 59 *MLR* 349.

[129] On the rationale of the Treaty based obligation see, e.g., Case 24/22, *Germany* v. *Commission* [1963] ECR 63, 69. Note that a Regulation is invalid if reasons are not given: Case 158/80, *Rewe-Handelsgesellschaft Nord mbH* v. *Hauptzollamt Kiel* [1981] ECR 1805.

[130] See respectively Council Decision 93/731 on public access to Council documents, OJ 1993 L340/43 and Commission Decision 94/90 on public access to Commission documents, OJ 1994 L46/58. And see now Art. 255 (ex 191a) EC.

[131] See, e.g., Case T-105/95, *WWF UK (World Wide Fund for Nature)* v. *EC Commission* [1997] ECR II-313.

founded in the Treaty and related Declarations and secondary acts, the reason giving obligation that impacts upon national authorities derives instead from the general principles of EU law.[132] The leading case on the obligation is *UNECTEF* v. *Heylens*.[133] In the case a Belgian football trainer was employed in France by the Lille Olympic Sporting Club. The individual possessed a Belgian football trainer's diploma, yet the French National Equivalence Committee, without giving any reasons for its decision, refused to accord it status comparable to its French equivalent. Heylens was subsequently asked to stop working as a football trainer in France by the French Minister for Youth and Sport (again, he was not given any reasons for the request). Despite these "decisions", Heylens continued to work at the Lille Club until criminal charges were brought against him. The French court hearing the proceedings thereupon referred to the ECJ the question of whether the requirement that a foreign diploma must be recognised as the equivalent of a French diploma by a committee which did not have to give reasons for its decision was contrary to the EU's free movement of workers provisions.[134] The ECJ, in response, stressed that the free movement of workers is a fundamental right in EU law and that there must, as such, be full and effective judicial protection of that right:

> "Effective judicial review, which must be able to cover the legality of the reasons for the contested decision, presupposes in general that the court to which the matter is referred may require the competent authority to notify its reasons. But where, as in this case, it is particularly a question of securing the effective protection of a fundamental right conferred by the Treaty on EU workers, the latter must also be able to defend that right under the best possible conditions and have the possibility of deciding with a full knowledge of the relevant facts, whether there is any point in their applying to the courts."[135]

The common law approach to reason giving is, as stated, premised on the alternative understanding that, while the law does not impose a general duty to give reasons, the variable considerations of "fairness" may require that reasons be given in a particular case.[136] In *R* v. *Civil Service*

[132] Case C-70/95, *Sodemare SA* v. *Regione Lombardia* [1997] ECR I-3395, 3405 (para. 17, A-G Fennelly).

[133] Case 222/86, [1987] ECR 4097.

[134] In particular Art. 39 (ex 48) EC.

[135] [1987] ECR 4097, 4117 (para. 15). Note that the ECJ only required that reasons be given when a final decision was being relayed. There does not exist an obligation to give reasons for opinions and other measures occurring during the preparation and investigation leading up to the final decision. See [1987] ECR 4097, 4117 (para. 16).

[136] The variable nature of the concept is apparent from Lord Bridge's comment that: "the so-called rules of natural justice are not engraved on tablets of stone. To use the phrase which better expresses the underlying concept, what the requirements of fairness demand when any body, domestic, administrative or judicial, has to make a decision which will affect the rights of individuals depends on the character of the decision-making body, the

Appeal Board, ex p Cunningham,[137] for example, the applicant had, on account of charges of misconduct, been dismissed from his job as a prison officer. He had appealed his dismissal to the Appeal Board which, having had its recommendation of reinstatement rejected by the Home Office, calculated the applicant's compensation sum to the value of £6,500. The Appeal Board provided no reasons for its final determination, this being despite the fact that the applicant's evidence suggested that he was entitled to between £14,500 and £16,500 compensation. The Court of Appeal thereupon considered that the Appeal Board was, in light of its judicial power to make decisions determinative of rights between the Crown and its employees, obliged to give reasons for its decision: "(J)udged by that standard the Board should have given outline reasons sufficient to show to what they were directing their mind and thereby indirectly showing not whether their decision was right or wrong, which is a matter solely for them, but whether their decision was lawful".[138] Indeed, the need for reasons was taken to be particularly pronounced as there was no right of appeal against the Board's decision: "(I)t seems obvious that for the same reason of fairness that an applicant is . . . entitled to know the reasons for an award of compensation, so that in the event of error he may be equipped to apply to the court for judicial review".[139]

The courts' determination to control "judicial" decisions which impact on individual interests was further evidenced in R v. *Home Secretary, ex p Doody*.[140] *Doody* raised questions about the procedure whereby mandatory life sentence prisoners had their term of imprisonment set by the Home Secretary and reviewed by the Parole Board.[141] The Home Office had, since 1983, pursued a policy under which the Home Secretary would, after consultation with the judiciary, set the penal element of a prisoner's sentence, thereby simultaneously establishing the date on which the Parole Board would review the prisoner's sentence. In the instant case, the applicant considered that the Home Office had increased the penal element of his sentence as originally recommended by the judiciary, with the consequence that his review date was delayed. The applicant thereupon argued

kind of decision it has to make and the statutory or other framework within which it operates". See *Lloyd* v. *McMahon* [1987] AC 625, 702–3. But note that the courts have also drawn upon other considerations by way of moderating the common law position. See generally Craig n 124 above and P Robertshaw, "Providing Reasons for Administrative Decisions" (1998) *Anglo-American LRev* 29.

[137] [1991] 4 All ER 310. See further J Herberg, "The Right to Reasons: Palm Trees in Retreat?" [1991] *PL* 340.

[138] [1991] 4 All ER 310, 319.

[139] [1991] 4 All ER 310, 323 (Leggatt LJ).

[140] [1994] 1 AC 531. On *Doody* see N R Campbell, "The duty to give reasons in administrative law" [1994] *PL* 184.

[141] Section 35 of the Criminal Justice Act 1991.

that he was entitled to know the judicial view of the penal element of his sentence; the reasons for the judiciary's recommendations; and the reasons for any departure from the judiciary's recommendations by the Home Secretary. The House of Lords agreed.

Judgment on behalf of their Lordships was given by Lord Mustill. His Lordship began by restating the orthodox position that there does not exist in domestic law a general duty to give reasons for an administrative decision. Nevertheless, and reflecting *Cunningham*, Lord Mustill stated that there may exist a duty to give reasons where the facts and circumstances of a particular case in fairness demand that this is so. This, he then suggested, was just such a case. In essence, his Lordship stated that where Parliament confers an administrative power there exists a corresponding presumption that the power will be exercised in a manner that is fair in all the circumstances.[142] Applying the logic of this understanding to the Home Office procedure governing mandatory life prisoners, Lord Mustill concluded that the "continuing momentum in administrative law towards openness of decision-making" obliged the Home Secretary to conduct a more transparent procedure:

> "It is not, as I understand it, questioned that the decision of the Home Secretary on the penal element is susceptible to judicial review. To mount an effective attack on the decision, given no more material than the facts of the offence and the length of the penal element, the prisoner has virtually no means of ascertaining whether this is an instance where the decision-making process has gone astray. I think it is important that there should be an effective means of detecting the kind of error which would entitle the court to intervene and in practice I regard it as necessary for this purpose that the reasoning of the Home Secretary should be disclosed."[143]

What, if anything, is the difference between the EU and domestic law approaches to the duty to give reasons? Certainly, there are striking similarities between Lord Mustill's approach in *Doody* and the ECJ's approach in *Heylens*. The judicial statements in both cases centred not only on the need to ensure effective protection of individual rights but also on the twin objective of administrative transparency, and there can be little doubt that the two approaches, at least as a matter of practice, will often achieve the same result.

Where the two approaches arguably depart from one another, however, is in relation to the institutional understandings that belie the duty to give reasons. The two approaches are, at source, separable by reference to the

[142] See further, e.g., *R* v. *Secretary of State for the Home Department, ex p Venables and Thompson* [1997] 2 All ER 97.

[143] [1994] 1 AC 531, 565. And see further, e.g., *R* v. *Home Secretary, ex p Duggan* [1994] 3 All ER 277; *R* v. *Home Secretary, ex p Follen* [1996] COD 169; and *R* v. *Home Secretary, ex p Murphy* [1997] COD 478.

fact that EU law prioritises the protection of individual interests[144] while UK law, at least as an historical observation, tends towards the prioritisation of administrative convenience. Recent case law has, of course, greatly moderated domestic law's historic preference, and the courts, consistent with developments in other areas of judicial review, now openly place an increased emphasis on the need to protect individual interests. But the fact that the revised approach continues to take as its staring point an understanding that the courts are departing from a rule rather than enforcing a new one might be said to be unsatisfactory. Although "the interests of fairness will very generally be found to require that a person affected by a decision . . . should know the reasons underlying a particular decision",[145] the inherently malleable nature of "fairness" may be argued to leave the parameters of the obligation ill-defined and open to unpredictable development.[146] In consequence, it may be preferable for the courts to redefine the common law approach, drawing upon EU law to emphasise that there is general duty to give reasons which can only be off-set by statute or by clearly stated and closely justified competing administrative interests.[147]

6. CONCLUSION

This chapter has developed in more detail the argument that the orthodox reception of EU law has created a dualist divide that has frustrated the deeper interaction of domestic and EU legal standards. Although the

[144] It may be doubted, on the basis of *Heylens*, whether the obligation to give reasons exists only with regard to fundamental EU law rights or more generally. Sir Patrick Neill, however, prefers a broad interpretation: "It may well be that this principle will be applied in all contexts where what is at stake, or what underlies national legislation, is a right created by EU law. The principle will, perhaps, not be confined merely to the effective protection of "fundamental rights" (such as the freedom of movement) conferred by the Treaty, but will range more widely". See n. 124 above, p 171.

[145] *Ibid*, p 183. See further, e.g., *R* v. *City of London Corporation, ex p Matson* [1997] 1 WLR 765; *R* v. *Secretary of State for the Home Department, ex p Fayed* [1997] 1 All ER 228 and *R* v. *Ministry of Defence, ex p Murray* [1998] COD 134.

[146] Sedley J attempted in *R* v. *Higher Education Funding Council, ex p Institute of Dental Surgery* [1994] 1 All ER 651, 672 to identify circumstances under which there would be a duty to give reasons (note that in the instant case, no duty was imposed): "One such case is where the subject matter is an interest so highly regarded by the law (for example, personal liberty), that fairness requires that reasons, at least for particular decisions, be given as of right . . . Another such class is where the decision appears aberrant. Here fairness may require reasons so that the recipient may know whether the aberration is in the legal sense real (and so challengeable) or apparent . . . it follows that this class does not include decisions which are themselves challengeable by reference only to the reasons for them. A pure exercise of academic judgment is such a decision".

[147] Note that EU law does not provide the only reference point against which the courts may wish to develop the duty to give reasons. See, e.g., JUSTICE/All Souls, *Administrative Law: Some Necessary Reforms* (Oxford, 1988) for a survey of the approach of other common law jurisdictions.

divide has not precluded integration, it has given rise to a perception that domestic and EU law should be seen as essentially distinct from each other. This understanding has led traditionalists to deny that EU principles of review should have any deeper role to play in the domestic order,[148] and it has also led some proponents of change to suggest that modification can be effected without recourse to EU standards.[149] The result has been for cross-fertilisation to remain unduly constrained, with the assimilation of domestic and EU principles of review occurring only when the courts have shown themselves willing to forego the dualist divide and to conceive of domestic and EU law as equal parts of an interlocking whole.[150]

The argument that the domestic order would benefit from an increased process of borrowing from EU law should not, of course, be read in isolation from related arguments about abstract and practical limits to integration.[151] EU law's historical and institutional characteristics are obviously different from those of UK law, and it would be erroneous to suggest that each and every principle of EU law should, or could, be transplanted into the domestic system. What the chapter has attempted to demonstrate, therefore, is not that EU law is in every respect superior to domestic law, but rather that EU law offers legal and institutional insights that *may* be of deeper relevance to the UK order. The elements of EU administrative law, while not beyond reproach,[152] clearly have greater domestic potential than the workings of the dualist divide suggest. Not only do they provide more structured and transparent means of review;[153] they also include established principles which the domestic order may be struggling to develop "internally".[154] It follows that, while integration may not always be appropriate or desirable, the courts' capacity to consider fully the informative value or otherwise of the principle and practice of EU law depends on their willingness to move beyond the strained and problematic language of orthodoxy.

148 See, e.g., Lord Hoffmann's judgments in *Stoke-on-Trent CC and Norwich CC* v. *B & Q plc* [1991] Ch 48 and *Tesco Stores Ltd* v. *Secretary of State for the Environment* [1995] 1 WLR 759, 771 *ff*. See also *R* v. *Secretary of State for the Home Department, ex p Brind* [1991] 2 WLR 588, 609–10 (Lord Lowry).

149 See, e.g., Laws J's judgments in *R* v. *Ministry of Agriculture, Fisheries and Food, ex p First City Trading Limited* [1997] 1 CMLR 250 and *R* v. *Secretary of State for Health, ex p Imperial Tobacco Ltd* [2000] 1 All ER 572 (as Laws LJ). And see also Sir John Laws at n. 12 above.

150 For example, *R* v. *Ministry of Agriculture, Fisheries and Food, ex p Hamble (Offshore) Fisheries Limited* [1995] 2 All ER 714 (Sedley J).

151 See further ch. 1.

152 Harlow n. 2 above.

153 Jowell and Lester at n. 11 above.

154 An, e.g., is equality. See further n. 45 above.

6

Remedies

1. INTRODUCTION

The inconsistencies of the orthodox reception of EU law also colour areas in which the courts have engaged in a more active process of harmonisation. UK courts have, despite their general reluctance to integrate principles of judicial review, been willing to allow some EU law remedies to "spill over" into domestic cases. Such spill-over has undoubtedly been facilitated by the fact that the common law itself has historically "fasten(ed) not upon principles but upon remedies".[1] There are many judicial statements to the effect that the "consideration which has first claim on the loyalty of the law is that wrongs should be remedied",[2] and the courts have openly alluded to the need to maintain symmetry between standards of remedial relief under EU and domestic law. This has led not only to particular remedies becoming available in novel institutional circumstances[3] but also to the modification of existing standards.[4] More significantly, it has demonstrated how UK courts can, when they consider integration desirable, react creatively and allow "superior standards" of EU law to cross the dualist divide.[5]

The difficulty with the courts' approach to the integration of domestic and EU remedial standards, however, lies in the point, developed at length in the preceding chapter, that it has not been accompanied by a more comprehensive recasting of the principle and practice of domestic law. Indeed, to the extent that the integration of remedies has sometimes had

[1] *Davy* v. *Spelthorne* [1984] AC 262, 276 (Lord Wilberforce).

[2] *X* v. *Bedfordshire CC* [1995] 3 All ER 353, 380 (Lord Browne-Wilkinson), although note that *X* is one case in which the courts famously declined to prioritise individual interests. For further judicial statements about domestic law's historic emphasis on remedies see, e.g., *Ashby* v. *White* [1703] 2 Ld Raym 938, 953 (Holt CJ); *Abbott* v. *Sullivan* [1952] 1 KB 189, 200 (Denning LJ); and *Kingdom of Spain* v. *Christie, Manson & Woods Ltd* [1986] 1 WLR 1120, 1129 (Browne-Wilkinson V-C).

[3] *M* v. *Home Office* [1993] 3 WLR 433, 443 (Lord Woolf), considered below.

[4] *Woolwich Building Society* v. *Inland Revenue Commissioners (No 2)* [1992] 3 WLR 366, 395–6 (Lord Goff), considered below.

[5] J D B Mitchell, "'What do you want to be inscrutable for, Marcia?'/The White Paper on the Legal and Constitutional Implications of United Kingdom Membership of the European Communities" (1967) 5 *CMLRev* 112, 122. See further J Bell, "Mechanisms for Cross-fertilisation of Administrative Law in Europe" in J Beatson and T Tridimas (eds.) *New Directions in European Public Law* (Hart Publishing, Oxford, 1998), pp 147, 161.

far-reaching implications, the courts' wider approach to legal integration might ultimately be said to militate against fully harmonised protection of an individual's EU and domestic law interests. The courts' willingness to allow spill-over has been limited to those circumstances where a particular form of remedial relief had previously only been available to protect EU law interests. While spill-over then ensures that comparable relief is available in both EU and domestic law proceedings, the courts' reluctance to permit a deeper enmeshing of the principle and practice that determines whether there is entitlement to the remedy might be said to maintain disparity. In other words, an individual who is able to argue a case on the basis of EU principle and practice may, depending on the nature of the case at hand, be in a stronger position than an individual who must rely upon the analogous principle and practice of domestic law. Full and far-ranging harmonisation, therefore, would seemingly require that the courts view protection of the individual as dependent not just upon the existence of particular forms of relief but also upon the means of access to them.

2. REMEDIES AND THE INDIVIDUAL

The body of EU law remedies that must be applied by domestic courts is designed to ensure that EU law provisions which ". . . impose obligations on individuals . . . (and) . . . confer upon them rights which become part of their legal heritage"[6] enjoy equal force throughout the Member States.[7] The ECJ's initial approach to the protection of EU law interests had, subject to relatively inchoate notions of equal treatment and effective protection, emphasised that EU law interests could best be protected in national courts through the application of domestic procedures and remedies.[8] The shortcoming with this approach, however, was that it failed to take account of systemic variations throughout the Member States. The co-existence of different legal traditions, different assumptions about the institutional role of courts, and different rules of procedure all combined to give rise to the possibility that EU law rights may be better protected in some Member States than in others. Such unequal protection of EU law rights would not only prejudice individuals but would also affect the equilibrium of the general integration process. Thus, it was through the introduction of EU law requirements that include interim protection for

[6] Case 26/62, *Van Gend en Loos v Nederlandse Administratie der Belastingen* [1963] ECR 1, 12. And see further Case 6/64, *Costa* v. *ENEL* [1964] ECR 585, 593.

[7] See ch. 3, p 59 *ff*.

[8] Case 33/76, *Rewe-Zentralfinanz eG and Rewe-Zentral AG* v. *Landwirtschaftskammer für das Saarland* [1976] ECR 1989; Case 45/76, *Comet* v. *Produktschap voor Siergewassen* [1976] ECR 2043; and Case 158/80, *Rewe Handelsgesellschaft Nord mbH* v. *Hauptzollamt Kiel* [1981] ECR 1805.

EU law rights;[9] the provision of effective sanctions[10]; the modification of domestic rules of procedure;[11] and the award of damages for breach of EU law[12] that the ECJ was able to elaborate its understanding of what "effectiveness" requires as a matter of practice.[13]

Restitution

The ECJ's concern for the effective protection of EU law rights can be illustrated by reference to restitution, this being the first area in which there was spill-over into UK law. Here, there is a well established EU law rule that money levied illegally should, prima facie, be repaid to the individual as of right. The leading case on the point is *Amministrazione delle Finanze dello Stato* v. *San Giorgio*.[14] In the case, an Italian company sought to recover charges paid pursuant to Italian legislation which had, on the ground that it was contrary to EU law, been declared unconstitutional by the Italian Constitutional Court.[15] The claim, which related to import duties paid over a three-year period, was successful at first instance. On appeal, however, the State Finance Administration argued that it was not obliged to reimburse San Giorgio because it had been acting pursuant to a legislative provision which protected it against claims such as that in the instant case. The legislation in question stated that "a person who has paid import duties . . . which have been unduly levied . . . is not entitled to the repayment of the sums paid when the charge in question has been passed on in any way whatsoever to other persons, except in cases of substantive

[9] Case C-213/89, *R* v. *Secretary of State for Transport, ex p Factortame* [1990] ECR I-2433.

[10] Case 326/88, *Anklagemyndigheden* v. *Hansen & Sons I/S* [1990] ECR I-2911 and Case C271/91, *Marshall* v. *Southampton and South West Hampshire Area Health Authority (No 2)* [1993] ECR I-4367.

[11] Case C-208/90, *Emmott* v. *Minister of Social Welfare* [1991] ECR I-4269. But see Case C-338/91, *Steenhorst-Neerings* v. *Bestuur van de Bedrijfsvereniging voor Detailhandel, Ambachten en Huisvrouwen* [1993] ECR I-5475.

[12] First introduced in Joined Cases C-6 and 9/90 *Francovich and Bonifaci* v. *Italy* [1991] ECR I-5357 and developed in a line of jurisprudence running through to Joined Cases C-178–179 and 188–190/94, *Dillenkofer* v. *Germany* [1996] 3 CMLR 469.

[13] See further M Hoskins, "Tilting the Balance: Supremacy and National Procedural Rules" (1996) 21 *ELRev* 365. Although note that the ECJ's endeavours have been subject to criticism. See, e.g., C Harlow, "*Francovich* and the Problem of the Disobedient State" (1996) 2 *ELJ* 199.

[14] Case 199/82, [1985] 2 CMLR 658. See also Case 240/87, *Deville* v. *Administration des Impôts* [1988] ECR 3513; Case C-62/93, *BP Supergaz* v. *Greek State* [1995] ECR I-1883; Joined Cases C-192/95 to C-218/95, *Comateb and Others* v. *Directeur Général des Douanes et Droits Indirects* [1997] ECR I-165; and Case 309/85, *Barra* v. *Belgium and Another* [1998] ECR 355.

[15] Regulation 804/68/EEC, JO 1968 L148/13 and Regulation 805/68/EEC JO 1968 L148/24.

error".[16] Given this, the Presidente Istruttore referred to the ECJ the question of whether a national law which, by way of exception to the general provisions concerning recovery of undue payments, permits that charges be repaid only where they have not been passed on to other persons is to be regarded as discriminatory and contrary to EU law. The reference also asked whether it was significant that the charges covered by the said national provision had been wrongly levied because their collection conflicted with a rule of EU law.

The ECJ, while not stating that individual entitlement to repayment of monies under EU law is absolute,[17] emphasised that national rules and procedures should not render the effective protection of EU law rights impossible or, indeed, treat claims arising under EU law less favourably than their national equivalents.[18] Although anxious to avoid imposing unnecessary burdens on national administrations, the ECJ's principal concern was to prohibit the erosion of EU law rights by national legislation. Highlighting how the general rule of entitlement to repayment is "a consequence of, and an adjunct to, the rights conferred on individuals by (EU) provisions", it concluded:

> "(A) Member State cannot make the repayment of national charges levied contrary to the requirements of EU law conditional upon the production of proof that those charges have not been passed on to other persons if the repayment is subject to rules of evidence which render the exercise of that right virtually impossible, even where the repayment of other taxes, charges or duties levied in breach of national law is subject to the same restrictive conditions."[19]

EU law's understanding that there exists a prima facie right to the repayment of unlawfully levied monies contrasted with the position in UK law. Although the historical understanding in UK law suggested that such right should exist,[20] there had emerged in the law a "shabby rule" whereby the individual would only succeed in a claim if he could establish that he had been subjected to illegitimate duress or had made a mistake of fact.[21] The

[16] Section 10 of Decree-Law 430 of 10 July 1982, Gazzetta Ufficiale No 190 of 13 July 1982.

[17] The ECJ qualified its approach, e.g., by stating that "(EU) law does not prevent a national legal system from disallowing the repayment of charges which have been unduly levied where to do so would entail unjust enrichment of the recipients". [1985] 2 CMLR 658, 688–9 (para. 13).

[18] See further the cases at n. 8 above.

[19] [1985] 2 CMLR 658, 688 and 690 (paras. 12 and 18).

[20] See Art 4 of the Bill of Rights 1689, cited in P Birks, "'When Money is Paid in Pursuance of a Void Authority. . .' – A Duty to Repay?" [1992] *PL* 580: "levying money for or to the use of the Crowne by pretence of prerogative without grant of Parlyment for longer time or in other manner than the same is or shall be granted is illegal".

[21] See further P Birks *ibid.*, 581. Birks cites the following cases: *Slater* v. *Burnley Corporation* [1888] 59 LT 636; *Slater* v. *Burnley Corporation (No 2)* [1889] 3 JP 535;

domestic case which saw the courts harmonise the EU and domestic approaches was *Woolwich Building Society* v. *Inland Revenue Commissioners (No 2)*.[22] The *Woolwich* litigation stemmed from a change in taxation policy whereby the government regulated the manner in which building societies compounded for the income tax liability of their members. Under the new policy, contained in the Income Tax (Building Societies) Regulations 1986,[23] building societies would be required to pay their annual composition payments in quarterly instalments. The Regulations also contained transitional provisions, and it was these which ultimately led to the *Woolwich* litigation. In essence, the Woolwich Building Society argued that the effect of the transitional provisions was to double the amount of taxation to be paid between the end of its own accounting year and the beginning of the tax year for 1985–6. Having registered a complaint on this point at the time of its first payment to the Inland Revenue, the Woolwich subsequently initiated two actions: an application for judicial review of the legality of the relevant Regulations and an action for recovery of the money paid over to the Inland Revenue. The application for judicial review was successful[24] and, in consequence of this, the Inland Revenue returned the capital sum in the private action with interest from the time of judgment in the judicial review proceedings. The Woolwich then initiated a further action for the amount of interest which had accrued in the period between the initial payment of the tax sum to the Inland Revenue and the date of judgment in the judicial review proceedings.[25] The Inland Revenue refused to pay over the additional sum, arguing that the payments under the void Regulations had not created restitutionary debts. The Woolwich in turn argued that it was entitled to restitution as of right at the moment when the Inland Revenue received the sums paid pursuant to the Regulations.

The Woolwich's action was dismissed in the High Court by Nolan J who held that there was no "support in the decided cases for the application of

Meadows v. *Grand Junction Waterworks* [1905] 21 TLR 538; *William Whitely* v. *R* [1910] 101 LT 101; *Brocklebank Ltd* v. *R* [1925] 1 KB 52; *National Pari-Mutuel Association* v. *R* [1929] 46 TLR 594; *Twyford* v. *Manchester Corporation* [1946] Ch 236; and *Sebel Products* v. *Commissioners of Customs and Excise* [1949] Ch 409.

22 [1992] 3 WLR 366. For commentary see P Birks n. 20 above; T Hill, "Restitution from Public Authorities and the Treasury's Position: *Woolwich Equitable Building Society* v. *IRC*" (1993) 56 *MLR* 856; and J Beatson, "Restitution of Taxes, Levies and Other Imposts: Defining the Extent of the *Woolwich* Principle" (1993) 109 *LQR* 401.

23 SI 1986/482 (introduced pursuant to S. 40 of the Finance Act 1985).

24 *R* v. *Inland Revenue Commissioners, ex p Woolwich Building Society* [1987] STC 654. This decision was successfully appealed before the CA ([1989] STC 463) before being upheld by the HL. The HL ruling can be found at *R* v. *Inland Revenue Commissioners, ex p Woolwich Building Society* [1990] 1 WLR 1400.

25 *Woolwich Building Society* v. *Inland Revenue Commissioners* [1989] 1 WLR 137. The action was for £7,000,000 (the initial amount paid over to the Inland Revenue by the Woolwich was almost £57,000,000).

a general restitutionary principle, operating in the absence of mistake of fact or duress upon claims by the subject against the Crown or public authorities".[26] Nolan J's ruling was subsequently overturned by the Court of Appeal, however, a decision which was upheld by the House of Lords.[27] Delivering the lead judgment of the House, Lord Goff noted how the Woolwich considered that it had suffered an injustice to such an extent "that it was prepared to back its conviction that the Revenue was acting ultra vires by risking a very substantial amount of money in legal costs establishing the fact". His Lordship thereafter addressed the traditional understanding that an individual should be entitled to restitution only where they can show that they acted under duress or by mistake of fact, finding that "logic" demanded that the traditional approach be by-passed in the instant case in favour of prima facie entitlement. Although Lord Goff openly acknowledged that the House was "reformulating the law",[28] he considered the decision justified by reason of the need to protect private interests against the abuse of power by a government department. Not only would the recognition of the new restitutionary standard deny the Inland Revenue "the benefit of a massive interest free loan as the fruit of unlawful action", it would likewise ensure that notions of "common justice" prevailed. Even more significantly for present purposes, his Lordship also considered that it would achieve parity between the standards of protection given to the individual both by EU law and domestic law:

> "There is a sixth reason which favours this conclusion. I refer to the decision of the ECJ in *Amministrazione delle Finanze dello Stato* v. *San Giorgio SpA* which establishes that a person who pays charges levied by a Member State contrary to the rules of Community law is entitled to repayment of the charge, such right being regarded as a consequence of, and an adjunct to, the rights conferred on individuals by the Community provisions prohibiting the relevant charges . . . *I only comment that, at a time when Community law is becoming increasingly important, it would be strange if the right of the citizen to recover overpaid charges were to be more restricted under domestic law than it is under European law.*"[29]

[26] [1989] 1 WLR 137, 144.

[27] [1992] 3 WLR 366. The CA ruling can be found at [1991] 3 WLR 790.

[28] [1992] 3 WLR 366, 391. Although various matters were left unresolved, e.g., procedural questions and more general considerations as to the proper scope of the "new" common law right to restitution. See further N Bamforth, "Restitution and the scope of judicial review" [1997]*PL* 603.

[29] *Ibid*, 395–6. Emphasis added. The HL ruling was to prove highly controversial. Indeed, even before the judgment was delivered the Government had introduced legislation designed to give the offending Regulations retrospective validity (see s. 53 of the Finance Act 1991; see also s. 64 of the Finance (No 2) Act 1992). The legislation, which was to limit the possibility of further retroactive claims against the Inland Revenue, eventually led to proceedings before the ECtHR: see *National Provincial Building Society and others* v. *United Kingdom* [1997] 25 EHRR 127.

Injunctive relief

The second, and seminal, instance of the integration of remedies occurred when the House of Lords decided that the EU law rule establised in *Factortame (No 2)*,[30] namely that interim injunctions should be available against ministers of the Crown, should be developed in a purely domestic case. The *Factortame* saga, as considered in chapter four, arose from an application for judicial review made by a group of Spanish fishing boat operators which wished to challenge the lawfulness under EU law of the Merchant Shipping Act 1988.[31] Part of the application requested that an interim injunction be granted to prevent the Secretary of State enforcing the Act until all issues were resolved. The request, which was initially refused by the courts on the ground that they did not have jurisdiction to grant the relief,[32] led to a reference to the ECJ on the question of whether national courts were obliged as a matter of EU law to set aside the rule that prevented them making an interim order. The ECJ, in a judgment which prompted wide-ranging debate about the constitutional implications of EU membership, replied that the full effectiveness of EU law would be impaired if interim relief was not available: "(I)t follows that if a court which, in those circumstances would grant interim relief, if it were not for a rule of national law, is obliged to set aside that rule".[33]

The spill-over of *Factortame* occurred in *M* v. *Home Office*.[34] *M* v. *Home Office* concerned an application for judicial review of a decision of the Home Secretary to deport a citizen of Zaire (M) who was claiming refugee status in the UK. Pending the outcome of the application, the Home Office had given an undertaking to the court to defer removal of the applicant. The undertaking was subsequently ignored and M was deported. The case thereupon raised two intertwined issues. First, there was the issue of whether a minister of the Crown could be held in contempt of court for failure to uphold an undertaking given to the court. Second, there was the question of whether injunctive relief should, under circumstances such as those of the instant case, be available against a minister of the Crown for the purpose of ensuring that any undertaking given to the courts is legally enforceable. Indeed, as the House made clear, the question of whether injunctive relief was available was logically prior to the issue of contempt: "If there were no power to make coercive orders, then the need to rely on the law of contempt for the purpose of enforcing the orders would rarely arise".[35]

[30] *R* v. *Secretary of State for Transport, ex p Factortame (No 2)* [1991] 1 All ER 70.

[31] See further p 86 *ff*.

[32] Lord Bridge considered that the courts were precluded from granting an injunction both by common law precedent and by s 21 of the Crown Proceedings Act 1947.

[33] Case C-213/89, *R* v. *Secretary of State for Transport, ex p Factortame* [1990] ECR I-2433, 2465 (para 21).

[34] [1993] 3 WLR 433.

[35] [1993] 3 WLR 433, 446 (Lord Woolf).

In deciding that injunctive relief should be available in domestic proceedings, Lord Woolf made immediate reference to the fact that ". . . while a citizen is entitled to obtain injunctive relief (including interim relief) against the Crown or an officer of the Crown to protect his interests under (EU) law he cannot do so in respect of his other interests which may be just as important".[36] Describing this as an "unhappy situation", his Lordship surveyed pre-existing domestic jurisprudence to determine whether the rule against relief need be sustained by reference to precedent. Although Lord Bridge had already decided in *Factortame* that it did,[37] Lord Woolf drew upon *dicta* in several other cases to reach the conclusion that injunctions should be available in purely domestic cases.[38] In doing so, his Lordship was careful to state that the jurisdiction to grant injunctive relief against officers of the Crown should only be exercised "in the most limited circumstances".[39] But beyond addressing executive concerns, his Lordship made clear that he considered it correct that the power to award such relief should rest with the courts, and, returning to the post-*Factortame (No 2)* anomaly, he concluded: "(I)t would be most regrettable if an approach which is inconsistent with that which exists in (EU) law should be allowed to persist if this is not strictly necessary".[40]

[36] [1993] 3 WLR 433, 448.

[37] *Factortame Ltd* v. *Secretary of State for Transport* [1990] 2 AC 85.

[38] Notably *R* v. *Secretary of State for the Home Department, ex p Herbage* [1987] QB 872 and *R* v. *Licensing Authority Established under the Medicines Act 1968, ex p Smith, Kline & French Laboratories Ltd (No 2)* [1990] 1 QB 574. In *Herbage*, Hodgson J considered the ambit of s. 21 of the Crown Proceedings Act 1947 and found obiter that applications for judicial review fall outside the Act's scope as they are "public law" rather than "civil" proceedings. The finding was endorsed by the Court of Appeal in *Smith, Kline & French* which further suggested that s. 31(2) of the Supreme Court Act 1981 could be read as conferring the power to grant injunctions (note that Lord Woolf was one of the judges in the Court). And see also *R* v. *Education Secretary, ex p Avon County Council* [1991] 2 WLR 702 wherein the CA attempted to circumvent the "domestic" ruling in *Factortame* by moving the debate away from injunctive relief towards the power of the Court to stay proceedings pending the outcome of an application for judicial review. Stays are similar in legal effect to injunctive relief, and in *Avon* the CA found *obiter* that the court can, under Order 53, r 3(10)(a), stay ministerial decisions.

[39] Note that the courts have long been cautious when granting injunctions against public authorities. Before granting interim relief, a court must, on the basis of *American Cynamid* v. *Ethicon Ltd* [1975] AC 396, be satisfied both that there is a "serious" issue for the court to resolve and that the respective interests/rights of the parties would not be satisfactorily protected by a subsequent award of a remedy. The court must also take into account "many other special factors" before deciding whether it should, on the "balance of convenience", grant the injunction. One such "other special factor" in proceedings against public authorities is the broader public interest in allowing public authorities to perform their duties – see, e.g., *Smith* v. *Inner London Education Authority* [1978] 1 All ER 411, 422. For post-*M* application of these considerations see, e.g., *R* v. *Ministry of Agriculture, Fisheries and Food, ex p Monsanto plc* [1998] 4 All ER 321, considered in N Bamforth, "Interim Relief in the Public Law Context" (1999) 58 *CLJ* 1.

[40] [1993] 3 WLR 433, 463. This dictum might usefully be compared with that of Lord

In one sense, *M* v. *Home Office* might be said to provide the most open and far-reaching example of the fusion of the respective dynamics of the EU and domestic legal orders. Not only did the case highlight how the reception of EU law can create pressure for change within a domestic order; it also provided an insight into the vibrancy of the "internal' process whereby the UK courts have developed judicial review by way of reasserting democratic controls. Carol Harlow has suggested that *M* v. *Home Office* might best be understood as one of a series of post-War cases "in which courts have moved to cut down to size prerogative powers asserted by government and subject them to controls appropriate in a modern democracy",[41] and the judgment has likewise been characterised as "a great loss to the government . . . the House . . . show(ed) that the rule of law is more than a constitutional nicety, and . . . established the law of remedies in a way that no government would have allowed in legislation".[42]

Yet, beyond the specific facts and context of the case, questions may be raised about how far *M* v. *Home Office* was truly representative of a process of harmonisation. The integration of the EU standard was, as Lord Woolf made clear, designed to "level-up" the domestic order to ensure that parallel forms of relief are available in both domestic and EU law cases. While *M* v. *Home Office* may have achieved the initial objective, the corresponding fact that domestic and EU proceedings continue to exist on either side of the dualist divide means that related issues may thereafter be resolved on the basis of contrasting principle and practice. An individual may, for example, obtain interim relief in an application for judicial review based upon their EU law rights. While the individual may likewise obtain interim relief in a "domestic" application, the outcome of the cases may be crucially affected by the principles of review used in the full hearing. In short, the fact that the individual in the EU law application can legitimately present argument on the basis of the proportionality principle may be said to place them in a potentially more advantageous position than the individual in domestic proceedings. Although the approach in the domestic proceedings may be adapted according to the subject matter of the application,[43] the domestic

Denning in *Abott* v. *Sullivan* [1952] 1 KB 189, 200: "I should be sorry to think that if wrong has been done, the plaintiff is to go without a remedy simply because no one can find a peg to hang it on". Note that, while an injunction (interdict) may be awarded against a minister of the Crown in Scotland for purposes of protecting EU law rights (*Millar & Bryce Ltd* v. *Keeper of the Registers of Scotland* [1997] SLT 1000), the remedy is not available in domestic judicial review proceedings (*McDonald* v. *Secretary of State for Scotland* [1994] SC 234).

[41] "Accidental Loss of an Asylum Seeker" (1994) 57 *MLR* 620, 626.

[42] M Gould, "*M* v. *Home Office*: Government and the judges" [1993] *PL* 568, 578. And see further Sir S Sedley, "The Crown in its Own Courts" in C Forsyth and I Hare (eds), *The Golden Metwand and the Crooked Cord* (Clarendon Press, Oxford, 1998), p 253.

[43] See the previous chapter's discussion of the courts' approach in judicial review proceedings that raise fundamental rights issues at p 115 *ff*. And see also the following ch.

order's apparent reluctance finally to depart from *Wednesbury* unreasonableness suggests that the case may be resolved on the basis of a principle that is historically conditioned to minimise court involvement in the decision-making process. It follows that, while both individuals may be able to obtain an interim injunction, their chances of ultimate success, for example in the form of obtaining final injunctive relief, may vary on account of the manifestation of different understandings about the institutional role of the courts.

3. REMEDIES, THE COURTS AND INSTITUTIONAL BALANCE

The difficulties presented by the co-existence of contrasting principle and practice have also been recognised in the context of damages actions against public authorities.[44] Judicial approaches to public authority liability, as with applications for judicial review, are structured around preferred understandings of the institutional balance of the State.[45] Although UK law views public authorities as theoretically subject to the same rules of civil liability as private persons,[46] there exists a series of requirements which reflect judicial assumptions about the need to protect exercises of administrative discretion and to safeguard against public authorities being unduly burdened by litigation.[47] Actions for loss caused by the unlawful exercise of statutory discretion, for example, may, on account of domestic law's understanding that an ultra vires act *per se* does not occasion liability,[48] require proof of negligence,[49] and negligence actions themselves may be frustrated by judicial assumptions about public policy and the broader public interest.[50] Likewise, it may also be said that

[44] P Craig, "Once More Unto the Breach: The Community, The State and Damages Liability" (1997) 113 *LQR* 67 and M Amos, "Extending the liability of the state in damages" (2001) 21 *LS* 1.

[45] For comparative analysis see B S Markesinis, J-B Auby, D Coester-Waltjen and S F Deakin, *Tortious Liability of Statutory Bodies* (Hart Publishing, Oxford, 1999).

[46] An observation consistent with the historical understanding that there is no public-private divide in UK law. But see now the modern understanding, the evolution of which is critically traced in JWF Allison, *A Continental Distinction in the Common Law: A Historical and Comparative Perspective on English Public Law* (Oxford University Press, Oxford, 2nd edn, 2000). And see also ch. 2, p 35 *ff*.

[47] See further S Arrowsmith, *Civil Liability and Public Authorities* (Earlsgate Press, Humberside, 1992).

[48] *Hoffman-La Roche* v. *Secretary of State for Trade and Industry* [1975] AC 295, 359 (Lord Wilberforce).

[49] See, e.g., *Larner* v. *Solihull MBC* [2001] LGR 255. The individual may alternatively seek to show that the circumstances give rise to a private law cause of action for, e.g., breach of statutory duty or misfeasance in public office. On the difficulties associated with the tort of breach of statutory duty, however, see, e.g., *O'Rourke* v. *Camden LBC* [1998] AC 188. On misfeasance in public office see n. 51 below.

[50] See, e.g., with regard to police liability when investigating crime, *Hill* v. *Chief*

the tort of misfeasance in public office, which requires proof that the public authority knowingly or maliciously exceeded its powers, is characterised by a concern to minimise the scope for liability.[51]

The understanding that the co-existence of different principle and practice can create difficulties has developed in light of the demands placed upon domestic orders by EU law's state liability doctrine. State liability obliges national courts to award damages to an individual as a matter of EU law when the Member State breaches the individual's EU law interests.[52] The doctrine does not, as such, require national courts to introduce new remedial procedures, but it does require that there is effective access to damages through existing domestic standards.[53] Paul Craig has thereupon argued that the courts should use their experience giving effect to the EU law doctrine to embellish existing domestic heads of liability, most notably those governing responsibility for unlawful administrative acts.[54] His arguments in this regard have, consistent with more general debates about legal integration, met with resistance from other commentators who have highlighted the existence of functional differences between the domestic and EU standards.[55] While the differences are not said to render the process of cross-fertilisation entirely problematic, they are taken to raise questions about how far borrowing of the kind urged by Craig is viable. Thus, the issue of integration and public authority liability, as with the *Wednesbury* v. proportionality debate, reduces to questions of institutional balance.

Constable of West Yorkshire [1989] AC 53; *Alexandrou* v. *Oxford* [1993] 4 All ER 328; *Metcalfe* v. *Chief Constable of the RUC* [1995] NI 446; and *Osman* v. *Ferguson* [1993] 4 All ER 344. But see also the ECtHR's judgment in *Osman* v. *United Kingdom* [1999] 1 FLR 193 as mediated by *Barrett* v. *Enfield LBC* [1999] 3 All ER 193, considered below.

[51] The scope of the tort was recently examined by the HL in *Three Rivers DC* v. *Bank of England (No 3)* [2000] 2 WLR 1220. On public authority liability see further HWR Wade and CF Forsyth, *Administrative Law* (Oxford University Press, Oxford, 2000, 8th edn) ch. 21.

[52] Introduced in Joined Cases C-6 and 9/90 *Francovich and Bonifaci* v. *Italy* [1991] ECR I-5357 and developed in a line of jurisprudence running through to Joined Cases C-178–179 and 188–190/94, *Dillenkofer* v. *Germany* [1996] 3 CMLR 469.

[53] For example, the House of Lords had, in *Bourgoin SA* v. *Ministry of Agriculture, Fisheries and Food* [1986] 1 QB 716, suggested that damages actions for breach of an individual's EU law rights should be taken under the tort of misfeasance in public office. However, in Joined Cases C-46 and 48/93, *Brasserie du Pêcheur SA* v. *Germany, R* v. *Secretary of State for Transport, ex p Factortame Ltd* [1996] 1 ECR 1029, 1154 (para. 73), the ECJ stated: "any condition that may be imposed by English law on State liability requiring proof of misfeasance in public office, such an abuse of power being inconceivable in the case of the legislature, is also such as in practice to make it impossible or extremely difficult to obtain effective reparation for loss or damage resulting from a breach of Community law". But note that the point had already been conceded by the domestic courts: see *Kirklees Borough Council* v. *Wickes Building Supplies Ltd* [1992] 2 CMLR 765, 785 (Lord Goff).

[54] Note 44 above.

[55] J W F Allison, "Transplantation and Cross-fertilisation" in J Beatson and T Tridimas (eds.), n. 5 above 1998, p 169.

State liability in EU law

The origins of the state liability doctrine can be traced to the *Francovich* case.[56] In the case, which is often associated with the ECJ's attempts to circumvent the difficulties created by its *Marshall* ruling,[57] it was held that a Member State can be liable in damages under EU law where its failure to implement a Directive causes loss to an individual. The scope of the doctrine has, however, since been greatly expanded[58] and it now covers potentially any breach of an individual's EU law rights by the legislative, administrative or judicial branches of the State.[59]

The central element in the doctrine is the concept of a "sufficiently serious" breach of an EU provision. The concept was first introduced by the ECJ in its *Brasserie du Pêcheur/Factortame III* judgment.[60] In *Brasserie/Factortame III* the issue for the ECJ was whether a Member State could be liable in damages for maintaining or introducing domestic legislation which contravenes an individual's EU law rights.[61] In ruling that it could, the ECJ stated that a Member State would be liable in damages for *any* of its actions where (a) there is an EU law provision conferring rights upon individuals; (b) there is a "sufficiently serious" breach of the provision by the State; and (c) an individual suffers loss as a direct result of the breach.[62] The question of whether a breach has been "sufficiently serious" is to be gauged by reference to all the facts of a case. Thus, where a Member State authority has a wide discretion in a particular policy area, for example the national legislature introducing national legislation, liability will rest only where the State "manifestly and gravely disregards

[56] Cases C-6 and 9/90, *Francovich and Bonifaci* v. *Italy* [1991] ECR I-5357, annotated in G Bebr, "Francovich v Italy, Bonifaci v Italy" (1992) 29 *CMLRev* 559.

[57] See further ch. 3, p 58 *ff*.

[58] See P Spink, "Contravening EC Law: The Liability of the Member State" (1997) 48 *NILQ* 111; E Deards, "'Curiouser and Curiouser'? The Development of Member State Liability in the Court of Justice" (1997) 3 *EPL* 117; and J Steiner, "The Limits of State Liability for Breach of European Community Law" (1998) 4 *EPL* 69.

[59] Joined Cases C-46 and 48/93, *Brasserie du Pêcheur SA* v. *Germany, R* v. *Secretary of State for Transport, ex p Factortame Ltd* [1996] ECR I 1029, 1145 (para. 34).

[60] [1996] ECR I 1029. Although the ECJ stated in *Dillenkofer* that the concept of a "sufficiently serious" breach was inherent in the original *Francovich* formulation. See Joined Cases C-178/94, C-179/94, C-188/94, C-189/94 and C-190/94, *Dillenkofer* v. *Germany* [1996] 3 CMLR 469, 495 (para. 23).

[61] *Brasserie du Pêcheur* concerned a claim for damages brought by a French brewery which had been unable to export its beer to Germany during 1981–1987 because its produce did not comply with the German beer purity requirements laid down in the Biersteuergesetz of 1952: these requirements were removed following the ECJ's ruling in Case C-178/84, *Commission* v. *Germany* [1987] ECR 1227. The claim in *Factortame III* was for loss incurred in consequence of the Merchant Shipping Act 1988.

[62] On the elements of the doctrine see further T Tridimas, "Liability for breach of community law: growing up and mellowing down?" (2001) 38 *CMLRev* 301.

the limits of its discretion".[63] By contrast, where a Member State has only very limited or no discretion, for example making an administrative decision in a policy area closely regulated by EU law, the "mere infringement" of an EU provision may be enough to occasion liability.[64] The resolution of cases "in between", for example the national legislature introducing national legislation to give effect to an EU Directive, will then depend upon the application of the ECJ's suggested list of criteria for identifying a sufficiently serious breach: was the EU provision which was breached clear? Was the breach/damage intentional? Was any error of law on the part of the State excusable? Had the Member State been adopting or retaining practices contrary to EU law?[65]

State liability and damages actions in domestic law

Craig's argument that the state liability doctrine might be used to develop domestic standards centres upon the insights provided by the "sufficient seriousness" element. Arguing that the state liability doctrine could in the first instance be accommodated within the domestic standard for breach of statutory duty,[66] he considers that the flexibility of the "sufficient seriousness" requirement might usefully inform domestic attempts to balance the protection of an individual's interests and the protection of areas of administrative discretion. Highlighting how the EU law approach centres upon the extent to which the Member State enjoys discretion, Craig argues that an increased awareness of, and openness to, the ECJ's approach might lessen some of the difficulties inherent in the domestic approach to liability

[63] [1996] I ECR 1029, 1150 (para. 55). The formulation is based upon the *Schöppenstedt* formula used in the context of Art. 288(2) (ex 215(2)) EC actions against the EU institutions. See Case 5/71, *Aktien-Zuckerfabrik Schöppenstedt* v. *Council* [1971] ECR 975.

[64] Case C-5/94, *R* v. *Ministry of Agriculture, Fisheries and Food, ex p Hedley Lomas (Ireland) Ltd* [1996] ECR I-2553 (para. 28).

[65] Joined Cases C-46 and 48/93, *Brasserie du Pêcheur SA* v. *Germany, R* v. *Secretary of State for Transport, ex p Factortame Ltd* [1996] I ECR 1029, 1150 (para. 56). An example of an "in between" case is Case C-392/93, *R* v. *HM Treasury, ex p British Telecommunications plc* [1996] ECR I-1631.

[66] Noting how the three-stage EU law test has parallels in the domestic standard ((a) the existence of a statutory duty; (b) breach of the duty; causing (c) damage to the plaintiff), Craig has "no doubt" that the domestic standard could be suitably modified in EU law cases. See n. 44 above, 93. It should further be noted that there is some pre-existing judicial support for the suggestion both that damages actions should be brought within the rubric of breach of statutory duty (*Garden Cottage Foods Ltd* v. *Milk Marketing Board* [1984] AC 130) and that damages actions on the basis of EU law be seen to found a new and independent source of action in domestic courts (*Application des Gaz SA* v. *Falks Veritas Ltd* [1974] 2 CMLR 75 (Lord Denning)). But see most recently the judgment of the High Court in *R* v. *Secretary of State for Transport, ex p Factortame (No 7)* [2001] 1 CMLR 1191, again suggesting that actions should be taken within the framework of breach of statutory duty (the duty being said to arise from relevant EU law provisions read in conjunction with s. 2 (1) of the European Communities Act 1972).

for unlawful administrative acts. The domestic standard, as stated above, proceeds from the starting point that an ultra vires act *per se* will not occasion liability in damages, requiring instead that any claim also satisfies the elements of a negligence action. Negligence actions, which are founded in the common law, require the individual to demonstrate that the public authority owed them a duty of care; breached the duty of care; thereby causing the damage complained of.[67] While the elements of the action, in particular the duty of care requirement, have been used to protect exercises of administrative discretion,[68] Craig wonders how far the action is able to take cognisance of the related concerns of the individual and the variable circumstances of different cases:

> "The jurisprudence of the ECJ may be of assistance here, in that it increases the options at our disposal. It shows a way of adding to the existing heads of liability, without thereby imposing excessive burdens upon public authorities . . . (I)t might be objected that this recasting of domestic doctrine has failed to reconcile the fact that UK law requires proof of negligence in addition to the seriousness of the breach, whereas (EU) law imposes no such condition . . . (W)hat would be lost if we dropped this stipulation? . . . (T)he principal difference in this respect is that the ECJ's concept of serious breach is richer and better worked out than its national counterpart."[69]

The criticisms of Craig's thesis, made by John Allison, draw upon an understanding that truly effective legal cross-fertilisation can only occur when the process is tempered by an awareness of doctrinal, institutional and functional differences between legal systems.[70] Finding Craig's "regard for the specific considerations crucial to cross-fertilisation . . . open to question"[71] Allison suggests that it would be difficult to transpose the EU law standard of "state" liability onto the "stateless (UK) legal tradition".[72] Allison likewise expresses reservations about the broader functional implications of Craig's approach, doubting whether domestic judicial institutions and procedures would be able to accommodate the procedure and practice of the ECJ. Stating that Craig's analysis neglects such issues, he argues that the ECJ's jurisprudence running from *Francovich* through *Brasserie du Pêcheur* was primarily concerned to ensure the effectiveness of EU law, while the function of UK rules on the

[67] See further M Brazier and J Murphy, *Street on Torts* (Butterworths, London) chs. 11–14.

[68] The point is developed more fully below.

[69] (1997) 113 *LQR* 90, 93–4.

[70] Note 55 above.

[71] *Ibid*, p 177.

[72] *Ibid*, p 178. Allison has pursued a similar argument elsewhere in the context of the introduction into the common law the "public–private" distinction associated with the French legal system. See n. 46 above.

liability of public authorities has been to ensure that the courts avoid "non-justiciable" questions and "determining the financial priorities of government": "(W)hether the balance encapsulated by the ECJ's test can be appropriate in both EU law and (UK) law despite significant functional differences is questionable".[73]

Allison's statement about the function of domestic law's rules on public authority liability may, given previous experience, be taken to imply that integration of the kind urged by Craig may not be immediately forthcoming. The courts have already demonstrated a general reluctance to integrate principles of judicial review which may upset core institutional assumptions, and it is difficult to see why their approach in other areas which are likewise reflective of institutional preferences should be different.[74] The remaining difficulty with such reluctance, however, is that it seemingly distinguishes between elements of legal proceedings which are of primary concern to individuals, namely the existence of particular forms of relief, and elements which impact upon institutional relations between different branches of the State, namely principles of review and standards governing liability. The distinction is, of course, false, and seen from this perspective, Craig's argument about integrating the concept of "sufficient seriousness" assumes a different value. His argument, if followed through, need not necessarily give rise to inter-institutional tensions, but rather may allow courts to develop more flexible means of reconciling the competing interests of the individual and the administration and, moreover, of the competing institutional roles of the courts and decision-makers. That is not to say that the development of the domestic order would be entirely without difficulty, but it is to suggest that such development could, through time, come to be beneficial. The issue, then, is whether the required change in judicial approach will ever occur.

Barrett *v.* Enfield, *public authority liability and the interim impact of the ECHR*

It is in this context that the significance of the Human Rights Act 1998 can again be highlighted as, even before the Act came into force in October 2000, it had already exerted an influence on the courts' approach to public authority liability. In *Barrett* v. *Enfield LBC*,[75] the House of Lords delivered a judgment, shaped in part by the ECtHR's ruling in *Osman* v. *United Kingdom*,[76] in which it modified its approach to public authority liability

[73] Note 55 above, p 178.

[74] Of course, not all judges are opposed to the modification of the domestic standards: see, e.g., Lord Woolf's judgment in the CA in *R* v. *Secretary of State for Transport, ex p Factortame (No 5)* [1998] EuLR 456, 469.

[75] [1999] 3 All ER 193.

[76] [1999] 1 FLR 193.

for the unlawful exercise of statutory powers.[77] The change effected essentially saw the House reconsider how far public authorities which have acted unlawfully can be said to owe a corresponding common law duty of care to a plaintiff. The courts' approach to the existence of common law duties of care had, in previous years, been very restrictive, with many actions being "struck-out" before going to a full hearing.[78] This approach, which was driven by the broader public policy considerations identified by Allison, was criticised by the ECtHR on the ground that it had the potential to militate against the proper protection of an individual's interests. The House of Lords ruling in *Barrett* v. *Enfield*, therefore, was representative of an attempt to accommodate the ECtHR's concerns in advance of them being formally enforceable in the domestic courts.

A common law duty of care is taken to be owed when it can be shown that the harm suffered by the plaintiff should have been reasonably foreseen by the defendant; there existed a sufficiently proximate relationship between the plaintiff and defendant; and the court considers it "just and reasonable" to impose liability.[79] The latter requirement, that it be just and reasonable to impose liability, had been central to the courts' restrictive approach in public authority cases. Proceeding on the understanding that authorities do not owe common law duties of care in relation to "policy" decisions, such decisions being regarded as "non-justiciable", the courts emphasised that duties of care would only be imposed in respect of ultra vires acts where the subject matter of the case was justiciable and a close examination of the wider context of the case permitted such imposition.[80]

[77] It should be noted that the ECtHR has since revised its findings in *Osman* – *Z* v. *United Kingdom*, judgment of 10 May 2001 (see n. 92 below). Consideration of the case remains apposite, however, both because it indicates how far ECHR jurisprudence may require UK courts to modify domestic principle and practice, and also because it is unclear whether the ECtHR's revised jurisprudence will now cause UK courts to rethink the domestic changes effected in light of the original *Osman* ruling. See further nn. 92 and 95 below.

[78] Cases are struck-out if it is considered that proof of all facts alleged would not sustain a cause of action.

[79] *Caparo Industries plc* v. *Dickman* [1990] 1 All ER 568, 573–4 (Lord Bridge).

[80] *Viz* the the "policy"/"operational" distinction introduced by the House of Lords in *Anns* v. *Merton London Borough Council* [1977] 2 All ER 492. The distinction sought to separate policy decisions from operational decisions on the basis that, while no duty of care could exist when an authority was making a "policy" decision, a duty could exist relative to "operational" decisions taken in light of the original policy preference. The obvious difficulty with the distinction, however, was that it left unresolved the issue of how policy issues may be identified and, moreover, how to determine where "policy" ends and "operational" begins. On the application of the distinction see, e.g., *Rowling* v. *Takaro Properties Ltd* [1988] 1 All ER 163 and *Lonrho plc* v. *Tebbit* [1991] 4 All ER 973. For criticism see, e.g., S H Bailey and M J Bowman, "The Policy/Operational Dichotomy – A Cuckoo in the Nest" (1986) 45 *CLJ* 430. For discussion of the meaning and uses of the related concept of justiciability, see AP Le Sueur, "Justifying Judicial Caution: Jurisdiction, Justiciability and Policy"

In *X* v. *Bedfordshire CC*,[81] for example, the issue for the courts was how far, if at all, a local authority could be said to owe a common law duty of care in respect of the exercise of its statutory powers to protect children from abuse.[82] The House of Lords, in finding that no common law duty was owed in the present case, noted that any decision to impose liability must be "profoundly influenced by the statutory framework within which the acts complained of were done".[83] Having examined the relevant statutory framework, the House struck-out the case because it considered that a finding of liability "would cut across the statutory system set up for the protection of children at risk", thereby further complicating an already "extraordinarily delicate" task and potentially causing local authorities to "adopt a more cautious and defensive approach to their duties".[84] This, the House reasoned, would not only frustrate the proper provision of public services but would also bring undue external pressure to bear on decision-makers who were best placed to make difficult choices: "In my judgment, the courts should proceed with great care before holding liable in negligence those who have been charged by Parliament with the task of protecting society from the wrongdoing of others".[85]

The ECtHR's criticisms in *Osman* of the domestic approach focused not upon the legitimacy of the courts' reasons for wishing to limit public authority liability, but rather on the negative impact the approach can have on an individual's rights of access to a court under Article 6 ECHR.[86] The *Osman* case itself had arisen in the analogous context of an action which alleged that the police had been negligent when investigating and suppressing crime (the action was brought by the family of a school pupil who was shot and injured by an obsessive teacher).[87] Although there was clear evidence in the case that the police knew both who the perpetrator

in B Hadfield (ed.), *Judicial Review: A Thematic Approach* (Gill & MacMillan, Dublin, 1995), p 228.

[81] [1995] 3 All ER 353.

[82] Under the terms of the Children and Young Persons Act 1969; the Child Care Act 1980; and the Children Act 1989. Note that the *X* case was joined with one other child abuse case and three further cases that alleged negligence in relation to the provision of education services. The following pages only refer to the judgment in respect of the child abuse cases, namely *X* and *M* v. *Newham London Borough Council*.

[83] [1995] 3 All ER 353, 371 (Lord Browne-Wilkinson).

[84] [1995] 3 All ER 353, 380-2 (Lord Browne-Wilkinson).

[85] *Ibid.* See further the courts' approach to the existence of common law duties of care when it is alleged that a local authority has been negligent in failing to exercise a statutory power in, e.g., *Stovin* v. *Wise* [1996] 3 All ER 801. Note also that *X* was to go to the ECtHR (as *Z* v. *UK*) – see n. 92 below.

[86] Article 6(1) states: "In the determination of his civil rights and obligations . . . everyone is entitled to a fair and public hearing within a reasonable time by an independent and impartial tribunal established by law". On *Osman* see further G Monti, "*Osman* v. *UK* – Transforming English Negligence Law into French Administrative Law?" (1999) 48 *ICLQ* 757.

[87] *Osman* v. *Ferguson* [1993] 4 All ER 344.

and victims of the crime were even before the crime was committed, the domestic courts had held that there could be no liability. Drawing on previous judgments, the Court of Appeal considered itself bound by the general rule of public policy that the police do not owe duties of care when investigating and suppressing crime.[88] Thus, even though the facts of the instant case could be easily distinguished from those in other cases, the existence of *de facto* blanket immunity for the police was taken to mean that the case should be struck-out before going to a full hearing: it was the legitimacy of this result which subsequently was in issue before the ECtHR.

The ECtHR began by stating that the broader public policy considerations that had underpinned the emergence of the domestic rule were recognised as valid by the ECHR. However, turning to the fact that the rule entailed seemingly "watertight" immunity from liability, the ECtHR considered that the *de facto*, if not *de jure*, position in domestic law represented a disproportionate restriction on rights of access to a fair and full hearing under Article 6 ECHR. Although the UK government had argued that the rule against liability was not absolute, the ECtHR was of the opinion that the domestic courts considered it "impossible to prise open (the) immunity which the police enjoy from civil suit".[89] For the ECtHR, this meant that the individual was, on account of the striking-out of the action, unable to raise before courts arguments which might contradict and overtake broader public policy considerations. It followed that, while the ECtHR did wish to diminish the significance of wider policy concerns, it considered that the automatic prioritisation of those concerns at the national level meant that no distinction could be made "between degrees of negligence or of harm suffered or any consideration of the justice of a particular case . . . these are considerations which must be examined on the merits and not automatically excluded by the application of a rule which amounts to the grant of an immunity to the police".[90]

[88] A rule associated with *Hill* v. *Chief Constable of West Yorkshire* [1989] AC 53, 63 (Lord Keith): "It would not be unreasonable to expect that if potential liability were to be imposed it would not be uncommon for actions to be raised against police forces . . . A great deal of police time, trouble and expense might then be expected to have to be put into the preparation of the defence . . . The result would be a significant diversion of police manpower and attention away from their most important function, the suppression of crime". For subsequent application see, e.g., *Alexandrou* v. *Oxford* [1993] 4 All ER 328 and *Metcalfe* v. *Chief Constable of the RUC* [1995] NI 446. But note also that there was no rule against findings of liability in cases which did not concern the investigation and suppression of crime. See, e.g., *Rigby* v. *Chief Constable of Northamptonshire* [1985] 2 All ER 985 (police liable for the negligent discharge of a CS canister); *Kirkham* v. *Chief Constable of Greater Manchester* [1990] 3 All ER 246 (officers liable for their failure to warn prison authorities that the plaintiff's husband was likely to attempt to commit suicide) and *Alcock* v. *Chief Constable of South Yorkshire* [1992] 1 AC 310 (police liable for allowing football fans to pour into a football ground thereby crushing to death a large number of other fans).

[89] [1999] 1 FLR 193, 231–2 (para 150).

[90] *Ibid*, paras. 151–152.

The ECtHR's ruling was immediately criticised by some senior members of the UK judiciary. Lord Hoffman, writing extra-judicially, stated that the ECtHR had "challeng(ed) the autonomy of the courts and indeed the Parliament of the United Kingdom to deal with what are essentially social welfare questions involving budgetary limits and efficient public administration",[91] and Lord Browne-Wilkinson suggested in *Barrett* v. *Enfield* that the ECtHR had misunderstood the nature of the relationship between Article 6 ECHR and domestic negligence actions.[92] Given his critcisms of *Osman*, however, it is something of a paradox that Lord Browne-Wilkinson then used the rest of his judgment in *Barrett* v. *Enfield* to effect the kind of change apparently required by the ECtHR.[93] The plaintiff in *Barrett* was a young man who had been taken into care at the age of ten months and who was now claiming damages for personal and psychiatric injuries suffered as a result of the negligence of Enfield Borough Council. The Council argued that the case should, on the authority of cases like *X* v. *Bedfordshire CC*, be struck out as disclosing no reasonable cause of action. But the House of Lords refused to do so. Although the House reiterated that local authorities cannot owe a duty of care when making policy decisions, it significantly modified its approach to the question of whether a duty of care could be owed in relation to justiciable decisions, stating that the matter could only be resolved with reference to the full factual and legal circumstances of a case.[94] In other words, the House pulled back from the practice of striking out, with the shift in emphasis clearly being consonant with the ECtHR's ruling in *Osman*:

[91] "Human Rights and the House of Lords" (1999) 62 *MLR* 159, 164. For a response see L Hoyano, "Policing Flawed Police Investigations: Unravelling the Blanket" (1999) 62 *MLR* 912, 920–3.

[92] Lord Browne-Wilkinson considered that Art. 6 ECHR guarantees apply only where an individual has a pre-existing right under domestic law, with the right thereafter being protected by recourse to the courts. As the Court of Appeal in *Osman* v. *Ferguson* had already determined that the plaintiff did not have a pre-existing right (in the sense that the police did not owe a duty of care), his Lordship thereupon deemed the ECtHR's judgment misguided – see [1999] 3 All ER 193, 198. His Lordship's comments in this regard subsequently led the ECtHR to modify its interpretation of Art. 6 ECHR relative to negligence actions brought in UK courts. See *Z* v. *UK* (previously *X* v. *Bedfordshire*), judgment of 10 May 2001, finding that the striking-out of the action did not violate Art. 6 ECHR. But note also that the Court further found in *Z* that the practice of striking-out could violate the Art. 13 ECHR effective remedy requirement if the individual is denied a full hearing where there is an arguable breach of one of the ECHR's substantive guarantees (in the instant case, Art. 3 ECHR).

[93] It should noted that Lord Browne-Wilkinson was the only Law Lord to consider explicitly the importance of *Osman* – the remaining Lords decided the case on the basis of common law principle and practice. On *Barrett* see further P Craig and D Fairgreave, "*Barrett*, Negligence and Discretionary Powers" [1999] *PL* 626.

[94] The HL also stated that the courts should examine the issue of whether a decision was justiciable in light of the full legal and factual circumstances of the case.

"In view of the decision in *Osman's* case it is now difficult to foretell what would be the result in the present case if we were to uphold the striking out order. It seems to me that it is at least probable that the matter would then be taken to Strasbourg. That court, applying its decision in *Osman's* case if it considers it to be correct, would say that we had deprived the plaintiff of his right to have the balance struck between the hardship suffered by him and the damage done to the public interest in the present case if an order were made against the defendant council . . .

For these reasons in my judgment this action should proceed to trial and when all the facts are known the difficult issues of law which arise may be confronted in the light of the real, as opposed to hypothetical facts."[95]

What is the significance of *Barrett* v. *Enfield* relative to the debate between Craig and Allison, and what does the case reveal about the manner in which the ECHR will impact upon the domestic order? Certainly, the fact that the courts will now examine more closely the competing merits of an individual's interests and those of the broader public interest raises afresh questions of how best to structure rules of liability. The debate between Craig and Allison had centred upon the value of the EU law model for state liability, with Craig arguing that it was of potential insight and Allison arguing that functional differences rendered integration problematic. But has the change effected by *Barrett* v. *Enfield* lessened the suggested functional differences? Allison's argument highlighted how domestic standards were centrally concerned with ensuring that the courts avoid "non-justiciable" questions and "determining the financial priorities of government" while the EU standard was concerned with the "effective" protection of EU law rights.[96] Although issues of justiciability and the need to limit liability will remain of central importance, it is clear that *Osman*, as mediated by *Barrett* v. *Enfield*, requires that the notion of "effective" protection of individual interests be afforded greater significance in domestic deliberations. Consequently, and given that the EU law model has already evolved to meet the competing demands of effective protection of the individual and the protection of

[95] [1993] 3 All ER 193, 199–200. On the courts' revised approach to striking out see further, e.g., *W* v. *Essex CC* [2000] 2 All ER 237 and *Phelps* v. *Hillingdon LBC* [2000] 4 All ER 504 (but see also, e.g., *S* v. *Gloucestershire CC* [2001] 2 WLR 909). It remains to be seen whether the ECtHR judgment in *Z* v. *UK* will cause UK courts to reassess the *Barrett* line of reasoning: while it might be argued that the ECtHR's more recent finding on Art. 6 ECHR vindicates the courts' original approach to striking-out, it might also be argued that the ECtHR's finding in *Z* of a violation of Art. 13 ECHR, when read with Art. 3 ECHR, would militate against a return to the previous position (the fact that Art. 13 ECHR is tied to Art. 3 ECHR is significant because, although Art. 13 ECHR itself does not have domestic effect under the terms of the Human Rights Act, it may have some impact through ECtHR jurisprudence on other Articles. On the Act and the provisions it gives effect to see further chpt 7).

[96] Note 55 above, pp 177–8.

public authority, or state, discretion, would it now be helpful to borrow from it for more general domestic purposes?

The answer to the question of what the case reveals about the likely future impact of the ECHR, meanwhile, would seem to be that the international standard will only place further demands on traditional institutional understandings. Although some senior judges were critical of the basis of the *Osman* ruling, the fact that the judgment ultimately prompted modification of domestic standards provided clear evidence that the ECHR will add a new and potentially vigorous element to the process of legal integration. Indeed, if *Osman*, as an interim judgment, could effect change, it may be that the process of adaptation can only become even more far-reaching as the Human Rights Act "beds in". The ECtHR's criticisms of the domestic order in *Osman* have been paralleled in other areas of law, notably judicial review,[97] and the courts have already indicated that accommodating the more exacting ECHR standards will require further adaptation.[98] Through time, therefore, the rather reluctant acceptance of ECHR jurisprudence in *Barrett* may come to be seen as the starting point in a new, challenging and beneficial process of interaction.

4. CONCLUSION

This chapter has further developed the argument that the manner in which EU law has been received into the domestic order has militated against a truly responsive approach to integration. Focusing on seminal instances of borrowing in the field of remedies, it has doubted how far existing instances of spill-over can ensure harmonised protection of the individual in the absence of deeper integration at the level of legal principle. More specifically, the chapter has cautioned that standardised protection of the individual will be frustrated while the courts continue to draw a distinction between those aspects of the legal process that are of primary importance to the individual and those aspects that are taken to raise issues of institutional balance. Although the integration of select forms of remedial relief has gone some way towards achieving parity of protection, it has not, of itself, gone far enough. Thus, fully standardised protection has been argued to require a process of cross-fertilisation that centres not just upon the existence of particular forms of remedial relief but also upon the principle and practice that determines whether the relief should be granted.

[97] See, e.g., *W* v. *UK* [1988] 10 EHRR 29 and *Smith and Grady* v. *UK* [2000] 29 EHRR 493.

[98] See, e.g., Lord Philips MR's judgment in *In Re Medicaments and Related Classes of Goods (No 2)* [2001] 1 WLR 700, modifying the domestic test for bias ("a real danger of bias" – *R* v. *Gough* [1993] AC 646) in light of the ECHR's objective test for impartiality (see, e.g, *Piersack* v. *Belgium* [1982] 5 EHRR 169).

The chapter has also had regard to the emerging relevance of the ECHR, suggesting that the Human Rights Act 1998 now adds a new and potentially vigorous element to the integration process. Taking as an example the interim impact that the ECHR had on the courts' approach to public authority liability, the chapter has shown how the courts have already modified domestic jurisprudence that corresponded with the institutional assumptions of *Wednesbury* review. Although the modification was not effected without reservation, it was taken to be significant not only because it demonstrated how the ECHR will create pressure for further change in domestic law, but also because it provided a new perspective on existing literature about the integration of domestic and EU law. The co-existence of domestic and EU liability standards had been accompanied by debate about whether domestic standards would benefit from the assimilation of EU law's standards, and the chapter suggested that the ECHR may now act as a catalyst for deeper integration. In other words, it was posited that the reception of ECHR jurisprudence could, at least at an abstract level, be taken to have lessened some of the presumed functional differences between domestic and European law and to have opened up the possibility of more far-reaching and beneficial integration.

The understanding that the Human Rights Act may create new opportunities for deeper integration does not mean, of course, that integration will follow a uniform, or set, pattern. The courts' prior reluctance to permit the deeper enmeshing of EU law and domestic law stemmed from a judicial reliance on orthodoxy relative to the reception of EU law, and some judges have already made clear that they will similarly rely on orthodoxy when elaborating the terms of the Human Rights Act.[99] However, where there is a judicial willingness to situate the reception of the ECHR within the alternative institutional framework of the common law model of review, this may, as is further argued in the following chapter, allow the domestic order to derive maximum benefit from the wider body of European law. Although the model can give rise to differing perspectives on the need for integration,[100] previous chapters have demonstrated that the institutional assumptions of the model better equip the domestic order to accommodate and engage European norms. As the Human Rights Act means that the courts must now facilitate the direct interaction of three, as opposed to two, bodies of law, it may be that the courts will wish to have increased

[99] See, e.g., Lord Hoffmann's judgments in *R* v. *Secretary of State for the Home Department, ex p Simms* [1999] 3 All ER 400, 412 and *R (on the application of Alconbury Developments Ltd)* v. *Secretary of State for the Environment, Transport and the Regions* [2001] 2 All ER 929 (although see also Lord Slynn's judgment in *Alconbury*, considered in the following chapter).

[100] Compare and contrast, e.g., *R* v. *Ministry of Agriculture, Fisheries and Food, ex p Hamble Fisheries* [1995] 2 All ER 714 (Sedley J) and *R* v. *Ministry of Agriculture, Fisheries and Food, ex p First City Trading Limited* [1997] 1 CMLR 250 (Laws J).

recourse to the common law model. While reliance on the model would not render the interaction of the bodies entirely unproblematic, it would provide the most effective means of pursuing harmonious and beneficial interaction. This may, on some occasions, then lead the courts to distinguish domestic standards from their European equivalents, and it may, on other occasions, equally lead the courts to permit the assimilation of selected standards. Either way, it will be seen that reliance on the model would allow the courts more freely to address the problem of co-existing legal principles and to engage in a process of harmonisation that takes the dynamics of UK public law and European law as mutually reinforcing rather than essentially distinct.

7

The Human Rights Act 1998 and Cross-fertilisation

1. INTRODUCTION

The impact that the ECHR had on the UK legal order prior to the passage of the Human Rights Act was, consistent with dualist orthodoxy, very limited. Ongoing government refusal to introduce implementing legislation meant not only that the ECHR could have no direct role in domestic proceedings[1] but also that the courts adopted a minimalist approach to its possible indirect influence.[2] Although the international standard could legitimately be used as an aid to the interpretation of ambiguous legislation[3] or to assist the development of common law standards for the protection of fundamental rights,[4] the courts were generally reluctant to have recourse to it. Indeed, the courts' reluctance was even apparent in EU law cases where it was argued that the courts were under an obligation to have regard to ECHR jurisprudence. The ECJ's understanding that domestic courts must give effect to the general principles of EU law, including those derived from the ECHR,[5] had the clear potential to influence domestic developments, yet the courts, with one notable exception, declined to use

[1] See, e.g., *R* v. *Secretary of State for Home Affairs, ex p Bhajan Singh* [1976] QB 198; *R* v. *Chief Immigration Officer, Heathrow Airport, ex p Salamat Bibi* [1976] 3 All ER 843; *Ahmad* v. *Inner London Education Authority* [1978] QB 36; *Malone* v. *Metropolitan Police Commissioner* [1979] 2 WLR 700; *Kaur* v. *Lord Advocate* [1980] SC 309; and *R* v. *Secretary of State for the Home Department, ex p Brind* [1991] 2 WLR 588.

[2] Note that government refusal to introduce legislation was often criticised because the UK had been central to the original drafting of the ECHR. See A Lester, "Fundamental Rights: The UK Isolated?" [1984] *PL* 46 and G Marston, "The United Kingdom's Part in the Preparation of the European Convention on Human Rights, 1950" (1993) 42 *ICLQ* 796.

[3] See, e.g., *R* v. *Secretary of State for Home Affairs, ex p Bhajan Singh* [1976] QB 198, 207 (Lord Denning); *R* v. *Chief Immigration Officer, Heathrow Airport, ex p Salamat Bibi* [1976] 3 All ER 843, 847 (Lord Denning); *R* v. *Secretary of State for the Home Department, ex p Phansopkar* [1976] QB 606, 626 (Scarman LJ); *Kaur* v. *Lord Advocate* [1980] SC 309, 326–7 (Lord Ross); and *R* v. *Secretary of State for the Home Department, ex p Brind* [1991] 2 WLR 588, 592 (Lord Bridge).

[4] See, e.g., *Derbyshire County Council* v. *Times Newspapers* [1992] QB 770 (CA). But see also the HL ruling in the same case at [1993] AC 534.

[5] Case 5/88, *Wachauf* v. *Germany* [1989] ECR 2609.

the intersecting bodies of law creatively.[6] An unincorporated international treaty, it seemed, was to be viewed as such even though membership of the EU rendered the understanding increasingly anachronistic.

The fact that the Human Rights Act now expressly obliges UK courts to "take into account" all relevant ECHR jurisprudence does, as indicated in the previous chapter, mean that judicial reluctance to have recourse to the ECHR will be considerably less pronounced in future years.[7] The *Barrett* v. *Enfield*[8] case demonstrated how the courts were prepared to facilitate realignment even in the interim period between the passage of the Act and its coming into force, and there now exist several more recent judgments which have seen the courts make use of the Act's institutionally novel provisions.[9] Judicial use of the provisions may, as was also indicated in the previous chapter, be taken to be entirely consonant with orthodox institutional understandings. Existing debate about the institutional role of the courts has focused on the extent to which the courts may be said to give effect to Parliament's express or implied intentions,[10] and judicial elaboration of the provisions of the Act could clearly be taken to coincide with orthodoxy.[11] But the corresponding difficulty with such an approach is that it not only ignores that some senior judges already reject several core orthodox assumptions;[12] it also denies that the wider social and political context of the Act increasingly militates against traditional public law understandings. The passage of the Human Rights Act has been accompanied by a more general programme of constitutional change that has

[6] See, e.g., *Allgemeine Gold-und Silberscheideanstalt* v. *Customs and Excise Commissioners* [1978] 2 CMLR and *R* v. *Immigration Appeal Tribunal, ex p Marchon* [1993] Imm AR 98. The exception is *R* v. *Secretary of State for the Home Department, ex p McQuillan* [1995] 4 All ER 400, considered below.

[7] The obligation is contained in s. 2, considered below. For a listing of ECHR arguments raised before the courts in England and Wales see E Martin Salgado and C O'Brien, "Table of Cases under the Human Rights Act" (2001) *EHRLR* 181 and 376. For commentary on Scotland see, e.g., G Moynihan, "Human Rights in Scotland – The Story So Far" (2000) 5 *JR* 274. On the wider context in Northern Ireland see M Gray, "The Northern Ireland Act 1998, Judicial Review and Human Rights" (2000) 5 *JR* 114.

[8] [1999] 3 All ER 193.

[9] For example, the s. 4 declaration of incompatibility in *Alconbury* v. *Secretary of State the Environment, Transport and the Regions* [2001] JPEL 291 (DC; overturned by the HL [2001] 2 All ER 929, considered below); *R (on the application of H)* v. *Mental Health Review Tribunal for North and East London Region* [2001] 3 WLR 512 (CA); and *Wilson* v. *First County Trust Ltd (No 2)* [2001] 3 WLR 42.

[10] C Forsyth (ed.), *Judicial Review and the Constitution* (Hart Publishing, Oxford, 2000).

[11] G Marshall, "On Constitutional Theory" in B Markesinis (ed.), *The Impact of the Human Rights Bill on English Law* (Clarendon Press, Oxford, 1998), p 15. And see also *R* v. *Secretary of State for the Home Department, ex p Simms* [1999] 3 All ER 400, 412 (Lord Hoffmann).

[12] Sir H Woolf, "Droit Public – English Style" [1995] *PL* 57; Sir J Laws, "Law and Democracy" [1995] *PL* 72; and Sir S Sedley, "Human Rights: A Twenty-first Century Agenda" [1995] *PL* 386.

included the devolution of power to Northern Ireland, Scotland and Wales.[13] Although it is unclear how the different elements of constitutional change will impact in practice, it is accepted that devolution will strain historical understandings about the locus of sovereign authority, thereby adding an "internal" dimension to the "external" challenge heralded by membership of the EU.[14] While it is possible to give the Human Rights Act a narrow reading that is consistent with orthodox understandings, therefore, it may be better to read it in light of emerging political structures and the growing challenge of overlapping sovereignties.

In suggesting that the institutional assumptions of the common law model of review would facilitate the required reading of the Human Rights Act, this chapter returns to the argument that the model allows the courts to forgo dualist distinctions between the spheres of influence of domestic and European law. Proceeding on the understanding that orthodoxy prevents the courts adopting an holistic view of the relationship between the bodies of law, the chapter argues that the common law model would situate the reception of the ECHR within a framework that is more responsive to emerging and existing legal realities. Although an orthodox reading of the Human Rights Act would not preclude realignment, it would, given the courts' previous approach to EU law, likely lead the courts to identify narrow categories of cases which would exist in virtual isolation from existing EU law and domestic law categories. This would, of course, inhibit legal cross-fertilisation and create further anomalies, and it would also see the courts continue to adjudicate on the basis of public law values that have long been, and will increasingly be, taken as ill-suited to the wider context of UK public law. By reading the Act in light of the common law model, therefore, it will be suggested that the courts would be able to adopt the approach that is best suited to addressing existing and emerging internal legal issues and to relating the issues to the wider process of European integration. The model's core value, as has been seen in previous chapters, is that it conceives of the courts developing the law on a reactive basis that takes account of changing institutional environments. While recourse to the model need not mean that the courts would diminish in their entirety the significance of pre-existing domestic values, it would

[13] The Northern Ireland Act 1998; the Scotland Act 1998; and the Government of Wales Act 1998. See further N Burrows, *Devolution* (Sweet & Maxwell, London, 2000).

[14] AW Bradley, "The Sovereignty of Parliament" in J Jowell and D Oliver (eds.), *The Changing Constitution* (Oxford University Press, Oxford, 4th edn, 2000), p 23. On devolution see further T Jones, "Scottish Devolution and Demarcation Disputes" [1997] *PL* 283; V Bogdanor, "Devolution: The Constitutional Aspects" in J Beatson, C Forsyth and I Hare (eds.), *Constitutional Reform in the United Kingdom: Practice and Principles* (Hart Publishing, Oxford, 1998), p 9; P Craig and M Walters, "The Courts, Devolution and Judicial Review" [1999] *PL* 274; and G Anthony and A Evans, "Northern Ireland, Devolution and the European Union" in C Harvey (ed.), *Human Rights, Equality and Democratic Renewal in Northern Ireland* (Hart Publishing, Oxford, 2001), p 53.

mean that the courts would be able to redraw the institutional parameters within which debate about integration is conducted. This may lead to an active process of cross-fertilisation which would then slow down after obvious questions of integration have been answered, or it may alternatively see the process of integration proceed much more slowly and deliberately. Crucially, however, it would see the courts adopt the more contextual approach to the significance of the Human Rights Act, thereby ensuring that the courts derive maximum benefit from the interaction and overlap of domestic law, EU law and the ECHR.[15]

2. DOMESTIC LAW, THE ECHR AND FUNDAMENTAL RIGHTS PRE-HUMAN RIGHTS ACT

The leading case on the pre-incorporation status of the ECHR is *R* v. *Secretary of State for the Home Department, ex p Brind and Others*.[16] In the case, considered in chapter five, questions were raised before the House of Lords about the compatibility with the ECHR of government restrictions on freedom of expression (the Home Secretary had introduced a ban on the simultaneous broadcast of interviews with the political representatives of various proscribed organisations in Northern Ireland).[17] In rejecting the arguments presented to it, the House of Lords demonstrated how orthodoxy can militate both against the deeper enmeshing of principles of judicial review and against creative use of select provisions of the ECHR. The application to the House had argued that the Home Secretary's initiative represented a disproportionate means to achieve the

[15] It should be noted that a much stronger argument about the need for the courts to forgo dualist orthodoxy has previously been made by Murray Hunt. Thus, while this ch. argues that the courts should adopt the more expansive approach when interpreting and applying the Human Rights Act, Hunt argued, before the passage of the Act, that the courts should draw upon the evolutionary qualities of the common law to give effect to international human rights standards (not just the ECHR) even in the absence of enabling legislation: "The (argument is) for a common law interpretive obligation on domestic courts, whereby they recognise that they must strive to give effect to the human rights norms contained in those international treaties to which the UK has committed itself". See *Using Human Rights Law in English Courts* (Hart Publishing, Oxford, 1997), p xi. Although Hunt's arguments may no longer be of immediate relevance in the context of the relationship between domestic law and the ECHR, they lend general support to this ch.'s argument, i.e. that the courts should take domestic law and European law (and, by association, other forms of international law) as mutually reinforcing bodies of law rather than bodies of law which are capable of interaction only within the confines of legislation as narrowly construed in accordance with orthodoxy.

[16] [1991] 2 WLR 588.

[17] See further B Thompson, "Broadcasting and Terrorism in the House of Lords" [1991] *PL* 346 and M Halliwell, "Judicial Review and Broadcasting Freedom: The Route to Europe" (1991) 42 *NILQ* 246.

particular end pursued, but the House of Lords declined to approach the case on that basis. Finding that the unincorporated status of the ECHR and the orthodox demands of *Wednesbury* precluded use of the principle,[18] the House emphasised that domestic and European principles of review pursue functionally and institutionally different objectives. Thus, even though some members of the House recognised the imperative of scrutinising more closely decisions which impact upon fundamental freedoms, the House was unanimous in its determination that the proportionality principle was of no application.[19]

The corresponding limitations that the judgment placed upon creative use of the ECHR arose from their Lordships' treatment of the applicants' arguments about the role and relevance of the Article 10 freedom of expression guarantee.[20] In essence, the applicants had argued that, as there exists a common law presumption that Parliament intends to legislate in conformity with the UK's Treaty obligations,[21] the House should likewise presume that Parliament intends that exercises of ministerial discretion conform with the ECHR. Although Lord Bridge confessed that he found "considerable persuasive force" in the argument, he ultimately decided that "the logic of it (was) flawed". Distinguishing the courts' approach to the interpretation of ambiguous legislation from the review of administrative action, his Lordship considered that it would "go far beyond the resolution of an ambiguity" for the courts to "impute to Parliament" the intention that exercises of administrative power should conform with the ECHR. In other words, Lord Bridge considered that, "where Parliament has conferred on the executive an administrative discretion without indicating the precise limits within which it must be exercised", it would amount to a "judicial usurpation of the legislative function" to assume that the discretion should be exercised in accordance with the international standard.[22]

The orthodox approach adopted in *Brind* was to be reflected in many subsequent judgments. Although it would be misleading to suggest that the

[18] See, respectively, the judgments of Lords Ackner and Lowry at [1991] 2 WLR 588, 605–6 and 609–10.

[19] Lord Bridge stated that where a decision impacts upon fundamental freedoms the courts are, "perfectly entitled to start from the premise that any restriction of the right to freedom of expression requires to be justified and nothing less than an important competing interest will be sufficient to justify it" – [1991] 2 WLR 588, 592. And see also Lord Bridge's judgment in *R* v. *Secretary of State for the Home Department, ex p Bugdaycay* [1987] AC 514, 531.

[20] Art. 10 reads: "1. Everyone has the right to freedom of expression. This right shall include freedom to hold opinions and to receive and impart information and ideas without interference by public authority and regardless of frontiers . . . 2. The exercise of these freedoms . . . may be subject to such . . . restrictions . . . as are . . . necessary in a democratic society . . . "

[21] *Salomon* v. *Commissioners of Customs and Excise* [1967] 2 QB 116, 143–4 (Lord Diplock) and *Garland* v. *British Rail Engineering Ltd* [1983] 2 AC 751, 771 (Lord Diplock).

[22] [1991] 2 WLR 588, 592.

ECHR was devoid of any influence on the domestic order – the courts sometimes used it as an aid to the interpretation of ambiguous legislation[23] and as a yard-stick against which to measure the reach of domestic fundamental rights guarantees[24] – the House of Lords' judgment established a forceful precedent. In *R* v. *Ministry of Defence, ex p Smith*[25] a challenge was made to the lawfulness of the ban on gay and lesbian persons serving in the military, with the case again raising issues about the relationship between *Wednesbury* and proportionality and about the potential role of the ECHR. While the High Court openly acknowledged that human rights considerations should be afforded added weight in judicial review proceedings and, moreover, that the policy in issue was likely to be contrary to the ECHR,[26] it considered itself bound by the language and logic of *Wednesbury* and by the understanding that the ECHR was of no relevance as it was not incorporated in domestic law. Finding this to be a matter of regret, the High Court nevertheless referred to *Brind* before concluding that the application to the court must fail.[27] Comparable outcomes were also taken as dictated in the context of challenges to the lawfulness of revised prisoner release dates[28] and to the lawfulness of regulations which limited the rights of expression of local government employees.[29]

The potential shortfall in the protection of fundamental rights which was created by the courts' inability to have recourse to the ECHR was to be off-set in part by some judges' efforts to elaborate more demanding common law standards for the protection of the individual. The common law has, of course, long emphasised the need to protect fundamental freedoms,[30] and several more recent judgments have explicitly enunciated a

[23] For example, *MacDonald* v. *Ministry of Defence* [2001] 1 All ER 620, considered below.

[24] See, e.g., *Attorney-General* v. *Guardian Newspapers Ltd (No 2)* [1988] 3 All ER 545, 660 (Lord Goff): "I can see no inconsistency between English law . . . and (Art. 10 ECHR). This is scarcely surprising since we may pride ourselves that freedom of speech has existed in this country perhaps as long, if not longer than, it has existed in any other country in the world. The only difference is that whereas Art. 10 of the ECHR, in accordance with its avowed purpose, proceeds to state a fundamental right and then to qualify it, we in this country (where everyone is free to do anything, subject only to the provisions of the law) proceed rather on the assumption of free speech, and turn to our law to discover the established exceptions to it". Note that this judgment was delivered pre-*Brind*. For post-*Brind* use, see, e.g., *R* v. *Chief Magistrate, ex p Choudhury* [1991] 1 All ER 306; *Derbyshire County Council* v. *Times Newspapers* [1992] QB 770; and *R* v. *Secretary of State for the Home Department, ex p Simms* [1999] 3 All ER 400.

[25] [1995] 4 All ER 427.

[26] An understanding subsequently confirmed by the ECtHR in *Smith and Grady* v. *UK* [2000] 29 EHRR 493.

[27] And see also [1996] QB 517 (CA).

[28] *R* v. *Secretary of State for the Home Department, ex p Hargreaves* [1997] 1 All ER 397

[29] *R* v. *Secretary of State for the Environment, ex p NALGO* [1993] Admin LR 785.

[30] *Entick* v. *Carrington* [1765] 19 St Tr 1030.

constitutional basis for the common law's standards.[31] The line of jurisprudence, which has been developed most vigorously by judges who eschew the justificatory force of orthodoxy,[32] has sought to limit the extent to which secondary legislation and administrative acts should be allowed to impact upon an individual's fundamental freedoms. In *R* v. *Lord Chancellor, ex p Witham*,[33] a challenge was made to the Lord Chancellor's decision to change a policy which exempted individuals on income support from having to pay court fees (the Lord Chancellor had introduced the changes pursuant to section 130 of the Supreme Court Act 1981).[34] When the application was heard in the High Court, Laws J quashed the Lord Chancellor's decision, ruling that the statutory provision did not expressly provide for measures which interfere with rights of access to the courts: "Access to the courts is a constitutional right; it can only be denied by the government if it persuades Parliament to pass legislation which specifically – in effect by express provision – permits the executive to turn people away from the court door. That has not been done in this case".[35]

Perhaps the most notable judicial statement about the common law's capacity to protect fundamental rights was made by Sedley J in *R* v. *Secretary of State for the Home Department, ex p McQuillan*.[36] Indeed, the *McQuillan* judgment is significant not only because it highlighted how the common law itself seeks to protect fundamental rights, but also because it provided the single and outstanding example of a court using EU law as the medium through which to allow the ECHR to influence domestic developments. The facts of the case concerned a challenge to the lawfulness of an exclusion order that prevented a former member of the

[31] See, e.g., in relation to prisoners' rights, *R* v. *Board of Visitors of Hull Prison, ex p St Germain* [1979] QB 425; *Raymond* v. *Honey* [1983] 1 AC 1; *R* v. *Secretary of State for the Home Department, ex p Anderson* [1984] QB 778; *R* v. *Home Secretary, ex p Leech* [1994] QB 198; and *R* v. *Secretary of State for the Home Department, ex p Pierson* [1998] AC 539. And see by analogy *R* v. *Cambridge Health Authority, ex p Child B* [1995] 25 BMLR 5 (DC – although see also the CA ruling at [1995] 2 All ER 129). Note also that there remained the problem of identifying the content of fundamental rights in the unwritten UK constitutional tradition, although, as Laws J stated in *R* v. *Lord Chancellor, ex p Witham* [1997] 2 All ER 778, 783, the problem likewise exists in the context of written constitutional traditions: "There may of course be other difficulties, such as whether on the constitution's true interpretation the right claimed exists at all. Even a superficial acquaintance with the jurisprudence of the Supreme Court of the United States shows that such problems may be acute".

[32] Note 12 above.

[33] [1997] 2 All ER 778.

[34] Section 130(1) reads: "The Lord Chancellor may by order under this section prescribe the fees to be taken in the Supreme Court, other than fees which he or some other authority has power to prescribe apart from this section". The changes were contained in the Supreme Court Fees Amendment Order 1996 SI 1996/3191.

[35] [1997] 2 All ER 778, 788. And see also *R* v. *Lord Chancellor, ex p Lightfoot* [1999] 4 All ER 583.

[36] [1995] 4 All ER 400.

Irish Republican Socialist Party taking up residence and employment in Great Britain. The applicant, who held dual British and Irish nationality, argued that as a citizen of Ireland, Britain and the European Union, he was entitled to move freely within the EU.[37] The applicant also argued that given his political affiliations and background, any derogation from his rights had to be rational, proportionate and sufficiently reasoned by reference to the risks he faced if being effectively barred from leaving Northern Ireland. By way of supporting the point, he relied upon Articles 2 and 3 ECHR (the right to life and the prohibition of torture).

Sedley J's approach to the applicant's arguments drew upon an understanding of the common law, EU law and the ECHR as inextricably intertwined and mutually reinforcing. Rather than proceed on the basis that common law standards for the protection of fundamental rights should be taken as separate from European standards, Sedley J demonstrated a willingness to relate common law developments to developments in the broader process of European integration. Emphasising how the ECHR informs the workings of EU law, thereby feeding into the domestic order, he made clear that the ECHR "can certainly be said to be a matter of which the law of this country now takes notice in setting its own standards". This, he then reasoned, rendered any assumed distinction between the scope of application of the respective bodies of law problematic:

> "Once it is accepted that the standards articulated in the (ECHR) are standards which both march with those of the common law and inform the jurisprudence of the European Union, it becomes unreal and potentially unjust to continue to develop (UK) public law without reference to them."[38]

Murray Hunt has described Sedley J's judgment in *McQuillan* as the "high-water mark of domestic law's permeability by the ECHR through (EU) law".[39] Although Sedley J was ultimately unable to find in favour of the applicant,[40] Hunt suggests that the ruling remains highly significant because it locates "the common law's development of a human rights jurisdiction in the wider context of the harmonisation of constitutional standards in an integrating Europe".[41] Sedley J's willingness to embrace

[37] Similar challenges to the legality of exclusion orders had previously been argued before the domestic courts, e.g., *R* v. *Secretary of State for the Home Department, ex p Adams* [1995] All ER (EC) 177. See further S Douglas-Scott and J A Kimbell, "The Adams exclusion order case: new enforceable civil rights in the post-Maastricht European Union" [1994] *PL* 516.

[38] [1995] 4 All ER 400, 422.

[39] Note 15 above, p 290.

[40] The Home Secretary stated in his affidavit evidence that national security interests were at stake. Sedley J, on the authority of various other cases, thereupon considered himself bound by precedent.

[41] Note 15 above, p 294.

the integration process has, of course, also been apparent in other cases.[42] While his receptive approach has sometimes been subjected to sharp rebuke (before being reinstated),[43] the passage of the Human Rights Act raises the question of how far the approach adopted in *McQuillan* might usefully inform future judicial reasoning. The confluence of domestic, EU and ECHR issues seen in *McQuillan* will doubtless become increasingly commonplace, and the challenge for the courts will be how to develop an approach that accommodates the plurality of standards that arise from the overlapping domestic and European orders. Will the courts continue to draw dualist distinctions between the respective spheres of application of domestic and European standards, or will they adopt the *McQuillan* template?

3. THE HUMAN RIGHTS ACT: AN OVERVIEW

Section 1 of the Human Rights Act identifies the ECHR provisions which are to be given effect in the domestic order.[44] The rights given effect to range across most of those in the original ECHR text[45] and various added by Protocol.[46] A court which is tasked with considering the scope of the

[42] *R* v. *Ministry of Agriculture, Fisheries and Food, ex p Hamble Fisheries* [1995] 2 All ER 714 and *R* v. *North and East Devon Health Authority, ex p Coughlan* [2000] 2 WLR 622. And see now also, albeit in the context of private law proceedings, *Douglas and others* v. *Hello Ltd* [2001] 2 WLR 992.

[43] See, e.g., *R* v. *Secretary of State for the Home Department, ex p Hargreaves* [1997] 1 All ER 397, criticising *Hamble Fisheries*, but now read in light of *R* v. *North and East Devon Health Authority, ex p Coughlan* [2000] 2 WLR 622. See further ch. 5, p 117 *ff*.

[44] On the Human Rights Act see further, e.g., J Coppel, *The Human Rights Act 1998: Enforcing the European Convention in the Domestic Courts* (Wiley, Chichester, 1998); S Grosz, J Beatson and P Duffy, *Human Rights: The 1998 Act and the European Convention* (Sweet & Maxwell, London, 2000); and J Wadham and H Mountfield, *Blackstone's Guide to the Human Rights Act 1998* (Blackstone, London, 2nd edn, 2000).

[45] Articles 2–12 and 14 ECHR. The Arts. cover the right to life; the prohibition of torture; the prohibition of slavery/forced labour; the right to liberty and security; the right to a fair trial; right to respect for private and family life; freedom of thought, conscience and religion; freedom of expression; freedom of assembly and association; the right to marry; and the prohibition of discrimination. Art. 1 (which obliges Member States to ensure the rights of everyone in their jurisdiction) is not recognised as creating legally enforceable rights for individuals and so was omitted from the Act. Art. 13 (which requires that a person whose rights are violated shall have an effective remedy) was omitted because the Government considered that the 1998 Act itself would provide for such remedies (see HL Debs, 3 November 1997, col 1308). On remedies see further D Feldman, "Remedies for Violations of Convention Rights under the Human Rights Act" (1998) *EHRLR* 692.

[46] Articles 1–3 of the First Protocol (protection of property; right to education; right to free elections) and Arts. 1–2 of the Sixth Protocol (abolition of the death penalty; and the retention of the death penalty in times of war). Each of these rights (and those noted above) are to be read subject to Arts. 16–18 ECHR (restrictions on the political activities of aliens; prohibition of abuse of rights; and limitation on the use of restrictions on rights).

rights in domestic proceedings is required by section 2 of the Act to "take into account" any relevant ECHR jurisprudence.[47] On this basis, sections 3–5 of the Act provide for the scrutiny of legislation relative to the terms of the ECHR. In the first instance, the Act imposes an obligation to attempt to construe primary and subordinate legislation in accordance with the terms of the ECHR, section 3 stating: "So far as it is possible to do so, primary legislation and subordinate legislation must be read and given effect in a way which is compatible with the Convention rights".[48] This formulation is, of course, one which the courts have already had experience with in other contexts,[49] and there is some judicial expectation that it will allow the courts to develop "a code of morals" and "to approach constitutional issues on a proper constitutional basis".[50] Indeed, the beginnings of such an approach may already be in evidence. In *MacDonald* v. *Ministry of Defence*,[51] a Scottish Employment Appeal Tribunal determined that the word "sex" in the Sex Discrimination Act 1975 could be read to include "sexual orientation" within its meaning.[52] The finding, which was made in a case that raised substantially the same issues as *R* v. *Ministry of Defence, ex p Smith*,[53] was obviously far-reaching and delivered without any apparent concern to reflect pre-existing domestic case law. Perhaps even more significantly, it was a judgment which drew upon ECHR jurisprudence to effect an outcome that went far beyond those previously achieved in like cases heard by the ECJ.[54]

[47] Section 2(1) reads: "A court or tribunal determining a question which has arisen under this Act in connection with a Convention right must take into account any – (a) judgment, decision, declaration or advisory opinion of the European Court of Human Rights, (b) opinion of the Commission . . . (c) decision of the Commission . . . or (d) decision of the Committee of Ministers . . . whenever made or given, so far as, in the opinion of the court or tribunal, it is relevant to the proceedings in which that question has arisen".

[48] See further A Lester, "The Art of the Possible – Interpreting Statutes under the Human Rights Act" (1998) *EHRLR* 665.

[49] See, e.g., with regard to the interpretation of ambiguous legislation in light of international Treaty obligations, *Salomon* v. *Commissioners of Customs and Excise* [1967] 2 QB 116 and *Garland* v. *British Rail Engineering Ltd* [1983] 2 AC 751. And see also with regard to the indirect effect doctrine in EU law, Case 14/83, *Von Colson and Kamann* v. *Land Nordrhein-Westfalen* [ECR] 1891 and Case C-106/89, *Marleasing SA* v. *La Commercial Internacionale de Alimentacion SA* [1990] ECR I-4135, considered at ch. 3, p 54 *ff* and ch. 4, p 92 *ff*.

[50] Lord Browne-Wilkinson, "The Impact on Judicial Reasoning" in B Markesinis (ed.) n. 11 above, pp 21, 22. Although see now also Lord Woolf CJ's judgment in *Poplar Housing* v. *Donoghue* [2001] 3 WLR 183 (re: the limits to the use of s.3).

[51] [2001] 1 All ER 620.

[52] Although see now also *Adv-Gen for Scotland* v. *McDonald*, [2001] SLT 819, overturning the EAT decision.

[53] [1995] 4 All ER 427.

[54] Case 249/96, *Grant* v. *South-West Trains Ltd* [1998] ECR I 621. It should be noted that *MacDonald* might best be descibed as an "interim" judgment rather than a judgment made within the terms of reference of the Human Rights Act. The EAT, which delivered its

If a court finds that it is unable to achieve harmonious interpretation, section 4 of the Act provides for a system of judicial declarations that will identify and isolate legislative provisions which are deemed incompatible with the international standard.[55] In this context, an important distinction is made between the review of primary legislation and the review of subordinate legislation.[56] The ultimate legality of primary legislation is vouchsafed by the fact that courts can go no further than making a declaration that a particular Act (or provisions therein) is incompatible with the terms of the ECHR.[57] Such declarations do not, consistent with orthodox institutional assumptions, affect the continuing validity of the Act in question,[58] and their impact will be political rather than legal in force (it is envisaged that declarations of incompatibility will prompt amendment of an offending Act/provision).[59] The position with regard to subordinate legislation differs in that the legislation can be quashed on the ground that it contravenes the ECHR and is, thereby, ultra vires.[60] The only exception to the position is when the subordinate legislation's enabling statute "prevents removal of the incompatibility":[61] here, the provision can only be subject

judgment just before the Human Rights Act came into force, did not make specific reference to the s. 3 obligation, but rather justified its approach with reference to traditional understandings that the ECHR may be used as an interpretative aid in the event of legislation being ambiguous. Nevertheless, the outcome achieved, coupled with the date of the judgment (25 Sept 2000), indicates how important s. 3 potentially will be.

[55] Section 4. For examples of declarations see n. 9 above. And note also that the courts have had some experience making comparable declarations in the context of EU law, e.g., *Equal Opportunities Commission and Another* v. *Secretary of State for Employment* [1994] 1 All ER 910.

[56] On the meaning of primary and subordinate legislation for purposes of the Act see s. 21.

[57] Section 4(2). See further N Bamforth, "Parliamentary Sovereignty and the Human Rights Act 1998" [1998] *PL* 572. Note that s. 4(5) provides a list of those courts which may make a declaration of incompatibility, namely the House of Lords; the Judicial Committee of the Privy Council; the Courts-Martial Appeal Court; in Scotland, the High Court of Justiciary sitting otherwise than as a trial court of the Court of Session; in England and Wales or Northern Ireland, the High Court or the Court of Appeal. Note also that, where a court is considering making a declaration of incompatibility, the Crown is permitted to make an intervention on the issues at hand – s. 5.

[58] Section 4(6).

[59] Section 10.

[60] As the Lord Chancellor has stated (583 HL Deb 544–5): "The position simply is that at present subordinate legislation may be struck down by the courts on the same grounds as in the case of other forms of administrative action . . . subordinate legislation which is incompatible will thus become susceptible to challenge on *vires* grounds in the ordinary way". Note that the legislative Acts of the Northern Ireland Assembly and of the Scottish Parliament can be quashed on the grounds that they contravene the terms of the ECHR (and EU law). See s. 6 of the Northern Ireland Act 1998 and s. 29 of the Scotland Act 1998. ECHR issues can also arise in the context of devolution proceedings involving the Welsh Assembly, i.e., "a question of whether a failure to act on the part of the Welsh Assembly is incompatible with any of the ECHR rights" – see Sch 8, 1(1)(d) of the Government of Wales Act 1998.

[61] Section 3(1)(c).

to a declaration, with subsequent change being effected through amendment of the primary Act.[62]

Section 6 of the Human Rights Act thereafter contains an umbrella provision whereby "It is unlawful for a public authority to act in a way which is incompatible with a Convention right". The section identifies public authorities for its purposes as including courts and tribunals and "any person certain of whose functions are functions of a public nature" (although the provision does not extend to either House of Parliament).[63] The phrase chosen approximates those used previously in the EU[64] and domestic orders,[65] and its place in the Human Rights Act will, as discussed in chapter two, resolve in part the issue of how to regulate the exercise of de facto governmental power. Although UK courts have reinvented the reach of judicial review, with their endeavours in this respect being central to the emergence of the ultra vires debate[66], it was suggested in chapter two that conceptual difficulties have prevented public law fully reacting to the challenge of privatisation and contracting-out.[67] This was taken to be particularly true of the public–private divide and the corresponding understanding that contractual relations fall outside the scope of judicial review.[68] Thus, while it was concluded that additional expansion of judicial review in light of the Human Rights Act may only further complicate the ultra vires debate, it was suggested that section 6 should, nonetheless, provide an additional reference point against which to effect greater control of the actions of "government".

[62] "The power to make a declaration of incompatibility should be, and is, reserved for those cases where it is needed because the courts have no power to anything else. The subordinate legislation is necessarily incompatible because the parent legislation causes it to be so. The rational outcome, therefore, is that both the parent and subordinate legislation are subject to a declaration of incompatibility" (583 HL Deb 544–5, Lord Irvine).

[63] Section 6(3). Note that the actions of public authorities will not be unlawful if they are expressly required by primary legislation – s. 6(2). Note also that, although s. 6 seemingly conceives of the Act having only vertical effect as against the State, it is now established that the Act will, on account of the s. 3 interpretative obligation and the fact that courts are public authorities under s. 6, have horizontal effect in proceedings between two private parties. See *Douglas and others* v. *Hello! Ltd* [2001] 2 WLR 992 and *Venables and Thompson* v. *News Group Newspapers and Others* [2001] 2 WLR 1038. On horizontal effect see further M Hunt, "The 'Horizontal Effect' of the Human Rights Act" [1998] *PL* 423 and G Phillipson, "The Human Rights Act, 'Horizontal Effect' and the Common Law: a Bang or a Whimper" (1999) 62 *MLR* 824.

[64] Case C-188/89, *Foster* v. *British Gas plc* [1990] ECR I-3313.

[65] *R* v. *Panel on Take-overs and Mergers, ex p Datafin plc* [1987] QB 815.

[66] D Oliver, "Is the *Ultra Vires* Rule the Basis of Judicial Review?" [1987] *PL* 543.

[67] M Freedland, "Government by Contract and Public Law" [1994] *PL* 86.

[68] See, e.g., *R* v. *Disciplinary Committee of the Jockey Club, ex p His Highness the Aga Khan* [1993] 2 All ER 853; *R* v. *Fernhill Manor School, ex p Brown* [1993] 5 Admin LR 159; and *R* v. *Servite Houses, ex p Goldsmith* [2001] LGR 55. For emerging judicial approaches see now *Poplar Housing* v. *Donoghue* [2001] 3 WLR and *Heather* v. *The Leonard Cheshire Foundation* [2001] EWHC Admin 429.

One further provision of the Act that is of note is section 7. Under section 7, a person who wishes to initiate proceedings on the basis of section 6 of the Human Rights Act may only do so where they are, or would be, a victim of an unlawful act within the meaning of Article 34 ECHR.[69] The ECtHR's approach to Article 34 ECHR is often characterised by a restrictive approach to the question of access[70] and there is, as such, some concern that section 7 could conflict with the approach in domestic law. UK courts have, in recent years, adopted a markedly liberal approach to the question of access to the courts, with their approach facilitating a series of high-profile public interest and representative applications.[71] Given that section 7 of the Human Rights Act requires that the domestic courts follow the more restrictive approach whenever ECHR provisions are in issue, some commentators have suggested that access will come to be governed by a set of competing tests which will "cause needless complexity" and, moreover, may lead to the "bizarre spectacle of cases in which representative applicants are held to have standing to argue non-human rights points, but not to argue human rights points".[72] In consequence, while the greater weight of opinion is that the Human Rights Act offers many opportunities for the positive development of domestic law, section 7 would appear to sit as an "exception" to the "rule".

4. THE HUMAN RIGHTS ACT AND THE LIMITS OF CROSS-FERTILISATION

The provision of the Human Rights Act that will be central to any increased process of borrowing is section 2. While section 3 will, as indicated, also be of importance to the process of realignment, the section 2 requirement that courts "take into account" all relevant ECHR jurisprudence will be logically prior to any revised approach either to the interpretation of legislation or to the more general development of domestic law. The nature of the section 2 requirement can, as such, be contrasted with the nature of the corresponding provisions of the European Communities Act 1972.[73] Although the deeper interaction of domestic and EU law has been

[69] Section 7(7).

[70] See, e.g., *X Union* v. *France*, Application No 9900/82 [1983] 32 DR 261. Although see also *Klass* v. *Germany* [1979–80] 2 EHRR 214.

[71] For example, *R* v. *Secretary of State for Foreign Affairs and Commonwealth Affairs, ex p Rees-Mogg* [1994] 1 All ER 457; *R* v. *Inspectorate of Pollution, ex p Greenpeace Ltd (No 2)* [1994] 4 All ER 328; *R* v. *Secretary of State for Foreign and Commonwealth Affairs, ex p World Development Movement Ltd* [1995] 1 WLR 386; and *R* v. *Secretary of State for the Home Department, ex p Fire Brigade's Union* [1995] 2 WLR 275.

[72] See J Marriott and D Nicol, "The Human Rights Act, Representative Standing and the Victim Culture" (1998) *EHRLR* 730, 741.

[73] Sections 2–3.

unduly frustrated by the orthodox reception of EU law, there is also the fact that the institutional dynamics of the process which the European Communities Act gives effect to differ from those of the ECHR.[74] In short, the historic objective of the European Communities Act has not been to enable the courts to use EU law to develop domestic law, but rather to ensure that the courts give effect to EU law insofar as is required to discharge the UK's obligations to the wider process of integration. This point of focus can easily be contrasted with that of the Human Rights Act as, to the extent that the European Communities Act pursues an "external" objective, the Human Rights Act clearly pursues an "internal" one. The point of emphasis in the Human Rights Act is, by virtue of sections 2 and 6, much more inward looking as it requires the courts to ensure that *all* daily activities of public authorities comply with the minimum fundamental rights guarantees of the ECHR. By providing for the much deeper permeation of ECHR jurisprudence, therefore, the Human Rights Act may, in some senses, be described as a domestic Act proper.

The area in which section 2 will be of most immediate significance is principles of judicial review. ECHR jurisprudence incorporates several key principles, including the proportionality principle,[75] and, although the courts have already emphasised that they will afford decision-makers an "area of discretion" in cases arising under the Human Rights Act[76], they

[74] See further ch. 3.

[75] M A Eissen, "The Principle of Proportionality in the Case-Law of the European Court of Human Rights" in R StJ Macdonald *et al* (eds.), *The European System for the Protection of Human Rights* (Martinus Nijhoff, Dordrecht, 1993), p 125 and J McBride, "Proportionality and the ECHR" in E Ellis (ed.), *The Principle of Proportionality in the Laws of Europe* (Hart Publishing, Oxford, 1999), p 23.

[76] The "area of discretion" has been developed as a domestic equivalent of the ECtHR "margin of appreciation" doctrine. As Lord Hope has said: "The doctrine of the "margin of appreciation" is a familiar part of the jurisprudence of the European Court of Human Rights . . . This doctrine is an integral part of the supervisory jurisdiction which is exercised over state conduct by the international court . . . This technique is not available to the national courts when they are considering Convention issues arising in their own countries. But in the hands of national courts . . . the Convention should be seen as an expression of fundamental principles rather than as a set of mere rules. The questions which the courts will have to decide in the application of these principles will involve questions of balance between competing interests and issues of proportionality . . . In this area difficult choices may have to be made by the executive or the legislature between the rights of the individual and the needs of society. In some circumstances, it will be appropriate for the courts to recognise that there is an area of judgment within which the judiciary will defer, on democratic grounds, to the considered opinion of the elected body or person whose act or decision is said to be incompatible with the Convention . . . It will be easier for such an area of judgment to be recognised where the Convention itself requires a balance to be struck, much less so where the right is stated in terms which are unqualified. It will be easier for it to be recognised where the issues involve questions of social or economic policy, much less so where the rights are of high constitutional importance or are of a kind where the courts are especially well placed to assess the need for protection. But even where the right is stated in terms which are unqualified the courts will need to bear in mind the jurisprudence

have equally recognised that the proportionality principle now has some application.[77] This is, of course, highly significant, and, coupled with the fact that there has long existed judicial agitation for the modification of standards of review in fundamental rights cases[78], it is clear that the central issue in future years will no longer be one of whether domestic law recognises the proportionality principle, but rather one of where the principle sits relative to *Wednesbury* unreasonableness. Will proportionality be subsumed within *Wednesbury*, or will proportionality supersede *Wednesbury*?[79] Will the operation of the proportionality principle be limited to "classic" fundamental rights cases, or will it extend to other cases, including those in the socio-economic field?

The proportionality principle that underscores ECHR jurisprudence is typically concerned with the need to balance individual interests against the broader public interest in permitting a state to place limitations on ECHR guarantees. The principle has, as such, given rise a series of related standards that require decision-makers to provide, among other things, relevant and sufficient reasons for a decision and evidence that identifies the social need that any restrictive measure seeks to address.[80] Although it is sometimes argued that the elements of the proportionality principle inhere in *Wednesbury* review,[81] the consensus opinion is, as discussed in chapter five, that the proportionality standard represents a more searching and

of the European Court which recognises that due account should be taken of the special nature of terrorist crime and the threat which it poses to a democratic society". See *R* v. *DPP, ex p Kebeline and others* [2000] 2 AC 326, 379. For subsequent recognition of the area see, e.g., *Brown* v. *Stott (Procurator Fiscal, Dunfermline)* [2001] 2 All ER 97; *In the Matter of An Application by "A" for Judicial Review*, judgment of the NI High Court, 20 June 2001; and *R (on the application of Alconbury Developments Ltd)* v. *Secretary of State for the Environment, Transport and the Regions* [2001] 2 All ER 929, considered below. For commentary see P Craig, "The Courts, The Human Rights Act and Judicial Review" (2001) 117 *LQR* 589.

[77] The most forceful statement to date was made by the HL in *R* v. *Secretary of State for the Home Department, ex p Daly* [2001] 3 All ER 433. For subsequent application see e.g., *R (on the application of Saadi)* v. *Secretary of State for the Home Department* [2001] 4 All ER 961.

[78] For example, *R* v. *Secretary of State for the Home Department, ex p Bugdaycay* [1987] AC 514, 531 (Lord Bridge); *R* v. *Coventry Airport, ex p Phoenix Aviation* [1995] 3 All ER 37, 62 (Simon Brown LJ); *R* v. *Ministry of Defence, ex p Smith* [1995] 4 All ER 427, 445 (Simon Brown LJ); *R* v. *Cambridge Health Authority, ex p B* [1995] 25 BMLR 5; and *R* v. *Lord Saville, ex p A* [1999] 4 All ER 860. See further M Fordham and T de la Mare, "Anxious Scrutiny, the Principle of Legality and the Human Rights Act" (2000) 5 *JR* 40.

[79] For the argument that the two principles may easily co-exist see M Elliott, "The Human Rights Act 1998 and the Standard of Substantive Review" (2001) 60 *CLJ* 301.

[80] See further J Coppel n. 44 above, p 160 *ff*, considered in ch. 3, p 69 *ff*.

[81] See, e.g., *R* v. *Secretary of State for Health, ex p US Tobacco International Inc* [1992] 1 All ER 212, 221 (Taylor LJ). See also Sir John Laws, "*Wednesbury*" in C Forsyth and I Hare (eds), *The Golden Metwand and the Crooked Cord* (Clarendon Press, Oxford, 1998), p 185 and Lord Hoffman, "The Influence of the European Principle of Proportionality upon United Kingdom Law" in E Ellis (ed.) n. 75 above, p 107.

structured means of inquiry.[82] David Feldman has suggested that this is true both of the core question asked in proportionality and *Wednesbury* inquiries (balance v. irrationality) and of the intensity of any related questions,[83] and it might, at an abstract level, be expected that formal recognition of the principle as a free-standing ground of review will impact on the domestic order in a number of ways. First, the principle might be expected to displace in its entirety the standard of *Wednesbury* review whenever ECHR issues are raised in court. This does not necessarily mean that *Wednesbury* would be rendered redundant in cases which do not involve ECHR issues, but it might raise questions about the desirability of retaining for some cases a standard that has been deemed unsuitable to the resolution of others. Second, and by displacing *Wednesbury*, the proportionality principle might also be expected to provide the core standard against which other principles of judicial review must be set. Paul Craig has noted that ". . . the adoption of proportionality may well require us to think again about . . . the unwillingness to accord discovery in review actions, and more generally about the way in which we regard reasons and evidence in such cases".[84] Given this, it could be argued that the proportionality principle will allow the courts to develop more fully in domestic law some of the other tests associated with the ECtHR's approach. The duty to give reasons, for example, while already being developed in domestic law,[85] could in future come to be seen as a minimum standard rather than something to be gauged with reference to the variable standards of fairness.[86] Likewise, it might be

[82] For example, J Jowell and A Lester, "Beyond *Wednesbury*: Substantive Principles of Administrative Law" [1987] *PL* 368 and M Hunt n. 15 above, ch. 6.

[83] ". . . the doctrine of proportionality requires the reviewing court to assess the fairness of the balance which the national authority has struck, not merely its reasonableness. This is a different test from asking the question which an English court would currently ask in judicial review proceedings: is the balance struck by the authority so wholly irrational that no reasonable authority properly understanding its legal responsibilities and the facts, could have reached it? Secondly, the proportionality test may go slightly further than the other related tests under *Wednesbury*, based on a failure to take account of relevant considerations, taking account of irrelevant considerations, or using a power for an improper purpose. An unfair balance may be struck even after all the relevant interests have been considered, irrelevant ones ignored, and the proper purpose of the power borne clearly in mind. The proportionality doctrine directs attention not only to the interests or considerations weighed against each other, but also to the relative weights which the primary decision-maker attached to the various interests or considerations". See, "Proportionality and the Human Rights Act" in E Ellis (ed.) n. 75 above, pp 117, 127–8.

[84] See, "Unreasonableness and Proportionality in United Kingdom Law" in E Ellis (ed) n. 75 above, pp 85, 106.

[85] See, e.g., *R* v. *Civil Service Appeal Board, ex p Cunningham* [1991] 4 All ER 310; *R* v. *Home Secretary, ex p Doody* [1994] 1 AC 531; *R* v. *Higher Education Funding Council, ex p Institute of Dental Surgery* [1994] 1 All ER 651; *R* v. *City of London Corporation, ex p Matson* [1997] 1 WLR 765; *R* v. *Secretary of State for the Home Department, ex p Fayed* [1997] 1 All ER 228; and *R* v. *Ministry of Defence, ex p Murray* [1998] COD 134.

[86] The extent to which domestic law's emphasis on fairness lends itself to variable

expected that the future protection of substantive legitimate expectations would be achieved with reference to the singular institutional assumptions of the proportionality principle rather than with reference to competing assumptions identified by the Court of Appeal in *Coughlan*.[87]

The abstract expectation that the Human Rights Act could foster such increased cross-fertilisation is, however, one that must be closely qualified. Although section 2 of the Human Rights Act envisages that borrowing will occur, the Lord Chancellor has emphasised that this need not entail every aspect of ECHR jurisprudence being introduced into the domestic order.[88] Stating that UK courts "will often be faced with cases that involve factors perhaps specific" to domestic law, he noted that, as the government is not "bound in international law to follow the (ECtHR's) judgments in cases to which it has not been a party . . . it would be strange to require the courts . . . to be bound by such decisions".[89] This understanding then raises the question of which factors will be taken to be specific to the UK legal order, with the answer being crucially affected by the institutional model of law that it is taken to underpin the domestic system and the role of the courts. Geoffrey Marshall has suggested that the Act could easily be read to conform with orthodoxy[90] and, although the orthodox approach would permit some degree of increased integration, it would surely establish largely inflexible limits to cross-fertilisation. Indeed, within the orthodox paradigm, it might be expected not only that the proportionality principle would be viewed merely as a correlate of *Wednesbury*,[91] but also that the courts would be reluctant to allow ECHR jurisprudence to have an influence in cases that do not fall immediately within the terms of reference of the Human Rights Act. The pattern of pre-existing case law that agitates for closer scrutiny of

standards with regard to the giving of reasons is evident in Sedley J's judgment in *R* v. *Higher Education Funding Council, ex p Institute of Dental Surgery* [1994] 1 All ER 651. For ECtHR criticism of the domestic standard see e.g. *Jordan* v. *UK*. judgment of 4 May 2001.

[87] *R* v. *North and East Devon Health Authority, ex p Coughlan* [2000] 2 WLR 622. But see also Elliott, n. 79 above at 315 *ff*.

[88] "We believe that s. 2 gets it right in requiring domestic courts to take into account judgments of the European Court but not making them binding . . . The (Act will) of course permit United Kingdom courts to depart from existing Strasbourg decisions and upon occasion it might well be appropriate to do so and it is possible they might give a successful lead to Strasbourg" – 583 HL 514, 515.

[89] 484 HL 1270, 1271.

[90] "The supremacy of Parliament is not, on the face of it, affected . . . Neither is the Separation of Powers, nor the accountability of the executive to Parliament". See n. 11 above. For an orthodox approach see further M Elliott, "Fundamental Rights as Interpretative Constructs: The Constitutional Logic of the Human Rights Act 1998" in C Forsyth (ed) n. 10 above p 269.

[91] Note 81 above and *R* v. *Secretary of State for the Home Department, ex p Mahmood* [2001] 1 WLR 840 (CA). But see now also *R* v. *Secretary of State for the Home Department, ex p Daly* [2001] 3 All ER 433 (HL), considering, but not endorsing in its entirety, *Mahmood* (although see further Laws LJ's judgment in *Gough* v. *Chief Constable of Derbyshire Constabulary* [2001] 4 All ER 289, 316 ff).

administrative decisions has been confined to cases that raise more traditional fundamental rights issues,[92] and it might be that the courts would, on the basis of orthodox considerations, decline to develop judicial review beyond that immediately mandated by a narrow reading section 2. In other words, the courts may choose to confine ECHR jurisprudence to closely defined categories of cases and to prohibit development of the law in socio-economic cases or those that raise analogous themes.[93]

The alternative common law model approach to delimiting the scope for integration may, however, see the courts interpret the Human Rights Act in light of its wider institutional context. Such an approach would, as argued in other chapters, not only enable the courts to adopt a more flexible approach to the harmonisation of principle and practice; it would also allow them to emphasise how orthodox assumptions have been overtaken by developments within and without the State. The fact that the ECHR will co-exist with EU law and the parallel challenge of devolution[94] would, seen from the perspective of the common law model, demand the reinvention of public law standards, and the courts may, on this basis, prefer to develop principles of law that are of potential application in any case that comes before the courts. The need for the wider approach was identified by Sedley J in his *McQuillan* judgment, and it is notable that a similar point of emphasis underscored Lord Slynn's judgment in *Alconbury*,[95] this being one of the first significant House of Lords' rulings on the relationship between domestic law and the ECHR.[96] Although the judgment of the House may be criticised as containing an unduly restrictive reading of ECHR jurisprudence,[97] Lord Slynn's judgment remains important insofar as it emphasised the need to forego dualist distinctions between the respective spheres of influence of domestic law and European law. Indeed, given that some subsequent judgments have openly alluded to the likely limited existence of *Wednesbury* review,[98] Lord Slynn's judgment in *Alconbury* may, through time, come to be regarded as synonymous with the beginnings of an intensified process of integration and adaptation.

[92] Note 78 above.

[93] On the courts' traditional reluctance to involve themselves in the review of decisions taken in areas of economic choice and preference see, e.g., *R* v. *Secretary of State for the Environment, ex p Nottinghamshire CC* [1986] 1 AC 240 (but see also *R* v. *Secretary of State for Foreign and Commonwealth Affairs, ex p World Development Movement Ltd* [1995] 1 WLR 386). And see further the potentially limiting influence of the "area of discretion", n. 76 above.

[94] See Bradley n. 14 above.

[95] *R (on the application of Alconbury Developments Ltd)* v. *Secretary of State for the Environment, Transport and the Regions* [2001] 2 All ER 929.

[96] Of course, there had already been significant pronouncements prior to the Act coming into force, e.g., *Barrett* v. *Enfield LBC* [1999] 3 All ER 193 and *R* v. *DPP, ex p Kebeline and others* [2000] 2 AC 326.

[97] I Loveland, "*Alconbury* in the House of Lords" 151 *NLJ* 713.

[98] *R* v. *Secretary of State for the Home Department, ex p Daly*, [2001] 3 All ER 433, 447 (Lord Cooke).

The *Alconbury* case concerned the compatibility with Article 6(1) ECHR of the Secretary of State for the Environment, Transport and the Regions' powers under the Town and Country Planning Act 1990 to call-in and recover planning appeals.[99] Article 6(1) ECHR guarantees that, in the determination of an individual's civil rights or obligations, the individual should have "a fair and public hearing . . . by an independent and impartial tribunal established by law". The issue for the House in *Alconbury* was whether judicial review of a planning determination of the Secretary of State would ensure that the elements of Article 6(1) ECHR are satisfied. The ECtHR has long recognised that there is no breach of Article 6(1) where either the original decision-maker complies with ECHR requirements or there is "subsequent control by a judicial body which has full jurisdiction".[100] On this point, it was argued before the House that, although the Secretary of State did not satisfy the requirements of independence and impartiality – the Secretary of State is largely responsible for formulating planning policy – recourse to judicial review prevented any violation. Such arguments had already failed before the Divisional Court which, having concluded that the limited reach of orthodox grounds of judicial review meant that the reviewing court could not be said to enjoy "full jurisdiction", made a declaration that the legislation in question was incompatible with ECHR guarantees.[101] But the Divisional Court's finding, which clearly reflected some of the ECtHR's more general reservations about the effectiveness of domestic review proceedings,[102] was overturned by the House of Lords. Stating that the question of whether judicial review proceedings satisfy the Article 6 ECHR requirements can only be answered in light of all the circumstances of a case,[103] the House held that, where a "policy" decision – as opposed to a decision based on fact – is being reviewed, the ordinary principles of judicial review will suffice.[104] This finding, the House

[99] Note that *Alconbury* was one of three conjoined appeals and that issues were also raised about the compatibility with Art. 6 ECHR of provisions of the Transport and Works Act 1992; the Highways Act 1980; and the Acquisition of Land Act 1981.

[100] *Albert and Le Compte* v. *Belgium* [1983] 5 EHRR 533, 542 (para. 29).

[101] *Alconbury* v. *Secretary of State the Environment, Transport and the Regions* [2001] JPEL 291, applying *Bryan* v. *UK* [1995] 21 EHRR 342.

[102] For example, *W* v. *UK* [1988] 10 EHRR 29 and *Smith and Grady* v. *UK* [2000] 29 EHRR 493.

[103] Reference was made to the EComHR's opinion in *Bryan* v. *UK* [1995] 21 EHRR 342, 354: "Whether the power of judicial review is sufficiently wide to satisfy the requirements of Art. 6 must, in my view, depend on a number of considerations, including the subject-matter of the dispute, the nature of the decision of the administrative authorities which is in question, the procedure, if any, which exists for review of the decision by a person or body acting independently of the authority concerned and the scope of the power of review" (Nicholas Bratza).

[104] The distinction between "policy" and "other" decisions is one that is notoriously difficult to make. See, e.g., in relation to the policy/operational dichotomy previously used to delimit the liability of public authorities, S H Bailey and M J Bowman, "The Policy/Operational Dichotomy – A Cuckoo in the Nest" (1986) 45 *CLJ* 430.

reasoned, was mandated by the reality that policy decisions will often fall within the area of discretion that requires judicial deference to the decisions of elected authorities.[105] Thus having emphasised that *Alconbury* fell squarely within the policy category, the House concluded that there had been no violation of ECHR guarantees: "'Full jurisdiction' does not mean full decision-making power. It means full jurisdiction to deal with the case as the nature of the decision requires".[106]

The *Alconbury* ruling may, as noted above, be criticised for giving too narrow a reading to ECHR jurisprudence and, moreover, for tending towards orthodox understandings of the courts' review jurisdiction.[107] Yet, whatever criticisms are made of their Lordships' collective ruling, there are within Lord Slynn's judgment several significant comments that suggest that orthodox understandings may be increasingly rejected by the courts. While his Lordship agreed that ordinary principles of review would suffice in the instant case, he departed from the rest of the House in making clear that he did not consider the courts' review jurisdiction to end there. Stating that "the time has come to recognise" proportionality as a part of UK administrative law "not only when judges are dealing with (EU) acts but also when they are dealing with acts subject to domestic law", Lord Slynn stated that "trying to keep the *Wednesbury* principle and proportionality in separate compartments seems to be unnecessary and confusing".[108] His comments in this regard built upon previous statements to the effect that orthodox concerns about the proportionality principle are overstated,[109] and they do, in light of the fact that the Human Rights Act will "often require (a court to ask) whether the principle of proportionality has been satisfied",[110] bring into sharp relief the potential value of viewing the intersecting bodies of law as one and allowing proportionality to become the central principle of administrative law.[111] This need not mean that the proportionality principle should be applied with equal vigour in each and every case as his Lordship emphasised that the degree of scrutiny involved in a proportionality inquiry can vary according to the subject-matter of an application, with socio-economic decisions receiving less anxious examination where appropriate.[112] But what his judgment does imply is that the courts should be open to appropriate adaptation of the

[105] On which see n. 76 above.

[106] [2001] 2 All ER 929, 985 (Lord Hoffmann).

[107] Loveland n. 97 above.

[108] [2001] 2 All ER 929, 976.

[109] *R* v. *Chief Constable of Sussex, ex p International Trader's Ferry Ltd* [1998] 3 WLR 1260, 1277.

[110] [2001] 2 All ER 929, 976.

[111] Although note that Mark Elliott cites Lord Slynn's comments as authority for the proposition that Wednesbury and proportionality should be seen as complementary principles which may easily co-exist within the domestic order. See n. 79 above (fn. 90).

[112] On the varied application of the proportionality principle in the EU law context see G de Búrca, "Proportionality in EC Law" (1993) 13 *YEL* 105.

domestic order either on the basis of EU law, or the ECHR, or both.[113] The adaptation may, as the House of Lords has since indicated, take the form of a dramatic departure from *Wednesbury* whenever the Article 8 ECHR rights of a closed class of individuals are in issue,[114] or it may take the form of a more cautious approach whenever socio-economic policy preferences are raised. Either way, and by taking the proportionality principle as their starting point, the courts should be able to conduct more structured inquiries and to lessen the influence of historical understandings that have long been challenged both from within and without the domestic order.

5. CONCLUSION

This chapter has argued that UK courts may, as a result of the coming into force of the Human Rights Act, now engage in a more active process of legal cross-fertilisation. Focusing on proportionality, it has considered the potential implications of the courts' recognition of the principle as a ground of review in some Human Rights Act cases. Although proponents of orthodoxy may be reluctant to develop the principle to the full, the chapter has suggested that a judicial determination to view domestic and European law as mutually reinforcing could allow proportionality to become an increasingly important – maybe even *the* – reference point within the domestic order. In other words, the chapter has argued that the courts' previous reluctance to have regard to the principle should now be punctuated at a number of levels, with those judges who tend towards the institutional assumptions of the common law model of review using the changing institutional environment to maximum effect.

[113] It may be, e.g., that ECJ jurisprudence would be of more assistance to the courts as they seek to delimit the parameters of their role relative to the review of socio-economic decisions. Compare and contrast the jurisprudence of the ECJ considered in de Búrca, *ibid*, with the decision of the ECtHR in *Hatton* v. *UK* [2002] 34 EHRR 1 (see in particular the dissenting opinion of Sir Brian Kerr).

[114] *R* v. *Secretary of State for the Home Department, ex p Daly* [2001] 3 All ER 433. In the case, a prisoner challenged the lawfulness under the common law and the ECHR of a prison policy which enabled prison officers to examine a prisoner's privileged correspondence whenever the prisoner was excluded from the cell. The policy was found to be unlawful at common law and under the ECHR. Having reached the decision, Lord Cooke considered the possible future role of *Wednesbury* review and stated: "(T)he view that (*Wednesbury* and proportionality) are substantially the same appears to have received its quietus in *Smith and Grady* v. *United Kingdom* [2000] 29 EHRR 493 . . . And I think the day will come when it will be more widely recognised that (*Wednesbury*) was an unfortunately retrogressive decision in English administrative law, insofar as it suggested that there are degrees of unreasonableness and that only a very extreme degree can bring an administrative decision within the legitimate scope of judicial invalidation. The depth of judicial review and the deference due to administrative discretion vary with the subject matter. It may well be, however, that the law can never be satisfied in any administrative field merely by finding that the decision under review is not capricious or absurd". See [2001] 3 All ER 433, 447.

Recognition of proportionality as the central principle of judicial review would, of course, doubtless intensify debate about how far the courts should allow other European constructs to be developed in the domestic order. Proportionality is one of several European principles of review, and it may be that existing domestic equivalents could better be adapted in light of, or even replaced by, related European standards. This is particularly true of the equality principle. While there is some evidence that UK courts have sought to develop a principle of substantive equality whereby discriminatory decisions and secondary acts may be deemed unlawful,[115] it is generally accepted that the domestic standard remains underdeveloped.[116] The equality principles which underpin the EU and ECHR orders are, in contrast, much more elaborate, and it may be that UK courts would wish to embellish the domestic order with reference to the supranational and international standards.[117] Likewise, it might be expected that the courts would wish to utilise the European language of "effectiveness" as they seek to ensure full protection of an individual's interests.[118]

In any event, the central point to be drawn from this chapter is that the courts should now seize the opportunity to remove barriers to truly harmonised protection of an individual's domestic and European interests. It was argued in the previous chapter that harmonised protection will only be achieved when the courts accept the need to integrate more generally the principle and practice of the domestic and European orders. Although the courts have attempted to harmonise domestic and European law through the recognition of specific forms of remedial relief, it was argued that existing endeavours can only be frustrated in the absence of a much deeper process of integration. While the passage of the Human Rights Act may not mean that such integration will be immediately forthcoming, it should mean that there is greater deliberation about the merits of a revised approach. That this is so is only to be welcomed.

[115] For example, *Kruse* v. *Johnson* [1889] 2 QB 291; *Board of Education* v. *Rice* [1911] 179; *Nagle* v. *Fielden* [1966] 2 QB 633; and *R* v. *Secretary of State for the Home Department, ex p Stroud* [1993] COD 75. Note also that there are various Acts of Parliament which seek to prohibit discrimination, e.g., the Race Relations Act 1976 and the Northern Ireland Act 1998 (s. 75).

[116] See further J Jowell, "Is Equality a Constitutional Principle?" (1994) *CLP* 1 and A Lester, "Equality and United Kingdom Law: Past, Present and Future" [2001] *PL* 77.

[117] Equality is a general principle of EU law and a value which finds expression in various Treaty Arts., e.g., Arts. 13 (ex 6a) and 141 (ex 119) EC. See further J Schwarze, *European Administrative Law* (Sweet & Maxwell, London, 1992) ch. 4. The ECHR's equality guarantee is found in Art. 14 ECHR, although note that it is not a free-standing provision. See further S Livingstone, "Art. 14 and the Prevention of Discrimination in the European Convention on Human Rights" (1997) *EHRLR* 25. But see now also Protocol 12, as yet not ratified by the UK Government.

[118] Although the fact that the Government expressly decided not to give to domestic effect to Art. 13 ECHR (the guarantee of an effective remedy) may militate against such development of the law. For the reason why Art. 13 ECHR was not given domestic effect see n. 45 above.

8

The Dynamics of Legal Integration?

The argument that has been made in this book is that UK public law potentially has much to gain from adopting a more open approach to the integration of domestic and European legal standards. The rationale for the argument has simply been that the co-existence of the standards, coupled with ongoing internal processes of change in UK public law, demand deeper consideration of the possible benefit of increased fusion. Although differences between the bodies of law entail limits to integration,[1] it has been argued that a greater willingness to engage in a process of cross-fertilisation would allow the courts to resolve a number of outstanding issues.[2] Previous approaches to integration have largely been structured around orthodox institutional considerations, and these have prevented the courts both from developing principles of judicial review that more accurately reflect their institutional role and from achieving the full and proper protection of the individual's domestic law interests. A more open approach to integration, therefore, has been argued to be desirable and, in some contexts, essential.

The book has also suggested that the more active assimilation of domestic and European standards may now be facilitated by the passage of the Human Rights Act 1998. The dynamics of legal integration were said in chapter one to be driven by a sequential process of interaction which, in the first instance, involved European law feeding into the domestic order and raising questions about the desirability, or otherwise, of adaptation. While EU law has long raised such questions, the fact that the ECHR could not have a direct impact on domestic proceedings greatly lessened its influence. The significance of the Human Rights Act was thereupon taken to lie in the section 2 obligation that the courts consider the relevance to domestic proceedings of ECHR jurisprudence. Not only does the obligation bring to an end the strained understanding that the ECHR is of no direct relevance to domestic law,[3] it also, and by so doing, requires that the

[1] R Dehousse, "Comparing National and EC Law: The Problem of the Level of Analysis" (1994) 42 *AJCL* 761.

[2] J Bell, "Mechanisms for Cross-fertilisation of Administrative Law in Europe" in J Beatson and T Tridimas (eds.), *New Directions in European Public Law* (Hart Publishing, Oxford, 1998) p 147.

[3] *R* v. *Secretary of State for the Home Department, ex p Brind* [1991] 2 WLR 588.

courts reconcile the contrasting institutional values of domestic law, the ECHR and, by analogy, EU law.[4] Even more significantly, the obligation likewise demands further reassessment of the related issue of how best to achieve protection of the individual's interests, with the courts recognising the point even before the Human Rights Act came into force.[5]

In making this argument, the book has not simultaneously assumed that any process of change prompted by the Human Rights Act will adopt a uniform pattern or be far-reaching in each instance. Chapter one also highlighted how the dynamics of legal integration are finally mediated by internal institutional considerations, and the emergence of a truly open approach to integration was taken to depend upon a judicial willingness to emphasise the institutional assumptions of the common law model of review. The contested legitimacy of the model means, of course, that integration will, at least initially, continue to be mediated by the contrasting institutional preferences that have informed the ultra vires debate.[6] Where the preferences tend towards the assumptions of the common law model, this may, as has already been evidenced, lead to the adaptation of the domestic order.[7] But where the preferences tend towards orthodox public law assumptions, change will be less far-reaching. Dualist orthodoxy has been seen to militate against harmonisation,[8] and it can only be expected that further reliance on orthodoxy would place undue constraints on the process of borrowing. The prospects for deeper integration, therefore, will, at least in the short term, likely continue to vary in accordance with preferred understandings of the institutional balance of the State.

The extent to which orthodox institutional considerations will mediate the process of integration in the longer term is, however, less clear. The Human Rights Act is, as has been stated several times, only one part of a much wider constitutional reform package that can, when juxtaposed with the demands of EU membership, only further strain the justificatory force

[4] See, e.g., *R* v. *Secretary of State for the Home Department, ex p Daly*, [2001] 3 All ER 433, 447 (Lord Cooke), considering the more exacting standard of review contained in the ECtHR's judgment *Smith and Grady* v. *UK* [2000] 29 EHRR 493. And see also *In Re Medicaments and Related Classes of Goods (No 2)* [2001] 1 WLR 700, modifying the domestic test for bias in light of, e.g., *Piersack* v. *Belgium* [1982] 5 EHRR 169.

[5] *Barrett* v. *Enfield LBC* [1999] 3 All ER 193.

[6] C Forsyth (ed.), *Judicial Review and the Constitution* (Hart Publishing, Oxford, 2000).

[7] *M* v. *Home Office* [1993] 3 WLR 433; *R* v. *Ministry of Agriculture, Fisheries and Food, ex p Hamble Fisheries (Off-shore) Limited* [1995] 2 All ER 714; *R* v. *Secretary of State for the Home Department, ex p McQuillan* [1995] 4 All ER 400; *R* v. *North and East Devon Health Authority, ex p Coughlan* [2000] 2 WLR 622; and *R (on the application of Alconbury Developments Ltd)* v. *Secretary of State for the Environment, Transport and the Regions* [2001] 2 All ER 929, 976 (Lord Slynn).

[8] Chs. 4–6. And see further I Ward, "Dualism and the Limits of European Integration" (1995) 17 *Liverpool LRev* 29.

of orthodox public law assumptions. This is particularly true in relation to devolution. Although the devolution legislation is couched in terms that reassert orthodox assumptions,[9] several commentators have suggested that the courts may have to develop new principles that are better suited to the resolution of devolution disputes.[10] Should new defining "constitutional" principles be forthcoming, these may, in turn, render the domestic order more generally receptive to the integration of external standards. It may be, for example, that the new principles would themselves be developed with reference to the comparative experience of European law and other common law jurisdictions,[11] and this would surely facilitate a more general and far-reaching process of borrowing at the level of administrative law. Indeed, a judicial willingness to situate constitutional developments within a framework that recognises the reality of overlapping sovereignties within and without the State would witness the courts foregoing the insular perspective of dualist orthodoxy in favour of the broader perspective envisaged by the common law model. Within that framework, integration would not only be more easily achieved; it would be inevitable.

The internal institutional considerations that structure the process of legal integration can, therefore, only be expected to become more responsive to the need for harmonisation. Many of the institutional assumptions that for so long sustained UK public law have, in the words of one Law Lord, now "received (their) quietus".[12] Although the elements of any "new orthodoxy" will doubtless be contested, ongoing and recent internal developments present the courts with the opportunity more fully to engage and accommodate the respective strengths of the domestic and European orders. The interface between UK public law and European law has long created pressure for adaptation and realignment. It is surely time to make fuller use of the insights offered.

[9] See, e.g., s. 28(7) of the Scotland Act 1998: "This section does not affect the power of the Parliament of the United Kingdom to make laws for Scotland".

[10] See further B Hadfield, "The Foundations of Review, Devolved Power and Delegated Power" in C Forsyth (ed.) n. 6 above, p 193 and AW Bradley, "The Sovereignty of Parliament – Form or Substance?" in J Jowell and D Oliver (eds.), *The Changing Constitution* (Oxford University Press, Oxford, 4th edn, 2000), p 23. On the magnitude of the challenge see N Walker, "Beyond the Unitary Conception of the United Kingdom Constitution?" [2000] *PL* 384.

[11] C Harlow, "Export, Import. The Ebb and Flow of English Public Law" [2000] *PL* 240. On the relevance of European experience to the challenge of devolution see N Burrows *Devolution* (Sweet & Maxwell, London, 2000). On the possible value of, e.g., Canadian constitutional experience see M D Walters, "Nationalism and the Pathology of Legal Systems: Considering the *Quebec Secession Reference* and its Lessons for the United Kingdom" (1999) 62 *MLR* 371.

[12] *R* v. *Secretary of State for the Home Department, ex p Daly*, [2001] 3 All ER 433, 447 (Lord Cooke, commenting on the future relevance of *Wednesbury* review).

Select Bibliography

Ajani, G, "By Chance and Prestige: Legal Transplants in Russia and Eastern Europe" (1995) 43 *American Journal of Comparative Law* 93.

Allan, T R S, "Parliamentary Sovereignty and the EEC" (1982) *Public Law* 562.

—— "Parliamentary Sovereignty: Lord Denning's Dextrous Revolution" (1983) 3 *Oxford Journal of Legal Studies* 22.

Allison, J W F, "Transplantation and Cross-fertilisation" in J Beatson and T Tridimas (eds), *New Directions in European Public Law* (Hart Publishing, Oxford, 1998), p 169.

—— *A Continental Distinction in the Common Law: A Historical and Comparative Perspective on English Public Law* (Oxford University Press, 2nd edn, 2000).

Amos, M, "Extending the liability of the state in damages" (2001) 21 *Legal Studies* 1.

Arnull, A, "The Duke Case: An Unreliable Precedent (1988) *Public Law* 313.

—— "Does the Court of Justice Have Inherent Jurisdiction?" (1990) 27 *Common Market Law Review* 683.

——"When is pregnancy like an arthritic hip?" (1992) 17 *European Law Review* 265.

—— "The European Court and Judicial Objectivity: A Reply to Professor Hartley" (1996) 112 *Law Quarterly Review* 411.

Arrowsmith, S, *Civil Liability and Public Authorities* (Earlsgate Press, Humberside, 1992).

Bailey, S H and Bowman, M J, "The Policy/Operational Dichotomy – A Cuckoo in the Nest" (1986) 45 *Cambridge Law Journal* 430.

Bamforth, N, "The Scope of Judicial Review: Still Uncertain" (1993) *Public Law* 239.

—— "Fairness and Legitimate Expectation in Judicial Review" (1997) 56 *Cambridge Law Journal* 1.

—— "Restitution and the scope of judicial review" (1997) *Public Law* 603.

—— "Interim Relief in the Public Law Context" (1999) 58 *Cambridge Law Journal* 1.

—— "The Application of the Human Rights Act 1998 to Public Authorities and Private Bodies" (1999) 58 *Cambridge Law Journal* 159.

Barendt, E, "Constitutional Law and the Criminal Injuries Compensation Scheme" (1995) *Public Law* 357.

Barnard, C and Hare, I, "The Right to Protest and the Right to Export: Police Discretion and the the Free Movement of Goods" (1997) 60 *Modern Law Review* 394, 403.

Beatson, J, "Restitution of Taxes, Levies and Other Imposts: Defining the Extent of the *Woolwich* Principle" (1993) 109 *Law Quarterly Review* 401.

Beatson, J and Tridimas T (eds), *New Directions in European Public Law* (Hart Publishing, Oxford, 1998).

Beatson, J, Forsyth, C and Hare I (eds), *Constitutional Reform in the United Kingdom: Practice and Principles* (Hart Publishing, Oxford, 1998).
Bell, J, "Mechanisms for Cross-fertilisation of Administrative Law in Europe" in J Beatson and T Tridimas (eds), *New Directions in European Public Law* (Hart Publishing, Oxford, 1998) p 147, 161.
Birks, P, "'When Money is Paid in Pursuance of a Void Authority . . .' – A Duty to Repay?" (1992) *Public Law* 580, 581.
Boyron, S, "Proportionality in English Administrative Law: A Faulty Translation?" (1992) 12 *Oxford Journal of Legal Studies* 237.
Brazier, R, "New Labour, New Constitution" (1998) 49 *Northern Ireland Legal Quarterly* 1.
—— "The Constitution of the United Kingdom" (1999) 58 *Cambridge Law Journal* 96.
Bridge, J W, "Judicial Review in Mauritius and the Continuing Influence of English Law" (1997) 46 *International and Comparative Law Quarterly* 787.
Brunell, T L and Stone Sweet, A, "The European Court and the national courts: a statistical analysis of preliminary references, 1961–95" (1998) 5 *Journal of European Public Policy* 66.
Burrows, N, *Devolution* (Sweet & Maxwell, London, 2000).
Callewaert, J, "Is there a Margin of Appreciation in Articles 2, 3 and 4 of the ECHR?" (1998) 19 *Human Rights Law Journal*
Campbell, N R, "The duty to give reasons in administrative law" (1994) *Public Law* 184.
Canor, I, "*Primus inter pares*: Who is the ultimate guardian of fundamental rights in Europe?" (2000) 25 *European Law Review* 3.
Carmichael P and Dickson B (eds), *The House of Lords: Its Parliamentary and Judicial Roles* (Hart Publishing, Oxford, 1999).
Chalmers, D, "Judicial Preferences and the Community Legal Order" (1997) 60 *Modern Law Review* 164, 189–90.
Convery, J, "State Liability in the United Kingdom After *Brasserie du Pêcheur*" (1997) 34 *Common Market Law Review* 603.
Coppel, J and O'Neill A, "The European Court of Justice: Taking Rights Seriously?" (1992) 29 *Common Market Law Review* 669.
—— "Rights, Duties and the End of Marshall" (1994) 57 *Modern Law Review* 859.
—— "Horizontal Effect of Directives" (1997) 26 *Industrial Law Journal* 69.
—— *The Human Rights Act 1998: Enforcing the European Convention in the Domestic Courts* (Wiley, Chichester, 1998).
Cotterrell, R, *Law's Community: Legal Theory in Sociological Perspective* (Clarendon Press, Oxford, 1995).
Craig, P, "Sovereignty of the UK Parliament after *Factortame*" (1991) 11 *Yearbook of European Law* 221, 251–3.
—— "Once Upon a Time in the West: Direct Effect and the Federalization of EEC Law" (1992) 12 *Oxford Journal of Legal Studies* 453.
—— "Legitimate Expectations: A Conceptual Analysis" (1992) 108 *Law Quarterly Review* 79.
—— "The Common Law, Reasons and Administrative Justice" (1994) *Cambridge Law Journal* 282.

—— "Substantive Legitimate Expectations in Domestic and Community Law" (1996) 55 *Cambridge Law Journal* 289.

—— "Once More Unto the Breach: The Community, The State and Damages Liability" (1997) 113 *Law Quarterly Review* 67.

—— "Directives: Direct Effect, Indirect Effect and the Construction of National Legislation" (1997) 22 *European Law Review* 519.

—— "*Ultra Vires* and the Foundations of Judicial Review" (1998) 57 *Cambridge Law Journal* 63.

—— and de Búrca, G, *EU Law: Text, Cases and Materials* (Oxford University Press, Oxford, 2nd edn, 1998).

—— *Administrative Law* (Sweet & Maxwell: London, 4th edn, 1999).

—— and de Búrca, G (eds), *The Evolution of EU Law* (Oxford University Press, Oxford, 1999).

—— and Fairgreave, D, "*Barrett*, Negligence and Discretionary Powers" (1999) *Public Law* 626.

—— and Schonberg, S, "Substantive Legitimate Expectations after *Coughlan*" (2000) *Public Law* 684.

Craighead, Lord Hope, "Mike Tyson Comes to Glasgow – A Question of Standing" (2001) *Public Law* 294.

Davies, P, "Market Integration and Social Policy in the Court of Justice" (1995) 24 *Industrial Law Journal* 49.

de Búrca, G, "Proportionality in EC Law" (1993) 13 *Yearbook of European Law* 105, 110.

—— "The Quest for Legitimacy in the European Union" (1996) 59 *Modern Law Review* 349.

—— "Proportionality and *Wednesbury* Unreasonableness: The Influence of European Legal Concepts on UK Law" (1997) 3 *European Public Law* 561.

Deards, E, "'Curiouser and Curiouser'? The Development of Member State Liability in the Court of Justice" (1997) 3 *European Public Law* 117.

Dehousse, R, "Comparing National and EC Law: The Problem of the Level of Analysis" (1994) 42 *American Journal of Comparative Law* 761.

Dicey, A V, *An Introduction to the Study of Law of the Constitution* (Macmillan, London, 10th edn, 1959).

Douglas-Scott, S and Kimbell, J A, "The Adams exclusion order case: new enforceable civil rights in the post-Maastricht European Union" (1994) *Public Law* 516.

Elliott, M, "The *Ultra Vires* Doctrine in a Constitutional Setting: Still the Central Principle of Administrative Law" (1999) 58 *Cambridge Law Journal* 129, 133.

—— "The Demise of Parliamentary Sovereignty? The Implications for Justifying Judicial Review" (1999) 115 *Law Quarterly Review* 119.

—— "*Coughlan*: Substantive Protection of Legitimate Expectations Revisited" (2000) 5 *Judicial Review* 27.

Ellis, E, "Supremacy of Parliament and European Law" (1980) 96 *Law Quarterly Review* 511.

—— "EEC Law and the Interpretation of Statutes" (1988) 104 *Law Quarterly Review* 379.

—— (ed), *The Principle of Proportionality in the Laws of Europe* (Hart Publishing, Oxford, 1999).

Evans, A, "Voluntary Harmonisation in Integration between the European Community and Eastern Europe" (1997) 22 *European Law Review* 201.

Everson, M, "Administering Europe" (1998) 36 *Journal of Common Market Studies* 195.

Ewald, W, "Comparative Jurisprudence (II): The Logic of Legal Transplants" (1995) 43 *American Journal of Comparative Law* 489.

Feldman, D, "Remedies for Violations of Convention Rights under the Human Rights Act" (1998) *European Human Rights Law Review* 692.

Fernandez Esteban, M L, "National Judges and EC Law: The Paradox of the Two Paradigms of Law" (1997) 4 *Maastricht Journal of European and Comparative Law* 143.

Fordham, M and Mare, T de la, "Anxious Scrutiny, the Principle of Legality and the Human Rights Act" (2000) 5 *Judicial Review* 40.

Forman, J, "The European Communities Act 1972: The Government's Position on the Meaning and Effects of its Constitutional Provisions" (1973) 10 *Common Market Law Review* 39.

Forsyth, C, "The Scope of Judicial Review: 'Public Duty' not 'Source of Power'" (1987) *Public Law* 356.

—— "The Provenance of Legitimate Expectations" (1988) 47 *Cambridge Law Journal* 238.

—— "Of Fig Leaves and Fairy Tales: The *Ultra Vires* Doctrine, the Sovereignty of Parliament and Judicial Review" (1996) 55 *Cambridge Law Journal* 122.

—— "Wednesbury protection of substantive legitimate expectations" (1997) *Public Law* 375.

—— (ed), *Judicial Review and the Constitution* (Hart Publishing, Oxford, 2000)

—— and Hare I (eds), *The Golden Metwand and the Crooked Cord: Essays on Public Law in Honour of Sir William Wade QC* (Clarendon Press, Oxford, 1998).

Foster, S, "Legitimate Expectations and Prisoners' Rights: The Right to Get What You are Given" (1997) 60 *Modern Law Review* 727.

Fredman, S and Morris, G S, "The Costs of Exclusivity: Public and Private Re-examined" (1994) *Public Law* 69.

Freedland, M, "Government by Contract and Public Law" (1994) *Public Law* 86.

Garner, J F "Administrative Law – A Step Forward?" (1968) 31 *Modern Law Review* 446.

Ganz, G, "Criminal Injuries Compensation: The Constitutional Issue" (1996) 59 *Modern Law Review* 95, 100.

Gould, M, "*M* v. *Home Office*: Government and the judges" (1993) *Public Law* 568.

Graham, C and Prosser, T (eds), *Waiving the Rules: The Constitution Under Thatcherism* (Open University Press, Milton Keynes, 1988).

Gray, M, "The Northern Ireland Act 1998, Judicial Review and Human Rights" (2000) 5 *Judicial Review* 114.

Grief, N, "The Domestic Impact of the Euroepan Convention on Human Rights as Mediated through Community Law" (1991) *Public Law* 555.

Griffith, J A G, "Judicial Decision-Making in Public Law" (1985) *Public Law* 564.
—— *The Politics of the Judiciary* (Fontana Press, London, 4th edn, 1991).
—— "The Brave New World of Sir John Laws" (2000) 63 *Modern Law Review* 159.
Grosz, S, Beatson, J and Duffy, P, *Human Rights: The 1998 Act and the European Convention* (Sweet & Maxwell, London, 2000).
Haas, E, *The Uniting of Europe: Political, Economic and Social Forces, 1950–57* (Stevens, London, 1958).
Hadfield, B (ed), *Judicial Review: A Thematic Approach* (Gill & MacMillan, Dublin, 1995).
Halliwell, M, "Judicial Review and Broadcasting Freedom: The Route to Europe" (1991) 42 *Northern Ireland Legal Quarterly* 246.
Harlow, C, "Accidental Loss of an Asylum Seeker" (1994) *Modern Law Review* 620.
—— "*Francovich* and the Problem of the Disobedient State" (1996) 2 *European Law Journal* 199.
—— "Export, Import. The Ebb and Flow of English Public Law" (2000) *Public Law* 240.
—— and Rawlings, R, *Law and Administration* (Butterworths, London, 2nd edn, 1997).
Harmsen, R, "A European Union of Variable Geometry: Problems and Perspectives" (1994) 45 *Northern Ireland Legal Quarterly* 109.
—— "The Europeanization of National Administrations: A Comparative Study of France and the Netherlands" 12 *Governance* 81.
Harris, D J, O'Boyle, M and Warbrick, C, *Law of the European Convention on Human Rights* (Butterworths, London, 1995).
Hartley, TC, "The European Court, Judicial Objectivity and the Constitution of the European Union" (1996) 112 *Law Quarterly Review* 95.
Harvey, C (ed), *Human Rights, Equality and Democratic Renewal in Northern Ireland* (Hart Publishing, Oxford, 2001).
—— and Livingstone, S, "Protecting the Marginalised: The Role of the European Convention on Human Rights" (2000) 51 *Northern Ireland Legal Quarterly* 445.
Hepple, B, "Social Values and European Law" (1995) 48 *Current Legal Problems* 39.
Herberg, J, "The Right to Reasons: Palm Trees in Retreat?" (1991) *Public Law* 340.
Herdegen, M, "Maastricht and the German Constitutional Court: Constitutional Restraints for an Ever Closer Union" (1994) 31 *Common Market Law Review* 235.
Heuston, R F V, *Essays in Constitutional Law* (Stevens and Sons: London, 1964).
Hill, T, "Restitution from Public Authorities and the Treasury's Position: *Woolwich Equitable Building Society* v. *IRC*" (1993) 56 *Modern Law Review* 856.
Himsworth, C M G, "Legitimately expecting proportionality" [1996] *Public Law* 46.
—— "Things Fall Apart: The Harmonisation of Community Judicial Procedural Protection Revisited" (1997) 22 *European Law Review* 291.

Hoffmann, Lord, "Human Rights and the House of Lords" (1999) 62 *Modern Law Review* 159, 164.
Hood Phillips, O, "High Tide in the Strand? Post 1972 Acts and Community Law" (1980) 96 *Law Quarterly Review* 31.
—— "A Garland for the Lords: Parliament and the Community Again" (1982) 98 *Law Quarterly Review* 524, 525.
Hoskins, M, "Tilting the Balance: Supremacy and National Procedural Rules" (1996) 21 *European Law Review* 365.
Hoyano, L, "Policing Flawed Police Investigations: Unravelling the Blanket" (1999) 62 *Modern Law Review* 912, 920–3.
Hunt, M, *Using Human Rights Law in English Courts* (Hart Publishing: Oxford, 1997).
—— "The "Horizontal Effect" of the Human Rights Act" (1998) *Public Law* 423.
Irvine, Lord, "Judges and Decision-Makers: The Theory and Practice of *Wednesbury* Review" (1996) *Public Law* 59.
Jaconelli, J, "Constitutional Review and Section 2(4) of the European Communities Act 1972' (1979) 28 *International and Comparative Law Quarterly* 65.
James, R and Longley, D, "Judicial review and tragic choices: *Ex parte B*" (1995) *Public Law* 367.
Jones, T, "Scottish Devolution and Demarcation Disputes" (1997) *Public Law* 283.
Jowell, J and Lester, A, "Beyond *Wednesbury*: Substantive Principles of Administrative Law" (1987) *Public Law* 368.
—— "Is Equality a Constitutional Principle?" (1994) *Current Legal Problems* 1.
—— "Is Proportionality and Alien Concept?" (1996) 2 *European Public Law* 401.
—— and Oliver D (eds), *New Directions in Judicial Review* (Stevens, London, 1988).
—— and Oliver D (eds), *The Changing Constitution* (Oxford University Press, Oxford, 4th edn, 2000).
JUSTICE/All Souls, *Adminstrative Law: Some Necessary Reforms* (Oxford, 1988).
Kahn-Freund, O, "On Uses and Misuses of Comparative Law" (1974) 37 *Modern Law Review* 1.
Keenan, P B, "Some Legal Consequences of Britain's Entry into the European Common Market" (1962) *Public Law* 327, 333.
Koopmans, T, "European Public Law: Reality and Prospects" (1991) *Public Law* 53.
—— "The Birth of European Law at the Cross-roads of Legal Traditions" (1991) 39 *American Journal of Comparative Law* 493, 500.
Laws, Sir John, "Is the High Court the Guardian of Fundamental Rights?" (1993) *Public Law* 59.
—— "Law and Democracy" (1995) *Public Law* 72, 81.
Le Sueur, A P, "The Judicial Review Debate: From Partnership to Friction" (1996) 31 *Government and Opposition* 221.
Legrand, P, "European Legal Systems are not Converging" (1996) 45 *International and Comparative Law Quarterly* 52.

—— "Against a European Civil Code" (1997) 60 *Modern Law Review* 44.

—— "The Impossibility of Legal Transplants" (1997) 4 *Maastricht Journal of European and Comparative Law* 111, 114.

Lester, A, "Fundamental Rights: The UK Isolated?" (1984) *Public Law* 46.

—— "*Pepper* v. *Hart* Revisited" (1994) 15 *Statute Law Review* 10.

—— "The Art of the Possible – Interpreting Statutes under the Human Rights Act" (1998) *European Human Rights Law Review* 665.

—— "Equality and United Kingdom Law: Past, Present and Future" (2001) *PL* 77

Levitsky, J, "The Europeanization of the British Legal Style" (1994) 42 *American Journal of Comparative Law* 347.

Leyland P and Woods T (eds), *Administrative Law Facing the Future: Old Constraints and New Horizons* (Blackstone, London, 1997).

Lindberg, L, *The Political Dynamics of European Economic Integration* (Stanford University Press , 1963).

Livingstone, S, "Article 14 and the Prevention of Discrimination in the European Convention on Human Rights" (1997) *European Human Rights Law Review* 25.

Loveland, I (ed), *A Special Relationship? American Influences on Public Law in the UK* (Clarendon Press, Oxford, 1995).

Luhmann, N, "Operational Closure and Structural Coupling: The Differentiation of the Legal System" (1992) 13 *Cardozo Law Review* 1419.

Lyell, N, "*Pepper* v. *Hart*: The Government Perspective" (1994) 15 *Statute Law Review* 1.

McAuslan, P and McEldowney J F (eds), *Law, Legitimacy and the Constitution* (Sweet and Maxwell, London, 1985).

McClean, H, "In Europe Part-time Workers Have Rights Too" (1994) *Cambridge Law Journal* 210.

Macdonald R StJ *et al* (eds), *The European System for the Protection of Human Rights* (Martinus Nijhoff, Dordrecht, 1993).

Macormack, N, "Beyond the Sovereign State" (1993) 56 *Modern Law Review* 1.

—— "The Maastricht-Urteil: Sovereignty Now" (1995) 1 *European Law Journal* 259.

Maduro, MP, *We the Court: The European Court of Justice & the European Economic Constitution* (Hart Publishing, Oxford, 1998).

Mahoney, P, "Judicial Activism and Judicial Self-Restraint in the European Court of Human Rights: Two Sides of the Same Coin?" (1990) 11 *Human Rights Law Journal* 57.

Markesinis, B S (ed), *The Gradual Convergence* (Clarendon Press, Oxford, 1994).

—— (ed), *The Impact of the Human Rights Bill on English Law* (Clarendon Press, Oxford, 1998).

—— Auby, J-B, Coester-Waltjen, D and Deakin, S F, *Tortious Liability of Statutory Bodies* (Hart Publishing, Oxford, 1999).

Marriott, J and Nicol, D, "The Human Rights Act, Representative Standing and the Victim Culture" (1998) *European Human Rights Law Review* 730, 741.

Marshall, G, *Constitutional Theory* (Oxford University Press, Oxford, 1971).

Marston, G, "The United Kingdom's Part in the Preparation of the European Convention on Human Rights, 1950" (1993) *International Comparative and Law Quarterly* 796.

Martin Salgado, E and O'Brien, C, "Table of Cases under the Human Rights Act" (2001) *European Human Rights Law Review* 181.

Mitchell, J D B, "'What do you want to be inscrutable for, Marcia?'/The White Paper on the Legal and Constitutional Implications of Membership of the European Communities" (1967) 5 *Common Market Law Review* 112, 122.

Monti, G, "Osman *v*. UK – Transforming English Negligence Law into French Administrative Law?" (1999) 48 *International Comparative and Law Quarterly* 757.

Moore, S, "Sex Discrimination and judicial review" (1994) 19 *European Law Review* 425.

Moravcsik, A, "Preferences and Power in the European Community: A Liberal Intergovernmentalist Approach" (1993) 31 *Journal of Common Market Studies* 473.

—— *The Choice for Europe: Social Purpose and State Power from Messina to Maastricht* (Cornell University Press, 1998).

Morison, J and Livingstone, S, *Reshaping Public Power: Northern Ireland and the British Constitutional Crisis* (Sweet & Maxwell, London, 1995).

—— "The Case Against Constitutional Reform" (1998) 25 *Journal of Law and Society* 510.

Mortelmans, K, "EC Law: More than a Functional Area of Law, Less than a Legal System" (1996) *Legal Issues of European Integration* 23.

—— "The Principle of Loyalty to the Community (Article 5 EC) and the Obligations of the Community Institutions" (1998) 5 *Maastricht Journal of European and Comparative Law* 67.

Moynihan, G, "Human Rights in Scotland – The Story So Far" (2000) 5 *Judicial Review* 274.

Nolte, G, "General Principles of German and European Administrative Law – A Comparison in Historical Perspective" (1994) 57 *Modern Law Review* 191.

O'Donnell, TA, "The Margin of Appreciation Doctrine: Standards in the Jurisprudence of the European Court of Human Rights" (1982) 4 *Human Rights Quarterly* 474.

Oliver, D, "Is the *Ultra Vires* Rule the Basis of Judicial Review?" (1987) *Public Law* 543.

—— " Fishing on the Incoming Tide" (1991) 54 *Modern Law Review* 442.

—— "*Pepper* v. *Hart*: A Suitable Case for Reference to Hansard?" [1993] *Public Law* 5.

—— "A Negative Aspect to Legitimate Expectations" [1998] *Public Law* 558.

—— *Common Values and the Public–Private Divide* (Butterworths, London, 1999).

Phelan, D R, "The Right to Life of the Unborn v. the Promotion of Trade in Services: The European Court of Justice and the Normative Shaping of the European Union" (1992) 55 *Modern Law Review* 670.

—— *Revolt or Revolution? The Constitutional Boundaries of the European Community* (Round Hall/Sweet & Maxwell, Dublin, 1997).

Plaza Martin, C, "Furthering the Effectiveness of EC Directives and the Judicial Protection of Individual Rights Thereunder" (1994) 43 *International and Comparative Law Quarterly* 26.

Public Law Project, The, *Judicial Review in Perspective: An Investigation of Trends in the Use and Operation of the Judicial Review Procedure in England and Wales* (London, 1993).

Rasmussen, H, *On Law and Policy in the European Court of Justice* (Martinus Nijhoff, Dordrecht, 1986).

Rawlings, R, "The Eurolaw Game: Some Deductions from a Saga" (1993) 20 *Journal of Law and Society* 309.

Richardson, G and Genn, H (eds), *Administrative Law and Government Action* (Clarendon Press, Oxford, 1994).

—— and Sunkin, M, "Judicial Review: Questions of Impact" (1996) *Public Law* 79.

Robertshaw, P, "Providing Reasons for Administrative Decisions" (1998) *Anglo-American Law Review* 29.

Schilling, T, "The Autonomy of the Community Legal Order – An Analysis of Possible Foundations" (1996) 37 *Harvard International Law Journal* 389.

Schonberg, S, *Legitimate Expectations in Administrative Law* (Oxford University Press, Oxford, 2000).

Schwarze, J, "Tendencies towards a Common Administrative Law in Europe" (1991) 16 *European Law Review* 3.

—— *European Administrative Law* (Sweet & Maxwell, London, 1992).

—— (ed), *Administrative Law under European Influence* (Nomos, Baden Baden and London, 1996).

Sedley, Sir Stephen, "The Sound of Silence: Constitutional Law without a Constitution" (1994) 110 *Law Quarterly Review* 270, 285.

—— "Human Rights: A Twenty-first Century Agenda" (1995) *Public Law* 386, 389.

—— *Freedom, Law and Justice* (Sweet & Maxwell, London, 1999)

Shaw, J, *Law of the European Union* (Macmillan, London, 2nd ed, 1996). (1998).

—— and More, G (eds), *New Legal Dynamics of European Union* (Clarendon Press, Oxford, 1995).

Sherlock, A, "The Applicability of the United Kingdom's Human Rights Bill: Identifying Public Functions" (1998) 4 *European Public Law* 593.

Simpson, R C, "Equal Pay in the Court of Appeal" (1980) 43 *Modern Law Review* 209.

Singh, R, Hunt, M and Demetriou, M, "Is there a Role for the 'Margin of Appreciation' in National Law after the Human Rights Act?" (1999) *European Human Rights Law Review* 15, 17.

Slaughter, A M, Stone Sweet A and Weiler, J H H (eds), *The European Courts & National Courts: Doctrine and Jurisprudence* (Hart Publishing, Oxford, 1998).

Spink, P, "Contravening EC Law: The Liability of the Member State" (1997) 48 *Northern Ireland Legal Quarterly* 111.

Steiner, J, "The Limits of State Liability for Breach of European Community Law" (1998) 4 *European Public Law* 69.

Styles, S C, "The Rule of Parliament: Statutory Interpretation after *Pepper* v. *Hart*" (1994) 14 *Oxford Journal of Legal Studies* 151.

Szyszczak, E, "Sovereignty: Crisis, Compliance, Confusion, Complacency" (1990) 15 *European Law Review* 480.

—— "Foster v. British Gas" (1990) 27 *Common Market Law Review* 859.

—— "European Community Law: New Remedies, New Directions" (1992) 55 *Modern Law Review* 690.

Taggart, M (ed), *The Province of Administrative Law* (Hart Publishing, Oxford, 1997).

Temple-Lang, J, "The Duties of National Courts under Community Constitutional Law" (1997) 22 *European Law Review* 3.

Teubner, G, "Legal Irritants: Good Faith in British Law or How Unifying Law Ends Up in New Divergences" (1998) 61 *Modern Law Review* 11.

Thomas, R, *Legitimate Expectations and Proportionality in Administrative Law* (Hart Publishing, Oxford, 2000).

Thompson, B, "Broadcasting and Terrorism in the House of Lords" (1991) *Public Law* 346.

Tranholm-Mikkelsen, J, "Neo-functionalism: Obstinate or Obsolete? A Reappraisal in the Light of the new Dynamism of the EC" (1991) 20 *Millennium* 1.

Tridimas, T, "Liability for breach of community law: growing up and mellowing down?" (2001) 38 *Common Market Law Review* 301.

Turner, S, "Horizontal Direct Enforcement of Directives Rejected" (1995) 46 *Northern Ireland Legal Quarterly* 244, 252.

Van Gerven, W, "Bridging the Gap Between Community and National Laws: Towards a Principle of Homogeneity in the Field of Legal Remedies" (1995) 32 *Common Market Law Review* 679, 700.

Volcansek, M L, *Judicial Politics in Europe: An Impact Analysis* (Peter Lang, New York, 1986).

Wade, H W R, "The Basis of Legal Sovereignty" (1955) 13 *Cambridge Law Journal* 172.

—— "What Has Happened to the Sovereignty of Parliament?" (1991) 107 *Law Quarterly Review* 1.

—— "Sovereignty – Revolution or Evolution?" (1996) 112 *Law Quarterly Review* 568.

—— and Forsyth, C F, *Administrative Law* (Clarendon Press, Oxford, 7th edn, 1994).

—— and Forsyth, C F, *Administrative Law* (Oxford University Press, Oxford, 8th edn, 2000).

Wadham, J and Mountfield, H, *Blackstone's Guide to the Human Rights Act 1998* (Blackstone, London, 1999). Walker, N, "Beyond the Unitary Conception of the United Kingdom Constitution?" (2000) *Public Law* 384.

Walters, MD, "Nationalism and the Pathology of Legal Systems: Considering the *Quebec Secession Reference* and its Lessons for the United Kingdom" (1999) 62 *Modern Law Review* 371.

Ward, I, "Dualism and the Limits of European Integration" (1995) *Liverpool Law Review* 29, 36.

Watson, A, *Legal Transplants: An Approach to Comparative Law* (University of Georgia Press, 2nd edn, 1993).

—— "Legal Transplants and Law Reform" (1976) 92 *Law Quarterly Review* 79.

—— "Comparative Law and Legal Change" (1978) 37 *Cambridge Law Journal* 313.

—— "From Legal Transplants to Legal Formants" (1995) 43 *American Journal of Comparative Law* 469.

—— "Aspects of the Reception of Law" (1996) 44 *American Journal of Comparative Law* 335.

Weiler, J H H, "A Quiet Revolution: The European Court of Justice and Its Interlocutors" (1994) 26 *Comparative Polticial Studies* 510.

—— and Lockhart, N J S, "'Taking Rights Seriously' Seriously: The European Court of Justice and Its Fundamental Rights Jurisprudence" (1995) 32 *Common Market Law Review* 51 and 579.

—— "Does Europe Need a Constitution? Reflections on Demos, Telos and the German Maastricht Decision" (1995) 1 *European Law Journal* 219.

Wiegand, W, "The Reception of American Law in Europe" (1991) 39 *American Journal of Comparative Law* 229.

Woolf, Sir Harry, "Public Law – Private Law: Why the Divide? A Personal View" (1986) *Public Law* 220.

Woolf, H, "Judicial Review: A Possible Programme for Reform" (1992) *Public Law* 221.

—— "Droit Public – English Style" (1995) *Public Law* 57, 63, 65, 69.

Wright, D, "Rethinking the Doctrine of Legitimate Expectations in Canadian Administrative Law" (1997) 35 *Osgoode Hall Law Journal* 139.

Wyatt, D, "New Legal Order or Old?" (1982) 7 *European Law Review* 147.

Yourrow, H, *The Margin of Appreciation Doctrine in the Dynamics of the European Human Rights Jurisprudence* (Kluwer, The Hague, 1996).

Index

Administrative law:
  control theories, 103
  EU law characteristics, 106–7
    see also Proportionality
  instrumental theories, 103
  UK law characteristics, 26–30, 105–6, 107–8
    see also Wednesbury
Allan, Trevor, 90–1
Allison, John, 13, 146–7, 152–3

Balancing interests, *see* Proportionality: Substantive Legitimate Expectations: *Wednesbury*
Bell, John, 12–13

Common law model of review:
  dualism, 159
  features, 24–30
  fundamental rights, 162–5
  Human Rights Act, 42–6, 159–60, 174–7
  legal integration, 45–6, 90, 124, 154–5, 159–60, 174–7, 180–1
  Parliament's intentions, 27–30
  Parliamentary sovereignty, 29, 45
Contracting-out, 36, 38, 41–2
Craig, Paul, 13, 29–30, 143, 145–6, 152–3
Cross-fertilisation, legal, 12–15
  Human Rights Act, 157–78

Damages, public authorities, UK law:
  misfeasance in public office, 142–3
  negligence:
    criticisms, 146
    elements, 146, 148
    impact of ECHR, 149–52
    problems, 142
    "spill-over" debate, 143–52
    striking-out and the duty of care, 148–52
  unlawful administrative acts, 142, 147–8
Declarations of incompatibility, Human Rights Act:
  instances, 158
  orthodoxy, 158, 167
  practical impact, 167
  subordinate legislation, 167
Devolution, 8, 45, 159, 181
Dualism:
  common law model of review, 159
  dualist divide, 18, 94, 100–1, 103–10, 130
  integration, limiting effect, 6–7, 180
  international law 6, 78, 157
  legal cross-fertilisation, 13
  Parliamentary sovereignty, 6
Dynamics:
  interacting, 15–17
  European law, 47–74
    see also European Convention on Human Rights; European Union law
  UK public law, 23–46
    see also Common law model of review; Judicial review; Ultra vires doctrine

European Convention on Human Rights:
  effectiveness doctrine, 67
  Human Rights Act,
    significance, 152–5, 158
    ECHR jurisprudence, 166
  institutional characteristics, 66–7,
    compared with EU process, 169–70
  integration, 5–6, 63–6
  legality doctrine, 68
  margin of appreciation, 71–2
    meaning, 71
    relevance in national courts, 72
  negligence, UK law, 147–55
  proportionality, 69–70, 171–2
    see also Proportionality
  UK law, pre-Human Rights Act, 157–65
European Court of Justice:
  activism, 49
  borrowing, 5, 51–3
  jurisprudence, 48–66

European Court of Justice (*cont.*):
national courts, 49
proportionality, 111
see also Proportionality
reference procedure, 49–50
use of principles of judicial review, 51–2, 106
see also European Union Law
European Union Law:
Charter of Fundamental Rights, 48, 66
direct effect, 1, 48, 54
effectiveness requirement, 60, 87, 134–6, 139
emanation of the State:
meaning, 56
purpose, 56
EU law paradigm, 3, 17, 50, 73–4, 77
French law, 51, 104
fundamental rights, 5–6, 51, 62–5, 157
German law, 51, 104
indirect effect:
criticisms, 57–8
Marleasing standard, 56–7, 96
modifications, 57, 96
origins, 54–6, 92–3
problems, 54, 57
purpose, 56
UK courts, 92–101
institutional characteristics, 48–9,
compared with ECHR process, 169–70
loyalty doctrine, 50
principles of judicial review, *see* Equality; Proportionality; Reasons; Substantive legitimate expectations
Remedies; Injunctions; Restitution; State Liability
criticisms, 61
evolution, 60–1, 134–5
features, 134–5
origins, 59–60, 134–5
rationale, 134–5
supremacy, 1, 48
Equality:
EU law, 51, 106, 108–10
UK law, 110, 178

Fundamental rights:
EU law:
Charter of Fundamental Rights, 48, 66
ECHR and, 5–6, 63, 65–6, 157–8, 163–5
evolution, 63–4
integration, 5–6, 65–6
point of conflict, 62–5
significance, 5–6, 51
UK law,
common law standards, 157, 162–5
increased judicial protection, 14, 44, 104
Wednesbury, modified, 18, 114–17

Hunt, Murray, 76–7, 85–6, 90, 98–9

Indirect effect, *see* European Union Law
Injunctions:
EU law understanding of national court obligation, 87, 139
original domestic rule re: ministers of the Crown, 87
"Spillover"/modification of domestic rule, 139–40
Irrationality/unreasonableness, *see* *Wednesbury*

Judicial Review, UK:
democratising function, 8, 23–4
growth, 8, 23–4, 30–9
Justiciability, 32–3, 148–53

Laws, Sir John:
common law model of review, 27–8
reach of EU law, 110
Wednesbury, 115–17
Legal integration:
common law model, 45–6, 159–60
cross-fertilisation, legal, 12–15
Human Rights Act, 157–78
fundamental rights, 5–6, 65–6
Human Rights Act, 19–20, 157–78
interacting dynamcis, 15–17
limits, 9–17
principles of judicial review, 5, 51–3
scholars, 2, 9–17
spill-over, 13, 133–4
transplants, legal, 9–12
UK orthodoxy, 77
Legitimate expectations, substantive:
definition, 118
EU law:
features, 104
protection, balancing, 118

role, 51, 106
UK law:
existence, 117, 120–25
heresy, 122
Human Rights Act and standard of protection, 173
protection, 119, 121–24
Legrand, Pierre, 11–12

Margin of appreciation:
area of discretion, UK law, 170, 175–6
ECHR jurisprudence, 71–2
meaning, 71
relevance to national courts, 72

National courts, reception of EU law:
German Constitutional Court, 62–4
Irish Supreme Court, 64–5
UK courts, *see* Dualism, Parliamentary sovereignty, Statutory interpretation
National law paradigm, 4
New Labour, constitutional reform, 7–8, 45

Orthodoxy, UK, *see* Parliamentary sovereignty, and UK Public Law

Parliamentary sovereignty:
challenges:
devolution, 45, 158–60, 180–1
EU membership, 18, 75–6, 79, 82–92, 158–60, 180–1
common law model of review, 27–30
Dicey, 75
dualism, 6, 78
juridical technique, 26, 77
meaning, 75
rule of recognition, 89–90
ultra vires doctrine, 24–30
Wednesbury, logic, 105–6
see also UK Public Law
Principles of judicial review:
EU law, 50–4, 106
function, 103
UK law origins, 27–8, 104
see also Proportionality; Reasons; *Wednesbury*
Proportionality:
definitions, 69, 110–11
ECHR, 69–70, 171
related tests, 69–70
EU law, 51, 104, 106:
balancing interests, 111
ECJ's application, 111
German law, 111
UK courts:
acceptance in Human Rights Act cases, 20, 170–1
difficulties, 111–13
previous rejection in domestic law, 114–17, 161
socio-economic cases, 174–7
Wednesbury, 18–19, 70, 113–4, 171–8
Privatisation, 35–6
Public authorities:
Human Rights Act, 40–2, 168
jurisprudence, UK, 35–8
liability, *see* Damages
Public-private divide:
Human Rights Act, 39–42
problems, 35–6

Reasons, duty to give:
Rationale, 125–6
EU law:
general principle, 127
national court obligation, 127
role, 51, 106, 125
Treaties, 126
UK law:
EU law compared, 129–30
historic understanding, 125, 127
Human Rights Act, 172
modified position, 127–9
Remedies, UK law:
historic emphasis, 22, 133
spill-over, 133
Restitution:
EU law, 135–6
effective protection requirement, 136
UK law:
historic understanding, 136
spill-over, 137–8
Royal prerogative:
amenability to review, 30–5:
description, 30
justiciability, 32–3
ultra vires doctrine, 34–5

Schwarze, Jürgen, 4, 16, 52–3
Sedley, Sir Stephen:
common law model of review, 27
integration, 124, 163–5

Spill-over, *see* Legal integration
Standing, UK law:
  liberalisation, 14, 24
  Human Rights Act, 168–9
State liability:
  criticisms, 61:
  elements, 59, 144–5
  origins, 58–9, 144
  relevance to UK liability standards, 143–52
  significance, 59–62
  see also European Union law; remedies
Statutory interpretation, UK courts:
  common law presumption, 78, 84–6, 98–100, 157, 162
  construction approach and EU law, 78–92
  Denning, Lord, 80–2
  Diplock, Lord, 84
  Human Rights Act and domestic legislation, 166
  indirect effect doctrine:
    acceptance of *Marleasing*, 96–8
    integration, 98–9
    problem of orthodoxy/dualist divide, 93–5
  literal interpretation, 77, 81

Transplants, Legal, 9–12

UK courts:
  evolving role, 14–15
  institutional role(s), 25–30
    see also Common law model, and Ultra vires doctrine
  institutional preferences and Human Rights Act, 173–7
  interpretation techniques, *see* Statutory interpretation
  reception, EU law, *see* Dualism, Parliamentary sovereignty, Statutory interpretation
    criticisms, 17–8, 76–7, 85–6, 90–1, 98–9
UK public law,
  orthodoxy:
    characteristics, 26, 77, 105–6
    integration, 17, 21, 77–101, 173–4
    limits, 26–30, 76–7, 85–6, 90–1, 98–100
  see also Dualism, Parliamentary sovereignty:
Ultra vires doctrine:
  debate, 26–30
  Human Rights Act, 42–4
  modified, 26–30
  Parliament's intentions, 26–9
  problems, 24–5, 27–30
  public-private divide, 35–42
  royal prerogative, 34–5
  traditional, 24, 26

Wade, Sir William, 88–90
Watson, Alan, 9–12
Wednesbury:
  criticisms, 117
  definition, 18, 105
  fundamental rights, 18, 114–17
  institutional logic, 18, 105–6
  margin of appreciation, 71–2
  proportionality, 18–19, 70, 113–14, 171–8
  review not appeal, 105, 116